P9-DFM-558

Abstract economic theory may be timeless and potentially universal in its application, but macroeconomics has to be seen in its historical context. The nature of the policy regime, the behaviour of the economy and the beliefs of professional economists all interact, and influence each other. This short historical account of monetary regimes since 1900 shows how the role of policy has changed, and how this has related to experience of inflation and the real economy, as well as to changes in political philosophies.

The narrative concentrates on developments in America, Britain, Germany, France and Japan. It begins with the era of the classical gold standard and ends with the 'neo-liberal' regimes of today. The decades in between saw much more active policy intervention, and much less faith in the stability of markets. The 'grand narrative' of the century is a journey 'to Utopia and back'. It is argued that no school of macroeconomics is right for all time; different theoretical models may be appropriate for different periods and regimes.

ANDREW BRITTON has been a Visiting Professor at the University of Bath since 1998. He was Director of the National Institute of Economic and Social Research between 1982 and 1995, when he left to join the Churches' Enquiry into Unemployment and the Future of Work. His other books include *Macroeconomic Policy in Britain 1974–1987*, *The Goal of Full Employment* and *The Trade Cycle in Britain, 1958–1982*.

THE NATIONAL INSTITUTE OF
ECONOMIC AND SOCIAL RESEARCH
XLII

2 DEAN TRENCH STREET, SMITH SQUARE, LONDON, SW1P 3HE

The National Institute of Economic and Social Research is an independent, non-profit-making body, founded in 1938. It has as its aim the promotion of realistic research, particularly in the field of economics. It conducts research by its own research staff and in cooperation with universities and other academic bodies.

Monetary Regimes of the Twentieth Century

ANDREW BRITTON

CAMBRIDGE
UNIVERSITY PRESS

PUBLISHED BY THE PRESS SYNDICATE OF THE UNIVERSITY OF CAMBRIDGE
The Pitt Building, Trumpington Street, Cambridge CB2 1RP, United Kingdom

CAMBRIDGE UNIVERSITY PRESS
The Edinburgh Building, Cambridge, CB2 2RU, UK http://www.cup.cam.ac.uk
40 West 20th Street, New York, NY 10011-4211, USA http://www.cup.org
10 Stamford Road, Oakleigh, Melbourne 3166, Australia

First published 2001

A catalogue record for this book is available from the British Library

ISBN 0 521 80169 9 hardback

Transferred to digital printing 2003

Contents

Contents

Tables

Figures

Preface

The turn of the century seems an appropriate time for reflection, interpreting the past so as to imagine the shape of the future. Often, in my career at the Treasury and at the National Institute I have tried to give an account of economic events in one country, in one year, or even in one month. But it is impossible to make sense of the detail unless one has some conception of the broader pattern to which it belongs. This book is my attempt to make that conception explicit.

Writing this book has been one of the most congenial tasks that I have set myself since I retired from the post of Institute director. I am very grateful to my successor, Martin Weale, for encouraging me to take it up, and providing assistance essential to carrying it out. I have been able to make full use of the Institute's library, including the many fascinating old books and periodicals hidden away in the basement. I am very grateful to Claire Schofield, the Institute's librarian, for her help in obtaining research material from this and other sources. One of my happiest hunting grounds was the library of the Bank of England; I would particularly like to thank Howard Picton for enabling me to make the most of that valuable collection.

Whilst working on this project, I was also, amongst other things, a visiting professor at the University of Bath. I was able to use draft chapters of the book as the basis for lectures to MBA students. I believe that they found both the historical perspective and the global context valuable to understanding economic conditions today. I am thankful for the encouragement that they gave me.

My warm thanks are also due to friends and colleagues who read my text in draft and commented on it: Martin Weale, Charles Goodhart and (especially) John Flemming. Responsibility for the finished product is, of course, my own. And, finally, I am very grateful also to Fran Robinson, who has done an excellent job in preparing the text for publication, as she has done for the other books that I have written for the Institute over the years.

Introduction: economics and history

This is a book about both history and economics. As a history book, it describes, in chronological order, the main monetary 'events' of the twentieth century, concentrating on the five major economies – the United States, the United Kingdom, Germany, France and Japan. The century is divided into eight periods of ten to fifteen years, and a chapter is devoted to each of them. Each chapter begins with a section that describes the behaviour of the major economies in respect of inflation, output growth, unemployment and interest rates.

A very broad overview of the century is provided by figures 1–4 at the end of this introduction (pp. 21–2).

At the beginning of the century inflation was low everywhere. In both world wars, and immediately after them, it was high, sometimes very high indeed. Between the wars it was sometimes negative. In the latter half of the century it was persistent, but not explosive. Towards the end of the century it was again generally low.

Growth rates varied greatly from year to year in the first half of the century. In the interwar period, output fell continuously for four years in America. There were recessions in the latter half of the century as well, but they were not so long, or so deep.

The peak rate of unemployment in the 1930s was much higher in America (and in Germany) than it was in Britain. Full employment was maintained in Europe for a generation after the Second World War. In the last two decades of the century, however, the rate was persistently higher in Europe than in the USA.

Interest rates remained low throughout the first half of the century, showing far less variation than there was in rates of inflation.

In the second half, on the other hand, they rose almost continuously for about thirty years, reaching double figures, before turning sharply down again.

These will be some of the story lines running right through this book. Whilst the meaning of the statistics does change from one period to another, it is often helpful to see the events of each decade, or regime, in the context of the longer-term trends.

The history of monetary regimes cannot properly be considered except in a broader political context. In each of the chapters, a second section will describe the evolution of economic policy in general, and of monetary policy in particular. The story is not quite the same in every country, but the broad trends are similar. There were relatively 'liberal' or 'free-market' regimes at the beginning and again at the end of the century, with relatively 'interventionist' or 'planned' regimes in between.

One cannot discuss the domestic policy regimes of nation states without considering how their external relations were conducted. The third section of each chapter is devoted, therefore, to international monetary systems. The first chapter describes the gold standard as it operated at the start of the century; the final chapter focuses on the formation of the European Monetary Union. In the intervening chapters some account is given of the turmoil between the world wars, of the Bretton Woods system from the 1940s to the 1960s, and of the subsequent experience with more or less freely floating exchange rates.

This is also a book about economics. It is about the interrelation between economic behaviour and the character of the monetary regime. There is, it will be argued, no general theory of macroeconomics which is independent of politics, social institutions and beliefs. One cannot, therefore, choose between alternative monetary regimes on the basis of 'the economic arguments' alone. A fourth section of each chapter will illustrate this interrelationship for each period and each policy regime. The remainder of this introduction will develop some related themes. It will look at the connections between economics and history from a number of different angles.

To Utopia and back

At the beginning of the twentieth century the freedom of action of central banks was constrained by the commitment to convert their currencies freely into gold. At the end of the century they were again inhibited by the need to maintain confidence in international capital markets. But in the middle decades of the century monetary regimes were of a quite different character. Monetary policy was one element in a scientifically designed strategy intended to maximise the economic well-being of an independent nation state. We have been to Utopia and back again.

In his introduction to the history of the world economy over these hundred years, Robert Skidelsky (1998) distinguishes four phases: 'liberal market (1900–13), autarkic (1914–50), managed market (1950–73) and neo-liberal (since 1973)'. In his conclusions he refers to the 'remarketization of economic life' in the closing years of the century as 'a modest movement back towards the world with which the century opened'. From a British perspective the phases are particularly easy to recognise, especially the sharp contrast between the role played by the state in the economy before and after the Second World War, and again before and after the change of government in 1979. But broadly the same grand narrative can be used to shape the history of America or western Europe, and indeed of the world as a whole. The sequence of monetary regimes, both national and international, relates to an accompanying succession of institutional and social developments.

The grand narrative tells how the nation state took increasing responsibility for the stability and prosperity of the national economy for a period of about sixty years, and then progressively abandoned that responsibility over the next forty years or so. The story can be told as a tragedy. Two generations of political leaders, public servants and applied economists overcame dark forces of ignorance and self-interest. They created, in the mixed economies of the mid-century, a system of economic management which gave the world a period of unprecedented prosperity. Then, perhaps because of some flaw in social organisation, or in human nature itself, their work was destroyed. The next two generations were unable, or unwilling, to sustain the system which gave us the 'golden age', and it fell apart.

Another way of telling the story is to condemn the attempt to manage economies as a dangerous attack on individual liberty. It was an attempt to copy the deceptive early achievements of economic planning and control in the totalitarian systems of Russia and Germany. The attempt to build the 'Great Utopia', as Hayek (1944) described it, was simply 'the Road to Serfdom'. It might be inspired by high ideals to begin with, but sooner or later 'the worst get on top'. The high road of human progress did not, on this view, lead through the regimes which were constructed in the middle years of the century. All that was just a diversion which led nowhere. It was necessary to retrace our steps.

It is not the purpose of this study to offer support to either side in this clash of ideals and historical interpretations, but it is important to recognise the strong feelings which lie just below the surface of much academic debate. Economics may seem to be a detached and scientific discipline, but it seldom is or has been. The history of economic thought can be seen as itself part of the same grand narrative. It justified successive changes of monetary, and indeed economic and political, regime. It supported – often tacitly – the values, and indeed the material interests, of some groups in society against others. The Keynesian revolution from the 1930s to the 1960s, and the counter-revolution which followed, were both expressions of changing political philosophies as well as shifts in the accepted explanatory paradigm. New evidence certainly played a part in changing the beliefs of economists, but what happened in economics cannot be fully understood in isolation from the political environment of the times.

It might seem therefore that economic history cannot be written without taking sides in the great controversies of political economy. One cannot avoid the need for a theoretical framework when describing economic behaviour and the consequences of monetary regimes. A mere catalogue of events would be superficial, and probably not in fact free from bias. Does one not therefore need at the outset to declare oneself a conservative or a radical? The contention of this study is that one can, and should, avoid making such a choice. Many different theories of behaviour may all be valid, each in the interpretation of a different regime. For example, classical economics may be appropriate to describe behaviour under a liberal regime, whilst what was called 'modern' economics may be right for a managed economy. Perhaps neither would qualify as a truly 'general' theory.

Macroeconomics and history

Clearly, there is a methodological question here of some importance, concerning the relationship of history and theory in economics. It was very familiar to students of the subject a hundred years ago and is not finally settled even now. There is an extensive discussion by J.N. Keynes (1891) (the father of the better known son). The historical school, especially in Germany, maintained that each country and each historical period had its own laws of economic behaviour, depending on its methods of production, its social structure and its institutions. The interesting questions to study concerned economic development and institutional change. The analytical school, on the other hand, in particular the British neoclassicals, sought to build economic theory on axioms of individual rationality which were supposed to be of general application. So-called 'economic man' is a model of human nature itself, not just of members of our own culture and society. It has been, in the main, the analytical approach which has prevailed. So far as what we now call 'microeconomics' is concerned, this may well be for the best, and this was what interested economists most at the start of the century, but it is a different matter when the focus is on what we now call 'macroeconomics'.

J.N. Keynes did recognise that social beliefs and interactions can influence economic behaviour, despite his general support for the axiomatic approach. Two examples that he gives are particularly relevant to this study, because they refer to two phenomena of particular concern for the design of monetary regimes, that is inflation and financial crises. The passage is worth quoting at length:

> Even in the case of a purely monetary question, such as the circumstances determining the amount of depreciation of an inconvertible currency, an important consideration may be the extent to which a people's distrust is aroused, and this in its turn may depend partly on their political sympathies, and on their knowledge and intelligence, or on the extent to which their power of moral restraint prevents them giving way to unreasoning panic. This last point is still more clearly important in connection with the phenomena that constitute a financial crisis. The theory, for example, of the recurrence of such crises at regular intervals, so far as it does not involve the operation of physical causes (as in Jevons' sun-spot theory), may require to be modified according to the stage of a nation's intellectual and moral development. (pp. 134–5)

The crucial question that faced macroeconomists in the twentieth century was the stability of the market system. Could the economy safely be left to stabilise itself? Or did the monetary authorities need to intervene, occasionally or all the time? Theory could point to mechanisms which should preserve or restore equilibrium. But how generally applicable was that theory? The evidence of the turbulent interwar years was that the system was fragile, or sluggish, or unreliable. How relevant was the experience of that period to others? If we are to gain a deeper understanding we must look at institutional change, at the framework of law and at the common beliefs which underlie the choices of individuals. This historical approach to macroeconomics may not result in many straightforward testable predictions, but it is nevertheless indispensable.

If we think of individual behaviour as rational and calculating, then it is clear enough that the nature of the monetary regime will affect behaviour. This is the favoured approach of present-day monetary theory, taking the theory of choice under uncertainty as its starting point. It follows that influencing rational expectations is the essence of monetary policy. A credible commitment to a fixed exchange rate, for example, will encourage stabilising capital flows. There will be little need for actual market intervention by government or central bank, because currency traders and speculators will anticipate such action. Similarly, a credible commitment to a money-supply target will discourage wage increases that are potentially inflationary. A credible commitment by government to maintain full employment may also encourage firms to initiate investment projects even in a time of recession. In all these cases rational individual behaviour will tend to preserve and validate the regime.

Commentators often use the more elusive concept of market 'confidence'. This is not just another word for expectations. It is a state of mind as well as a view of the future. It may be particularly significant when views of the future are most difficult to form rationally. Under great uncertainty people have to put their trust in something, even when they do not have the information on which an estimate of probabilities might be based. Confidence is not just an individual conviction; it is a shared belief, reinforced much of the time by social contact.

The ability to think rationally was seen by J.N. Keynes as a mark of moral development, the ability to keep one's head. But, if so, there has been little development since his time. Markets can still behave like herds of cattle or flocks of birds. Economists are reluctant to introduce crowd behaviour into their theories of economic behaviour, but clearly it is crucial to the understanding of events such as bank failures or stock market booms. It may also be important to the explanation of business cycles, and to the success or failure of monetary regimes. We shall keep an open mind.

A liberal regime is more likely to be viable if people believe that it is so, if people read neoclassical economists and trust central banks to observe the rules of the game. Equally a managed regime is viable, and indeed necessary, if people have been taught to rely on government intervention to keep the economy on course. It might seem, then, that whichever monetary theory is generally believed becomes, in that context, correct. This is too simple and too sweeping a conclusion. The relationship between the behaviour of the economy and the choice of monetary regime is more complex than that. It involves institutions as well as beliefs.

Clearly the behaviour of an economy must reflect its social organisation. For example, the equilibrium level of unemployment may depend on social security provision; the equilibrium real interest rate may depend on the normal age of retirement; the amplitude of cyclical fluctuations may depend on the degree of industrial concentration, unionisation and tariff protection. The role of the state in economic life generally is part of the institutional setting of the monetary regime. It interacts with the institutions of the private sector, for example when protection favours cartelisation, or incomes policies enhance the influence of trades unions.

Monetary regimes

We need a definition of a monetary regime, so as to distinguish it from the day-by-day policy measures taken by the monetary authorities, and also from the role of government more generally in relation to the economy. A monetary regime is defined both by law and by custom. The law will say what is legal tender and may regulate its creation and convertibility into other currencies or precious metals. The law may constrain the balance- sheet position of the central bank and some financial institutions in the private sector. There may also be international agreements and treaties which limit the independence of each national central bank.

But the definition of a regime is not only a matter of law and it may not all be set out unambiguously in black and white. The central bank will have some discretion within the law and the way that it uses its freedom of manoeuvre is also part of the definition of a regime. It may, for example, set monetary targets or exchange rate zones. It will have customary methods of operation, for example setting its discount rate at monthly intervals or varying the required reserve ratios of commercial banks. The nature of the monetary regime will interact with the behaviour of the economy and its institutional structure both as cause and as effect.

A particular monetary regime may be set up because it is thought to be appropriate to a particular institutional setting. The story of the twentieth-century regimes could be told that way. A liberal regime had been established in the nineteenth century because legislators understood this to be appropriate to the competitive economy of the time. Later on, however, a managed regime had to be introduced instead because markets became less flexible. Later still, the neo-liberal regime at the end of the century may be seen as a necessary response to the globalisation of finance.

It is also possible to tell the story with causation running in the other direction. Perhaps regimes determine institutions. There are some situations where we can quite clearly observe this happening. The growth of off-shore banking is, of course, a response to national regulation. The index-linking of contracts is a response to persistent inflation accommodated by a relaxed monetary regime. Perhaps we should see cartelisation and unionisation as being, amongst other things, the consequences of a regime which permits fluctuations in the levels of prices and nominal wages.

It is, then, interesting to consider whether adaptation of this kind tends to preserve an existing regime or to undermine it. To simplify greatly, a liberal or classical monetary regime would seem to work best when markets are competitive and prices are flexible; a managed regime would seem to require the cooperation of organised labour and big business. To what extent will the existence of either kind of regime maintain the conditions necessary for its own survival? Alternatively, does the existence of one kind of regime encourage the development of institutions and behaviour more appropriate to the other?

These are some of the questions which will be addressed in this study. There is, in the century, a great variety of experience on which to draw. There are periods of falling prices, stable prices, persistent and slow price increases and explosive hyperinflations. There are periods of steady growth in output, with or without full employment, sharp recessions and deep depression. There are banking crises and stock market crashes, commodity price booms and administered price hikes. There are examples of fixed exchange rate systems and of free floating, as well as various experiments with intermediate regimes. There are, of course, two world wars, and many lesser conflicts. As a result, economists today have no difficulty in writing a natural history of the monetary economy. We have developed plenty of what might be called expert knowledge; we can recognise certain patterns and recurrent combinations of events. Whether this has resulted in any deeper comprehension is another question. The system we observe may evolve more rapidly than we can learn to understand it.

A regime can be described in various ways. For the purpose of this study we identify four characteristics which will be of central concern. The first is the degree to which the behaviour of the monetary authorities is bound by preset rules. The second (which is related, but not the same) is the extent of reliance on market mechanisms. The third is the degree of national autonomy. The fourth identifies the main instruments of policy, especially the role of administered interest rates. We shall discuss each of these briefly in turn, adopting the timeless analytical approach of economic theory, before embarking on our account of history.

Rules versus discretion

Essentially there are two models of economic policy, whether it is conducted by governments or central banks. Either the 'authorities' act as referee or they are players in the game. In the first case the purpose of government is to uphold the rule of law. Those who exercise delegated authority must themselves be governed by rules. In the second case the duty of government is to enhance the well-being of the nation, assuming such powers as this task requires. Provided that public servants act in a disinterested way, they should be allowed full discretion to monitor events and act accordingly. The right balance between rules and discretion is a matter of perennial debate in political theory, as well as the central issue in the choice of a monetary regime in our own times.

As long ago as the days of the Roman republic it was recognised that dictatorial powers may be needed in times of war or other national emergency. This was certainly the case during the world wars of the twentieth century and I shall argue that the power given to governments to control the economy in wartime had a profound effect on the development of peace-time regimes as well. But, what constitutes a national emergency? This question has to be answered again and again in relation to economic policy. Postwar reconstruction may require that special powers are given to government, but what about more chronic economic backwardness or loss of international competitiveness? A long and deep economic depression may be sufficient reason for special measures to combat unemployment, but should governments seek to iron out the normal fluctuations of the business cycle? Different political philosophies will draw the line in different places.

In monetary theory the case for rules against discretion has been argued rigorously in recent decades. The first argument favours simplicity and predictability. Governments themselves are uncertain about the behaviour of the economy, and averse to risk, so they should not intervene too vigorously, trying to be too clever; they could make the instability worse. Moreover, they will confuse agents in the private sector who might otherwise behave in a stabilising way – sudden and unexpected changes in the rate of interest, for example, will bankrupt otherwise sound businesses. It was arguments of this kind which led Milton Friedman in the 1950s to advocate a regime in which the growth of the money supply was slow and constant year after year. A case for a fixed exchange rate regime could be constructed on similar lines.

The second, and more powerful, argument is about what is called 'time inconsistency'. This is not just a technical issue in the design of monetary regimes, but a problem which besets social control of almost any kind. The policy action which seems best 'before the event' will not seem best 'at the time'. The authority which controls behaviour by threats and promises will not in general wish to carry them out. The criminal law may threaten capital punishment, for example, but popular opinion may nevertheless plead for a reprieve. Economists have rediscovered and formalised this fundamental dilemma in the context of monetary policy.

A central bank which has its hands bound may be better at maintaining price stability than one which is able to react to events. In this respect controlling the economy is not like controlling a physical or mechanical system. The behaviour of the economy depends on expectations, which are formed intelligently. The market can sometimes foresee that the authorities will not really be prepared to raise interest rates to the level required to hit their declared target for the money supply or the exchange rate. Their commitment to a monetary rule may only be credible if their discretion is entirely taken away.

There is also a third and very well-known argument against executive discretion of any kind: power corrupts. Economists too easily assume that governments, or for that matter central banks, are altruistic servants of the public good. An older, more cynical, tradition has been revived in the contemporary theory of public choice. This assumes that politicians and public officials are inspired by the same motives as traders in a market – they seek their own advantage.

Governments in a democracy seek re-election. If they have discretion in the management of monetary policy they will seek to win favour by cutting interest rates as the date of the election approaches. Central bankers are not subject to this temptation if they have security of tenure, but some would say that they show a rather different bias. Their constituency is the financial community – the City of London or its equivalent. They may keep interest rates and exchange rates too high for the good of manufacturing industry or the economy as a whole. If governments and central bankers cannot be bound hand and foot, then they should at least be made accountable and made to work within clear guidelines and a policy framework.

Laissez faire and monetary policy

The general proposition that governments should not intervene in the operation of a market economy has long born the name of 'laissez faire'. The classical case rests, not only on the three arguments for rules already described, but also on a favourable view of the market as a system for allocating scarce resources. Individuals know best what is good for them; governments should let well alone. This argument clearly applies to microeconomic questions like those involved in trade policy or the regulation of industry. It has been extended, rather more speculatively, to the subject matter of macroeconomics as well. Those who believe that all economic behaviour is governed by rationality will argue that the degree of instability observed in a free market is the best that can be achieved. If price adjustment is slow, and if employment is not continuous for all workers, that, it is said, is because people prefer it that way, or at least prefer that outcome to any feasible alternative. The economy will always be subject to shocks of one kind or another, but the authorities should leave it to absorb them in its own way – the market knows best.

Nevertheless there are many who would say that the general preference for non-interference does not apply to monetary policy with the same force as it applies elsewhere. Lionel Robbins (1976), in his history of political economy, draws a distinction between intervention in particular markets and concern for 'the stability of the system as a whole'. He sees the origins of macroeconomic policy in the responsibilities accepted by central banks in the nineteenth century. There was, he wrote, 'no question of laisser faire' in responding to a banking crisis.

This view is not uncontroversial. There are historical examples of economies which seem to have functioned perfectly well without central banks to look after them. Even today there are those who advocate free banking (for example, Dowd, 1989). A truly competitive banking system, the theory says, would not need policing. If the banks were not well run, their customers would desert them. They should be left free to protect themselves from bank runs, for example by printing lots of banknotes with the option of immediate convertibility attached to them. If one or two small banks failed, that would not matter too much; the problem is that individual banks have been allowed to get too large. They are encouraged to behave irresponsibly because central banks exist and are expected to bail them out if they get into difficulties. The argument for free banking is thus constructed on the same lines as the case for competition policy in general, and against industrial planning of any kind. Laissez faire could in principle apply even to the monetary regime itself.

The case against laissez faire also has a long history. In the nineteenth century the governments of most industrial countries were introducing more controls on industry in the interests of efficiency, or indeed of humanity. The arguments about the under-provision of 'public goods' were already familiar. As the scope of legislation widened, it seemed more and more archaic to base the monetary system on the mystical appeal of gold. The discovery of new gold fields or new processes of extraction could disrupt the industries of the world. Surely a modern progressive society could not be expected to tolerate that! In the twentieth century science and technology extended our ability to control many aspects of our environment. Why not the economic environment as well? The improvements in public health showed how much benefit could flow from the intelligent application of knowledge, backed up by the power of the state. Could not the same approach be applied to the alleviation of poverty and unemployment? The combination of concern for the welfare of the poor and advances in knowledge had achieved so much in other areas of social policy.

More and more of the data on which economic control could be based have been collected: price indices, trade statistics, national income accounts. Econometric models have been estimated and used to forecast the economy several years ahead. The control theory developed by electrical engineers has been applied to analogous problems in applied macroeconomics – all this made possible by advances in computing and information technology. The problem was not a lack of resources devoted to economic research or a reluctance to use them.

One might question whether these models, or the data on which they were based, were sufficiently accurate for the purposes of control. The record of economic forecasting is not very encouraging. The control of the price level or output requires projections more than a year ahead. At that range the aim cannot be good. Even so, is it not right to use such information as one has? The deeper question is whether the mechanical analogy is appropriate at all.

The argument that really persuaded governments that they had to intervene in the economy was simply that the market system had broken down. Even those who attached great importance to individual liberty, economic efficiency and the private profit motive found themselves compelled, in the 1930s at least, to do something about the collapse of output and the hardships of the unemployed. This was the period when macroeconomics, and the policy principles that go with it, were first developed systematically. It was intended to save the free market, not to replace it.

The argument was that the state could take responsibility for aggregate demand, savings and investment, whilst not interfering with individual decisions about either consumption or production. It went well beyond the reform of central banking and the monetary regime, because it enlisted government spending and taxation as instruments of policy as well, but it was not intended to be comprehensive. This was the prescription put forward by Keynes (1936) in the *General Theory*.

In the concluding note at the end of that book, on 'the social philosophy towards which the general theory might lead', Keynes wrote:

> The central controls necessary to ensure full employment will, of course, involve a large extension of the traditional functions of government . . . But there will still remain a wide field for the exercise of private initiative and responsibility. Within this field the traditional advantages of individualism will still hold good.

After a paragraph in praise of individualism, he continued:

> Whilst, therefore, the enlargements of the functions of government, involved in the task of adjusting to one another the propensity to consume and the inducement to invest, would seem to a nineteenth-century publicist or to a contemporary American financier to be a terrific encroachment on individualism, I defend it, on the contrary, both as the only practicable means of avoiding the destruction of existing economic forms in their entirety and as the condition of the successful functioning of individual initiative.

It would appear from this passage that the state can be an umpire in relation to industry, trade and the labour market, standing back from direct intervention, whilst at the same time being a player in relation to aggregate demand, savings and investment, interest rates and the price level. Two contradictory models of government are thus combined. It seems to achieve the best of both worlds.

As we shall see in following the development of monetary regimes through the century, this is one proposal which was never really put into practice. Those governments which attempted to manage aggregate demand believed in planning and intervention in other spheres as well. Perhaps it is just that powers once taken will always be used. If the government is empowered to regulate the total of credit or the total of investment, it will soon start to take a view as to the right direction of credit and investment as well. Perhaps, also, the attempt to control one aspect of the economy is always prone to create new problems elsewhere, which will then need to be addressed by further intervention. In particular, success in achieving full employment creates wage inflation, for which wage restraint seems the only cure – and that surely implies control of profit margins as well. In any case, the governments which took up the challenge of controlling demand tended to be sceptical of the merits of the free market generally. Ironically, the very interventionist regimes of the 1950s and 1960s are what most people now understand as 'Keynesianism'.

Nation states and the global economy

There is no world government, nor any world authority capable of economic management. There is therefore a close connection between liberal regimes and international integration, between autarky and government intervention. The project of demand management and the mixed economy at mid-century was necessarily national in its scope. It was implemented independently in each country, along distinct lines, even if governments did learn from one another. The aim was clearly to serve the national interest, not the common good of the world as a whole. Sometimes the policies of one country came into conflict with the interests of others. It was the relatively liberal regimes at the beginning and the end of the century that did most to encourage globalisation and international trade.

Any history of the twentieth century must recognise the force of nationalism. National identity, loyalty and pride often proved stronger than any religious or political creed. Patriotism inspired devoted service and great personal sacrifice. Nationalism provoked two world wars and numerous other conflicts, from the start of the century right to its end. It is not too surprising therefore that economic policy sometimes adopted words like 'competitiveness' to describe its objectives.

It is well to remember the historical connection between monetary policy and war. Often the only means by which defence, or indeed aggression, can be financed is by depreciating the currency. That was true in the twentieth century as in ancient times. One reason for having a central bank is to make this process easier. International monetary regimes are unlikely to survive intact through any major conflict. The gold standard was suspended during the Napoleonic Wars, The Franco-Prussian War and the American Civil War. It was well understood that national commitments to a regime of convertibility did not cover events of this kind. This is one reason why those who value national sovereignty oppose the formation of monetary unions. It is difficult to see how one member of a monetary union could engage in a major war if the other members did not; still more difficult to imagine a war in which member states fought on opposite sides.

The choice of monetary regime is a matter for national decision. It is convenient, of course, if nations which trade extensively with one another or allow mobility of capital and labour, maintain easy convertibility between their currencies. It is even more convenient if their currencies have fixed exchange rates; best of all if there is just one currency in use. It is not only the annoyance of having to do a certain amount of arithmetic, or pay a small commission at the bureau de change. More important is the uncertainty of relative movements in currencies in the future. This can make a great difference to the profit margin between costs incurred in one country and sales revenue earned in another.

Despite all the obvious advantages of having fixed exchange rates, few countries in the twentieth century in fact maintained a regime of that kind for long periods. They valued their independence and sought to use monetary policy to achieve domestic objectives. Under a really fixed exchange rate system, in the absence of restrictions on trade or capital movements, the scope for an independent national monetary policy is very restricted indeed. The prices of standard goods which are traded internationally must be the same in all countries, or at least tend rapidly to equality. Prices of goods and services which are not traded, and the level of wages, will also tend towards equality, but more slowly, especially if the economy is large. Whatever happens, the price levels at home and abroad cannot diverge further and further. Thus all the countries in a fixed-rate system must on average over the years experience similar rates of inflation – even if they differ from one another in most other respects.

A really and truly fixed exchange rate system also means that interest rates for assets with the same risk and maturity characteristics have to be the same everywhere. If exchange risk has really been eliminated then arbitrage across money markets will keep rates in line – otherwise unlimited gains could be made by borrowing in one country to lend in another. One may question, however, whether anything short of a monetary union can ever abolish exchange risk altogether. So long as more than one currency exists, the possibility of exchange rate changes must remain, whatever commitments are made. In practice, fixed-rate systems have always had explicit or tacit 'let-out clauses' attached to them; and there have been realignments from time to time. The markets have always taken account of that possibility, and interest rates in practice have not been exactly the same. Real-life systems have also permitted flexibility of exchange rates within margins, sometimes wide enough to affect the calculations of arbitrageurs.

Not-quite-fixed exchange rate systems do allow interest rates to differ across countries, but they do not necessarily give monetary authorities any useful independence. On the contrary, the need to dispel fears of devaluation can come to dominate policymaking. The level of interest rates needed to reassure speculators that a devaluation is not intended – or to compensate them for the possibility that it is – may be totally inappropriate to the achievement of domestic objectives. The exchange markets seem to be dominated by speculators rather than traders or long-term investors. Experience, especially towards the end of the century, was that the expectation of an exchange rate move often proved self-fulfilling. Central banks cannot often mobilise the volume of foreign exchange they would need in order to prove the expectations wrong.

In principle a floating exchange rate system allows each nation state to decide its own monetary policy. As between any two countries, the exchange rate will move so as to offset differences in their rates of inflation. If one country chooses to inflate its currency – for example to fight a war – it is free to do so. If other countries prefer price stability, they do not have to import inflation from abroad. If capital is mobile between countries, then real interest rates for similar assets will be the same everywhere, but nominal rates will differ by the amount of relative inflation or currency depreciation. It would seem as if the national central bank was the master in its own house.

Theories of exchange rate determination now suggest that the conduct of independent monetary policy is not quite as easy as that. Experience with floating rates confirms that the job of the central bank can be more difficult than it sounds. Exchange rates do not move gradually from one equilibrium position to another: they tend rather to jump abruptly up or down. These jumps, according to the theory, typically overshoot the new equilibrium, and have to be gradually in part reversed.

Suppose that the central bank in one country raises its discount rate by two percentage points, and that this increase is expected to be maintained for five years. To maintain parity of real interest rates with the rest of the world, the expected depreciation of the domestic currency over those same five years must also be 2 per cent per annum. The exchange rate must therefore jump up immediately to a rate which is 10 per cent above the rate which is expected to hold in five years' time. Any news which changes market perceptions of where the long-run equilibrium lies will have a similar effect; the rate will fall too far in response to bad news, and rise too far when the news is good. The result could be a rough ride for the economy, especially for traders whose margins depend on relative prices at home and abroad.

Sometimes the exchange rate will jump on the basis of false rumours or market fads. It is very difficult to guess where the market equilibrium actually lies. It depends crucially on the monetary policies that will be followed in the future – how long, for example, an interest rate increase will be maintained. The main subject of speculation is what those policies will be, but in fact the pressure in the exchange market may influence what those policies are. In any event the market will be watching carefully to see who is appointed to run monetary policy, what are likely to be the results of the next election and how credible are any commitments that may be made.

Speculators will also be watching one another carefully because they know that expectations can help to fulfil themselves; foreign exchange markets, like any other speculative markets, can have 'bubbles', which rise simply by their own momentum, although everyone is behaving in a perfectly rational way. They are not always possible to detect, until the point when they burst. For any economy, but especially for a small open economy, this is a very difficult environment in which to conduct a coherent monetary policy at all.

Monetary theory and monetary practice

Neoclassical economic theory, as it developed in the nineteenth and twentieth centuries, is timeless and abstracted from history. It deduces the character of a market equilibrium from axioms of rational behaviour claiming to be of universal application to all market systems. One might question its relevance to the real world, but one cannot doubt its rigour and its elegance. In its simplest form it explains how consumer preferences and production possibilities together determine the price ratios of all commodities, and the quantities bought and sold.

This concept of equilibrium is fundamental to what is called 'mainstream' economic theory, but it is does not go unchallenged. Its use in macroeconomics in particular is disputed both by neo-Keynesians and by Marxians (see, for example, Dow, 1985, especially ch. 5). It seems to deny completely the relevance of history to market outcomes, but one needs to look more closely at precisely what is meant by 'equilibrium' in the different contexts in which the word is used. In common use the term means that at least three different conditions hold: prices clear markets; the quantities produced and consumed are held to be optimal at these prices; and expectations are not systematically proved wrong.

On closer examination these all turn out to be very difficult conditions to meet. Trading itself is not costless, and negotiations may take a long time to complete. There may be good reasons for negotiating fixed-price contracts of quite long duration; goods and services will then change hands today at prices reflecting yesterday's market conditions. So the concept of market clearing is not entirely straightforward: it may refer to a process that takes a long time to complete.

Quantity adjustment also takes place gradually when more rapid changes, for example in the stock of fixed capital, are especially costly to undertake. In the very, very long run, perhaps, the outcome does depend only on tastes and technologies, as the theory implies; but in the meantime it depends also on the initial conditions, that is on the existing stocks of such things as machines, or skills, or accumulated debt. In a world full of disturbances the economy may always be trying to move towards some theoretical long-run equilibrium, but it will never get there. That is one reason why history matters as well as economic analysis.

The fulfilment of expectations is, of course, a very strict criterion as well. One must doubt whether it is ever met. The theory requires everyone in the market to attain a better knowledge of economics than economists themselves would ever claim. Moreover, expectations, even if they are based on mistaken economics, will still affect actual behaviour. As we have already suggested, they can be to some degree self-fulfilling. Nevertheless, it is essential to make a distinction between the 'market fundamentals' on the one hand, and 'confidence factors' on the other. In equilibrium, only the fundamentals matter. In real time confidence may be crucial.

An even broader definition of equilibrium would embrace institutional change. We have suggested that regimes and institutions interact with one another. In 'normal times', they may be mutually supportive and the behaviour of the authorities may be known and trusted, but in periods of transition this is not the case. A theory of institutional evolution might have its own concept of equilibrium – but that takes us well beyond the agenda of mainstream economic theory. Here also history matters: if periods of excess supply or demand can change institutions, then permanent results can be caused by temporary disturbances.

At its very high level of timeless abstraction, general equilibrium theory provides one very important conclusion about the effects of monetary policy on the economy. Assume that money consists of banknotes, having no intrinsic value at all (and not of precious metals which might have other uses). Suppose that we compare one equilibrium position with another. Preferences and production techniques are the same in both; the only difference is that in one case the quantity of money is double that in the other. The conclusion is that the price level will also be doubled, and all else will be the same; there will be no difference in any output, or relative price or real rate of interest. In this context, money is neutral, and the economic system is a dichotomy as between real and nominal magnitudes. It would seem to suggest that monetary policy is easy to understand, and fundamentally unimportant.

Yet most of what is interesting about monetary policy concerns the effects it has on the real economy when its equilibrium is disturbed. It is one thing to conduct a thought experiment in which the quantity of money is doubled; quite another to trace through the consequences of an actual monetary expansion as it might be brought about by a government or a central bank.

In the simplest theoretical accounts of monetary expansion the authorities can increase the money supply directly. They are described as printing more banknotes and scattering them from the sky. The price level does then duly rise in proportion. The adjustment mechanism is no different from that assumed in any other market; when there is an excess demand for goods, that is to say an excess supply of money, then the price level is bid up. In a slightly more realistic scenario, the government prints the extra banknotes to pay for a war. Its own demand for munitions bids up the price level in the first instance. Importantly, though, prices do not fall back to their original level when the war is over; the money issued to pay for the war remains in circulation, and the price level must rise to the point where people will hold it willingly.

A slightly more complicated model includes the market for (private sector) loans as well as the market for goods. An excess supply of money will initially reduce the rate of interest, before the prices of most goods have had time to complete their adjustment. The fall in interest rates will then itself add to the excess demand for goods and help to speed up their price increases. But the introduction of borrowing and lending into the model does not change the long-run result. Eventually, the price level must rise in proportion to the monetary injection and the interest rate will be restored to its original level. The effect of excess money creation on the rate of interest is part of the transmission mechanism, not a permanent change. The rate of interest, as the classical economists knew, depends not on monetary policy, but on 'productivity and thrift'.

In this simple model it really makes no difference whether the authorities use their monopoly power to set the quantity of money or the rate of interest. They can bring about a monetary expansion, not by fiscal policy as in wartime, but by reducing the discount rate of the central bank. They cannot alter the real rate of interest in the long term, but they can hold the discount rate down for long enough to increase the stock of money by the amount they choose. This, in theory, gives them the ability they need to control the quantity of money, and hence the level of prices.

So much for the textbook; what do central banks actually do? Central banks can certainly influence interest rates in the market, long rates as well as short. One way of doing this is by means of actual transactions in various financial markets, but this is not the only or even the main method of operation. It might often require very large transactions indeed in order to change market rates to the extent intended; central banks may not find it easy to undertake actual transactions on the scale required; it is much easier just to threaten to undertake them. What central banks mainly do is to send signals to the market; they seek to provide leadership, and markets are usually content to follow them. If their signals are not being acted on, then central banks can strengthen them, and possibly back them up with sanctions of some kind; ultimately they can ask government to give them the powers they need. Often, however, central banks do little more than lead the markets in the direction which they in any case would want to go.

Central banks can influence, or even control, interest rates from month to month, or even from year to year. The question remains as to how, in the longer term, the level of real interest rates is determined. Does it really equate the desired levels of savings and investment, as the theory would require? If the central bank were not involved, then the market would balance supply and demand, with speculators day by day examining the 'market fundamentals' to form a view of the equilibrium rate. But if the central bank really sees itself as controlling interest rates, then it will have to form its own view of where the equilibrium lies; it will have to take over the role of the market speculators, using its own expertise.

If the central bank gets it wrong then it will eventually discover its mistake by observing either persistent excess supply or excess demand in the economy as a whole – but it could take many months, or even several years, for that to happen. Alternatively, the central bank could somehow stand back and let the market find its own level, abdicating for a time its leadership role. In doing this, however, it will want to make it clear that it is still able, if need be, to take control. This is not an easy message to convey. Central banking, as actually practised, is properly described as an art, indeed as something of a mystery.

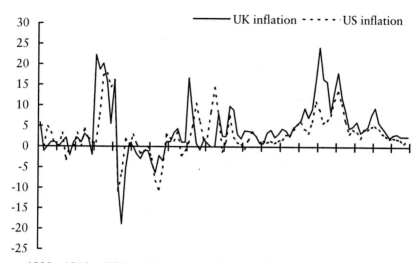

Figure 1. Inflation
Sources: 1900–1965: Mitchell (1998); 1966–1991; OECD 1992–1999:
National Institute Economic Review.

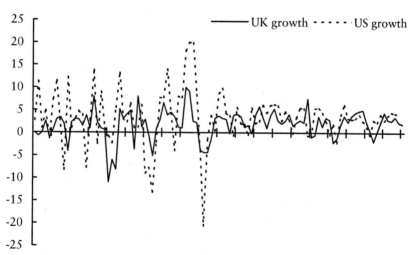

Figure 2. Output growth
Sources: 1900–1965: Maddison (1995); 1966–1999: as figure 1.

Figure 3. Unemployment
Sources: as figure 1.

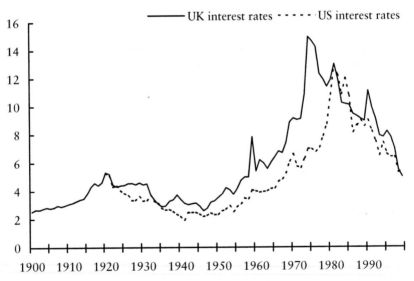

Figure 4. Interest rates (long-term government bond yields)
Sources: 1900–1989: Homer and Sylla (1991); 1990–1999: as figure 1.

1   Before the First World War (1900–1914)

The world under the gold standard

At the start of the century the currencies of almost all countries were linked to gold. In Britain, France, Germany and the United States, gold coins were in wide circulation; in other countries notes and coin were convertible into gold at a fixed price on demand. It had not always been so; the gold standard had grown and flourished in the final decades of the nineteenth century, replacing silver or inconvertible paper. Indeed, when people in later years looked back with nostalgia to the stability and prosperity of the old regime, they were remembering mainly the years from 1900 to 1914.

Between 1900 and 1914 consumer prices, as now estimated, rose by about 10 per cent in France and in Britain, by about 20 per cent in the United States and by a little over 30 per cent in Germany. Something quite close to price stability was the norm. In the preceding decade the price level was virtually unchanged in France, in Britain and in Germany, whilst it tended to fall a little in the United States. There was some movement up or down in individual years, at most about 5 per cent.

Exchange rates were fixed: there were always $4.87 to the pound, 25.4 French francs and 20.7 German marks; these were almost like 'constants of nature'. Discount rates in the money markets were quite volatile, but long-term interest rates were stable. The yield on government bonds was rising slowly, but showed little change from one year to another. In Britain, consols yielded 2.5 per cent in 1900; even as war approached in 1913, the figure was only 3.4.

Output and living standards were generally rising: gross domestic product was rising by about 1 to 2 per cent a year in France and in Britain, by about 3 per cent a year in Germany and by over 4 per cent a year in the

23

Table 1.1 *Consumer prices, 1900–1913, 1913/14 = 100*

	USA	UK	France	Germany
1900	84	91	91	77
1901	84	90	91	78
1902	88	90	91	78
1903	91	91	90	78
1904	91	92	90	79
1905	91	92	90	82
1906	91	93	91	87
1907	94	95	92	88
1908	91	93	93	88
1909	91	94	93	90
1910	94	96	94	92
1911	94	97	98	95
1912	98	100	98	100
1913	100	102	98	100

Source: Mitchell (1998).

United States. This is not to imply that the monetary regime was responsible for such economic growth, but it is understandable that, looking back from the troubled interwar years, the gold standard and prosperity should have been seen as associated with one another.

Growth was not uninterrupted. At the beginning of our period, output fell in 1901 in both France and Germany; in 1908 there was a sharp fall in America and Britain, an episode which deserves to be counted as a 'major recession' (Dow, 1998). The years of greatest prosperity were those immediately preceding the war.

It was a matter of increasing concern at the time that these fluctuations in output resulted in 'inconstancy of employment'. The data on unemployment rates are not comparable across countries, nor with rates today, but they indicate movements through the cycle well enough. In America a rate as low as 1.7 per cent is given for 1906, and as high as 8.0 per cent for 1908 – yet this was much lower than the rates quoted for most years in the 1890s. In Britain, the cyclical pattern was similar, but the trend seemed to be up rather than down. The figures for France and Germany show less volatility, with the exception of the high rate in Germany during the downturn of 1901.

Contemporary observers were uncertain what role monetary conditions played in these fluctuations in output and employment. The phenomenon

Table 1.2 *Indices of GDP, 1900–1913, 1913 = 100*

	USA	UK	France	Germany	Japan
1900	60.4	82.3	80.8	68.4	72.6
1901	67.2	82.3	79.5	66.8	75.2
1902	67.9	84.4	78.2	68.4	71.3
1903	71.2	83.5	79.9	72.2	76.3
1904	70.3	84.0	80.5	75.1	76.9
1905	75.5	86.5	81.9	76.7	75.6
1906	84.2	89.4	83.4	79.0	85.5
1907	85.5	91.1	87.0	82.5	88.2
1908	78.5	87.4	86.5	83.9	88.8
1909	88.1	89.4	90.1	85.6	88.7
1910	89.0	92.2	84.6	88.7	90.1
1911	91.9	94.9	92.9	91.7	95.0
1912	96.2	96.3	100.6	95.7	98.4
1913	100.0	100.0	100.0	100.0	100.0

Source: Maddison (1995)

of the business cycle had been quite thoroughly documented in several countries during the nineteenth century; most of the theories that are current today had already been proposed. Some emphasised real variables, such as the weather or the introduction of new technologies – electricity or motor transport for example; others thought that the causes were mainly psychological; others again saw the instability of the banking sector as an essential ingredient (Mitchell, 1913). For some, the cycle was a natural feature of a market economy, which might even contribute to its healthy development; for others it was a problem which better monetary management might be able to solve.

Noone could deny that the transition from boom to slump typically involved a 'crisis'. Often, if not invariably, this crisis was accompanied by the failure of some banks. Even today, with so much more experience to draw on, it is hard to tell whether these specifically financial problems should be seen as causes of a cycle in output and prices, or simply as amongst its common results. In any case, this association of industrial and financial crises made it inevitable that the stability of prices from year to year, as well as their trend, came to be an issue for central banks.

One can see how real and monetary events were interrelated by looking a little more closely at what happened in the years 1907 and 1908. Although they were far from typical of the period as a whole, they illustrate very well how the gold standard operated when it came under stress. The story begins with a moderate contraction of activity in the United States (Timberlake, 1978). There was also at the time some speculative excitement in the copper market. The banking system was more vulnerable than usual because of the development of so-called 'trusts', as a way of getting round the regulations placed on 'national banks'. One of these, the Knickerbocker Trust, failed in 1907 and panic soon spread across the country.

The United States at this time had no central bank, although the Treasury did sometimes seek to give some stability to the money markets. On this occasion it was the New York clearing house which did most to mitigate the effects of the crisis. Loans were made to support vulnerable banks and certificates were issued which came to be treated almost like currency. The temporary suspension of payments by some banks during the run may have helped to avert further and unnecessary failures (a view expressed in Friedman and Schwartz, 1963) – they might not have immediate access to cash on the scale demanded, but given a little time they could meet their obligations. Meanwhile the demand for liquidity was pulling gold across the Atlantic.

The crisis spread from New York to London. The gold reserves of the Bank of England were not adequate to support the American banking system. To protect them, the bank rate was raised from a moderate 4.5 per cent in August 1907 to a crisis level of 7 per cent in November. This was supposed to bring in gold both from the commercial banks in Britain and also from other central banks around the world. On this occasion, this market mechanism on its own might not have been enough; the situation required more explicit cooperation between central banks. The Banque de France and the Reichsbank both assisted the transfer of gold from their reserves, via London, to the United States (Eichengreen, 1995).

Thus the system of convertibility and fixed exchange rates weathered the storm. But the disturbance originating with the troubles of the American banks and speculation in copper shares had repercussions for output and employment, thanks to the international linkages between financial markets. In 1908 the index of commodity prices fell abruptly by 11 per cent. This illustrates one route by which interest rates affected prices under the gold standard. The prices of manufactured goods were, even then, slow to adjust, but the effect on raw materials was much quicker. An increase in the bank rate could always hit the merchants (Ford, 1989).

The Economist magazine conducted a survey, asking companies how they had been affected by the rise in interest rates. On this occasion, as on others, the response was that investment plans were little affected by the cost of finance. Nevertheless, the increase was a shock to confidence which had

a pervasive effect on trade. The bank rate, whatever else it might or might not do, sent a clear signal. It would certainly appear that the severe, if short-lived, recession of 1908 was a consequence of monetary measures taken to preserve the fixed exchange rate system when it was threatened by financial instability. It may be, however, that the fragility of the American banks, and of business confidence in Britain, was due to incipient recession in both countries, resulting from quite different developments. One must beware of telling too simple a story.

By 1909 the whole episode was nearly over. Short-term interest rates were low again in both Britain and America. Consumer prices were steady and commodity prices were resuming their rise; output was recovering in Britain, and leaping ahead in America; unemployment was already falling back; even the Knickerbocker Trust was back in business. The system had survived. There was, however, continuing anxiety in America at the weaknesses that the crisis there had exposed. The experience, as we shall see, did result in important institutional change.

The gold standard proved itself to be reasonably robust on a number of occasions. It had been severely tested by the Barings crisis at the start of the 1890s, when a British bank had been overexposed in Latin America. America and Spain had been at war. A candidate for the American presidency had campaigned on a platform of bimetallism, threatening to re-introduce silver as an alternative to gold. In the early years of the century the system survived the Boer War, despite the disruption of gold production. Russia and Japan both managed, with some difficulty, to maintain convertibility during their conflict in Manchuria. The stability of the system was not just the result of living in relatively quiet times.

One factor which favoured the survival of the gold standard in this period was the increase in the supply of gold itself. The stock of gold 'above ground' more than doubled between 1890 and 1914. This was partly the result of new discoveries, but also of new techniques of extraction. Gold was becoming an industry. Perhaps the increase in production was, in fact, a response to the rise in the price of gold in the nineteenth century as the demand for money increased. By the beginning of the twentieth century transactions were not so tightly linked to gold, as the use of cheques and bank deposits made it possible to economise on the holding of notes and coin. Popular support for silver fell away as the trend of the price level began to rise, and as the industrial stagnation of the mid- to late nineteenth century gave way to buoyant growth.

Nevertheless, there were some very eminent critics of the gold standard, even in the years of its greatest popularity and success. Irving Fisher is probably the most famous monetary economist of that era. He was not content with the performance of the world economy; he wrote about 'The problem of making purchasing power more stable'. He regarded the gold standard as no more than the result of a historical accident, but one that it would now be difficult to change. He wrote:

> Now that we have adopted a gold standard, it is almost as difficult to substitute another as it would be to establish the Russian railway gauge or the duodecimal system of numeration. (Fisher, 1911, p. 324)

He thought that a properly managed paper standard would be better, since the quantity of money could be varied so as to keep the price level stable. He recognised that this might mean that rates of exchange between currencies would need, from time to time, to be altered. He thought that more stable prices would mean less fluctuation in output.

In retrospect, perhaps, Fisher missed the main point of the gold standard. The belief in the value of gold was not just a convention or convenience like the standard layout of a typewriter keyboard; it was more a matter of faith. People trusted gold, more indeed than they trusted central banks or their own governments. They trusted gold precisely because it was not being managed. History told them that management was always associated with exploitation. That has been the judgement of some more recent economists, for example Friedman and Schwartz (1963). They wrote:

> The blind, undesigned, and quasi-automatic working of the gold standard turned out to produce a greater measure of predictability and regularity – perhaps because its discipline was impersonal and inescapable – than did deliberate and conscious control exercised within institutional arrangements intended to promote monetary stability.

Laissez faire

John Stuart Mill (1848), writing 'On the influence of government', laid down a guiding principle: 'Laisser-faire, in short, should be the general practice: every departure from it, unless required by some great good, is a certain evil.' His arguments were libertarian in character, as well as utilitarian or pragmatic. He realised that he was expressing a view shared by most of his contemporaries:

Few will dispute the more than sufficiency of these reasons, to throw, in every instance, the burthen of making out a strong case, not on those who resist, but on those who recommend, government interference.

It was the conventional wisdom of his day, and of most of the century in which he wrote. In the opening years of the twentieth century, it was still the received opinion, but it was increasingly open to challenge.

In the nineteenth century Britain led the way in introducing legislation to protect workers from ill-treatment by their employers. In Germany the state introduced compulsory insurance for workers against sickness, accident and old age. In the early twentieth century the scope of such laws was widened, and they were imitated in many other countries. Thus the role of the state was being substantially increased, and the principle of non-interference was being compromised. In political terms this is easy to explain. The industrial workers were gaining in numbers and in power. Either the state would recognise their interests or they would combine to subvert it. Even in France, where the political influence of the trades unions was weak, a Ministry of Labour was set up in 1906, and a *code de travail* enacted in 1912.

Political economists might preach the merits of free trade, but in the early years of the century their words were not being heeded. British exporters of manufactured goods faced high levels of duty when they sold in the home markets of their industrial competitors. Figures quoted for 1904 are as follows: Germany, 25 per cent; Italy, 27 per cent; France, 34 per cent; Austria, 35 per cent; the United States, a steep 73 per cent; and for Russia, an almost prohibitive 131 per cent (Clapham, 1928). The purpose of these tariffs was in part to raise revenue in an age when income taxes were regarded as especially oppressive and difficult to collect. But, of course, they were also instruments of commercial policy, intended to encourage domestic production and to win market share from competitors. In France there was the Meline tariff in 1892, in the United States the McKinley tariff of 1891. There was much pressure for Britain to follow suit.

The political influence of big business was increasing. In Germany, the Kartell movement was open and explicit in its aims. It wanted prices to be higher, and also more stable and predictable. It wanted foreign competition to be excluded. As union membership increased, collective bargaining became the norm. The increase in industrial concentration came later in France, but it was proceeding fast in Britain and especially in America. The more powerful the barons of industry became, the greater the need to strengthen the hand of central government, either to resist them or to cooperate with them. The big firms often saw themselves as 'national champions' and identified their own interests with those of the nation.

In Europe, the banking systems developed along parallel lines. The bigger banks absorbed the smaller ones, and developed close links with their corporate customers. This was especially true in Germany, but there were similar trends in Britain and France as well. In America the growth of individual banks was restricted, and perhaps for that reason, individual shareholding was prevalent. Nevertheless, the most powerful financiers in New York could bargain with European central bankers on a basis of equality. This concentration of financial power invited government intervention. The intellectual case for laissez faire depended on there being effective competition, in production, in finance and in the labour market; it was not meant to be an abdication of the right to economic management in favour of a few over-mighty subjects.

The philosophical basis of much writing in political economy at this time was utilitarianism. Economic behaviour was thought to be motivated by the maximisation of individual utility or happiness. (It was said of the economist Edgeworth that for him utility 'was as real as his morning jam'; see Hutchison, 1953). The justification for laissez faire was that it served the common interest, understood as the sum total of national utility. But, if the case was presented in this way, it could also be claimed that a different regime would increase the sum of well-being, for example (as Edgeworth himself believed) by the redistribution of income from the rich to the poor. The calculations of economists would not always lead them to recommend a regime which respected the liberty of the individual; utilitarianism could be the basis for a great expansion of the role of the state.

The leading intellectual challenge to laissez faire came from the socialists. This is how it was described in an economics textbook of the time (Nicholson, 1906):

> The form of socialism that at present is most in favour is state socialism or collectivism . . . From this standpoint the ideal aimed at may be described as the substitution of collective for private ownership and management of the means of production (land and capital), and the displacement of competition by organisation under state control. Under the present system, indeed, capital is often collected in large masses, and there is also, to a great extent, organisation of labour. But aggregation and organisation of this kind are the effects of the voluntary actions of individuals – voluntary, that is to say, in the sense that they are not due to the initiative or direc-

tion of the state. If, now, we seek to carry to its logical conclusions the proposal that the state should control and organise production, the first result is that there would be involved a similar control of distribution.

It is interesting to note how the author concedes that the concentration of power in capital and in labour is a step in the direction of a planned economy. He goes on to argue that the logical implication of state socialism is the abolition of trade, exchange and money. He identifies the use of money as one of the distinguishing features of a market economy, and he notes the antipathy to money expressed by socialist writers. 'The individualist emphasises the advantages of a money economy; the socialist, its disadvantages and abuses.' It does not seem to have occurred to anyone as yet that the control of money itself could be made into a powerful instrument of collective action.

In fact what Marx had to say about money was neither very original, nor central to his thesis. He recognised, as did many others, that there was a stage in the economic cycle when money itself could become scarce, contributing to a commercial crisis. What many of his followers in the early twentieth century believed and hoped was that the violence of the cycles would increase, and that the sufferings of the unemployed in the recessionary phase would become so severe that eventually the market system would be destroyed by its own 'contradictions'. Hearing that said, the defender of the status quo might wish that the role of the state could be extended to include some kind of counter-cyclical intervention.

It is, however, anachronistic to speak of monetary policy before the First World War. There were no policies, either of governments or of central banks, in the sense that the word came to be used later on. Noone claimed to control the national money supply, because gold could flow freely between countries; the world total of money was dependent on the supply of gold from the mines or from hoards held in the East. Policy, at best, might determine how much of the national money consisted of gold, how much of banknotes or deposits.

It was recognised, of course, that the government, with or without the help of a central bank, could cause inflation if it suspended convertibility and financed its spending by creating money. But that was regarded as an abuse of power. Responsible governments, except in the gravest of national emergencies, were urged to balance their budgets; where debts had been incurred in the past, they should be redeemed by means of a sinking fund. Money, in essence, was not the creation of the state; it had come into existence spontaneously as markets had developed. Its status as legal tender was not really necessary – at least according to the Austrian school of the time. It was best for governments to leave well alone.

The role of central banks was in fact in transition during the era of the gold standard. The Bank of England could not effectively control short-term interest rates in the market until late in the nineteenth century. Its bank rate had to follow the market, as often as lead it. The payment of dividends to its private shareholders was still an important consideration, making it reluctant to undercharge interest on its deposits. Later, it developed techniques which more or less ensured that the market had to follow changes in either direction when they were announced.

It has been said that the role of the Bank evolved naturally out of its responsibilities as a bankers' bank, supporting the system in a crisis (Goodhart, 1988). The relationship inevitably changed as a few large commercial banks came to dominate the market. It became partly a matter of personal relationships: the dropping of hints, the raising of eyebrows, what is sometimes called 'moral suasion'. The Bank became a kind of intermediary between the government and the City, conveying information and views in both directions. This is not the same as exercising monetary control.

The Banque de France was privately owned, like the Bank of England, but it was effectively under state control from its foundation by Napoleon. Its task included issuing notes and supporting the banking system in times of crisis. It had a large branch network and did much to provide a national payments system. Unlike the Bank of England it was able to hold its discount rate steady and low – almost unchanged at 3 per cent through good times and bad, thanks to the extensive gold reserves that it accumulated after it reluctantly abandoned silver. This was monetary policy of a kind, perhaps, certainly a policy designed to shelter the French economy from international storms and to foster its industrial development. It was not, however, a discretionary policy, reacting to events as they occurred.

In Germany, the Reichsbank claimed to have 'a patriotic duty to preserve the credit of the Empire'. It too was under state control although it had private shareholders. It was required to provide liquidity to the banking system as a whole, as in the crisis of 1901 when the Leipziger Bank failed; but it was not responsible for regulating individual institutions. Neither did it at all times effectively control domestic interest rates. It used its discount rate actively, its annual average level varying from a low of 3.3 per cent in 1903 to a high of 8.0 per cent in the crisis year of 1907. This seems to have been designed mainly as a means of stabilising its level of reserves in the face of international disturbances.

The United States managed without having a central bank at all. That in itself confirms that monetary policy had not yet begun at this time. However, America was beginning to feel the need for some kind of central monetary control. There was too much seasonal variation in interest rates, as money flowed west at harvest time. The US Treasury was having to exceed its proper function in the money markets, if only because the uneven flow of taxes and government spending would otherwise be disruptive. The crisis of 1907 was seen as a warning. Congress set up a commission of enquiry, which took evidence about the conduct of central banks all around the world – now a valuable source of historical information. After much deliberation, the Federal Reserve System was set up in 1913, just as the old regime of the gold standard was coming to an end.

As the First World War approached, two economists in Britain were both writing about the causes of 'industrial fluctuations' and what might be done to mitigate them. Denis Robertson (1915) was clear what the aim should be: 'maximising the community's aggregate of net satisfaction through time' – a very explicit, and for its time sophisticated, definition of welfare economics. He did not see 'monetary influences' as the main problem, although he was prepared to support Irving Fisher's proposals for currency reform. He thought that the growth of monopoly would make the economy more stable – an interesting contrast with views expressed by many at a later date. He thought that employers might be persuaded not to lay off their workers during a recession. He also supported the recommendation of a minority on the Poor Law Commission that government itself could help by bringing forward public works at times when unemployment was high.

Ralph Hawtrey (1913), by contrast, did believe that the economic cycle was mainly a monetary phenomenon. He suggested either credit controls enforced by all central banks around the world acting in concert, or else that each country should go its own way. He recognised that a cooperative solution was difficult when one of the main players, America, did not as yet have a central bank at all. He believed in monetary, but not in fiscal, policy. He did not accept that public works could raise total employment, because the extra government borrowing would raise interest rates and deter private investment – an argument which would become more familiar at a later date.

Thus the debate about the efficacy of what came to be called demand management was already getting under way before the First World War. Laissez faire was being more and more qualified as a principle of good government. It may seem to us now that the monetary regime was working rather well, but it was thought by some at the time to be capable of improvement. Hawtrey wrote:

> There is no reason why an inconvertible paper currency should not
> be successfully administered in an enlightened and advanced com-
> munity without any undesirable consequences.

Those who thought of themselves, and of their governments, as enlightened and advanced could have little respect for a monetary regime which
relied on a primitive and mystical reverence for gold.

Hegemony and cooperation

The international gold standard has been the subject of much retrospective analysis ever since its demise (Bayoumi *et al.*, 1996). How did it manage
to survive for so long? How did it preserve balance of payments equilibrium? How did each country reconcile internal and external balance? Was
there one dominant player, or did all cooperate on equal terms? Whose
interests did it serve? A variety of answers have been given to such questions, ever since the Cunliffe Committee on currency and foreign
exchanges first addressed some of them in Britain at the end of the war
(Cunliffe Committee, 1918).

The evidence given to that committee suggested that, in the first instance,
it was actual flows of gold between countries resulting from a trade imbalance which stabilised the system. The second line of defence, to which
great importance was attached, was the use of the discount rate to draw
gold to the countries in which it was becoming scarce. That was the reaction which was required from central banks, according to what were later
called the 'rules of the game'. This would help to stabilise the trade balance by depressing demand and output in the country which was
experiencing a deficit. This version of events was criticised in later studies,
which demonstrated that movements in discount rates in this period did
not in fact appear to be well correlated with changes in gold reserves
(Bloomfield, 1959).

What actually happened was more complicated. Exchange rates were not
absolutely fixed: the cost of gold transactions, and the delays involved in
actual shipments, allowed small fluctuations to occur. The dollar price of
a pound sterling could vary between \$4.895 and \$4.835, 1.2 per cent
either side of the mint parity. Then there were various 'gold devices' which
central banks could use to encourage or discourage transactions. Many central banks held some foreign exchange reserves as well as gold, and these
could be built up or run down to preserve balance in the market. Most significant of all was the possibility of stabilising action by private banks; if

there was no real danger of exchange rates changing, then it would pay banks to buy any currency that was falling close to its lower gold point. As Bloomfield in particular emphasised, there were no cases of destabilising speculation on a large scale in the years before the First World War. The system worked because it was believed that it would.

In a fixed exchange rate system, with no restrictions on capital flows, one would expect to see the same interest rate movements in all countries. There was indeed a tendency for rates to move together under the international gold standard. In 1890, at the time of the Barings crisis, interest rates generally rose to a peak, although not in France; in 1901 the increase in Germany is matched by some similar movements elsewhere; most noticeably, the 1907 crisis produced another peak in rates in almost all the markets for which we have data. One must not, however, imagine a world of perfect arbitrage. As we have seen, the French discount rate was almost unchanged throughout this period, and the French money market was relatively undeveloped and isolated from the rest of the world.

It has been suggested that the stability of the system was untested, since the business cycle was approximately in phase in the major countries most of the time. According to Mitchell's classification, Britain, France and Germany showed much the same pattern between 1900 and 1914. The same can be said of the United States, except for the years 1901 and 1902, which he considered to be years of prosperity in America and of depression in Europe. But this may have been no accident. As we saw in relation to the 1907 crisis, there was an international transmission process through capital flows and interest rate responses which must have contributed to synchronisation. Trade flows would have reinforced that: many of the fluctuations in output in Britain can be traced to variations in export demand. We can also identify some common causes, influencing output in all countries, for example changes in the prices of imported commodities.

If interest rates, output and prices all seemed to follow rather similar paths worldwide, this does not necessarily imply that they were deliberately coordinated, or that any institution was acting as a central bank for the world as a whole. We are familiar now with fixed exchange rate systems in which the central bank of one country is the leader and the rest follow; in rather different ways, this was true of America under the Bretton Woods system and also of Germany under the European Exchange Rate Mechanism. Under the international gold standard noone was in a position to set world interest rates, to determine the world money supply or the world rate of inflation; no country could pay for its imports by adding to world liquidity.

London, it is true, had a unique position as a financial centre. It was dominant in the capital markets, especially short term. It raised the capital to develop Latin America, as well as the British Empire. (France however raised the capital for development in Russia.) London was also the location of the main commodity markets, and the market for gold itself. British firms had once dominated trade in manufactures, but that was no longer the case by the beginning of the twentieth century; both Germany and America were rapidly gaining market share. But London still provided most of the shipping and the insurance. All this did give the Bank of England a special importance in the world money markets; but to call that 'hegemony' would be to overstate the case.

The prewar gold standard depended on the willingness of central banks to cooperate with one another. This is well documented by Eichengreen (1995), in the early chapters of his study called *Golden Fetters*. He has written:

> Though it is important to acknowledge that Bank of England leadership as well as international cooperation figured in the functioning of the prewar system, to concentrate on the leadership and neglect the cooperation is to fundamentally misunderstand its operation.

To control the world money market the Bank would have required, above all, immediate access to adequate reserves of gold, and that it never had. In a crisis it had to rely on other central banks, as in the events of 1907. The special position of the Bank of England was partly the consequence of the fact that America had no central bank of its own; its claim to leadership would surely have been much diminished if the international gold standard had remained in uninterrupted operation for any length of time after the Federal Reserve System had been set up.

It is true that the gold standard system developed during the nineteenth century at a time when the political power of Britain was still at its height. It has even been suggested that the system was 'a product of the British Empire' and doomed to fail as the power of Britain waned (de Cecco, 1989). This view identifies the overseas Empire, and especially India, as an essential stabiliser of the system. It is certainly true that developing countries and primary producers were especially exposed to turbulence in world markets. The gold standard was indeed asymmetric as between the countries which could lend and the countries that had to borrow. Moreover the independent Latin American countries had the possibility of devaluation, for what that was worth, whilst the monetary regime for the British Empire was decided with the interests of Britain itself as an important consideration. But none of this means that the gold standard was really made in Britain. It was genuinely international, and preserved by a consensus, not by political pressure. Countries were keen to join it because they saw it as being in their own economic interests to do so.

This is not to say that there were no countries that found membership at times a burden. There was always an asymmetry between the countries which were losing gold and those which were gaining it. The gainers did not need to reduce their interest rates to stop the flow, whilst the losers had to increase theirs, whether it suited their domestic situation or not. There could be said, in that sense, to be a deflationary bias at least latent in the system. The total quantity of money was not under the control of anyone, but a central bank that simply allowed its gold reserves to build up, without increasing the active circulation in its country, was in effect preventing some of the world money supply from affecting activity and prices. The system did not put much pressure on France, for example, to stop accumulating gold. All that it meant was that the shareholders of the Banque de France were obliged to forgo some of the return that they might have earned on their assets.

It is possible that the countries that were hoarding in this way saw themselves as collecting a war chest, or at least a reserve against political emergencies. Fortunately, however, this was a time when gold was in plentiful supply. The gradual rise in interest rates may not have had much to do with the monetary regime itself, but may rather have reflected the growing demand for loans in the private sector, both for infrastructure and for industrial investment.

It would be wrong to describe the workings of the international gold standard in political terms, as if it were the result of negotiations between nation states. It was not the product of international relations in that sense at all. There was no treaty setting it up, and no intergovernmental authority to supervise it. It was outside politics, and hence outside the rivalry of the great powers. In the early years of the century, that rivalry was intense, with governments everywhere adopting a bellicose attitude if they thought that the commercial interests of their nations were under threat. Capital flows were affected: Japan had financial links with Britain, and Russia with France, for strategic as well as business reasons. But the question of the monetary regime never seems to have been caught up in these manoeuvres. Noone seems to have contemplated, for example, forming currency blocs corresponding to military alliances. If the system had really been perceived as a British hegemony, then it is hard to see how an increasingly hostile Germany could have remained loyal to it. Fortunately for the stability of the system, gold was seen as politically neutral.

In the years leading up to the war, successive political crises and an accelerating arms race did not trouble the foreign exchanges. Noone in the markets seems to have foreseen the implications of the deepening divide in Europe. If they had known the scale of the coming conflict they could not have expected the monetary regime to survive intact. But, if they expected only increased tension and local conflicts, then they may have been right to suppose that the regime was sufficiently robust to ride out the storm. It did not really require cooperation between governments at all. It did not matter if the great powers were unfriendly. The system rested rather on firmly held prejudices and well established conventions. Traders and bankers were used to doing business with foreigners, however much their governments might distrust one another. Such attitudes could not survive a total war.

Neoclassical economics

Economics at the beginning of the century was establishing itself as an academic discipline. The American Economics Association had been founded in 1885, under the leadership of Richard Ely. Its first statement of principles had referred to the reform of society rather than the advancement of knowledge. It said for example, 'the conflict of labor and capital has brought into prominence a vast number of social problems, whose solution requires the united efforts, each in its own sphere, of the church, of the state, and of science'. This creed was regarded by many in the economics profession as too partisan and too interventionist, so in 1892 Ely had to resign as secretary of the Association. In Britain the Royal Economic Society was founded in 1890, the London School of Economics in 1895 and the Cambridge economics tripos in 1903. The British Association for the Advancement of Science had, and still has today, a section devoted to economics.

The twenty-five years prior to the First World War were a very fertile period for economic theory of the neoclassical school. This was the age of Marshall, Edgeworth, Sidgwick, Wicksteed, Bohm-Bawerk, Walras, Pareto, Fisher and Pigou. The theory of value and distribution, and of general equilibrium, as we know it now, was taking shape, built on the foundations of the classical writers. It developed, not so much in response to contemporary events, as in accordance with its own logic. It was indeed the very timelessness of the theory that alienated the historical or institutional school.

The focus of attention was not on what we would now call macroeconomics. Perhaps there was little in the events of the time to provoke interest in such matters. Monetary theory was being refined, and there was some

speculative writing about the causes of the business cycle, but this was not where reputations were being made. Indeed, some of those who were writing on these subjects were viewed with suspicion. Some of those now seen as precursors of Keynes were condemned as heretics in their day. In Britain, J.A. Hobson, who believed in 'under-consumption', lost his job as a lecturer as the price of his beliefs. His views gave support to the socialists, who taught that the market system was doomed.

It would be wrong to attribute to the neoclassical economists of this period the fully developed models of the economy produced by their disciples today. It would be anachronistic to call them 'monetarists', because they did not claim that the quantity of money could be measured or controlled. It would be misleading to suggest that they believed in rational expectations or continuous market equilibrium. These ideas have come as answers to questions which were not yet being asked.

A convenient way of illustrating the economics which was popular in the early years of the century is to quote from a textbook of the time. J.S. Nicholson, then Professor of Political Economy at the University of Edinburgh, was a prolific author, his major work being *The Principles of Political Economy*, in three volumes. The quotations which follow come from his shorter book, *The Elements of Political Economy*, intended for university students. It was first published in 1903, with a second edition in 1906.

Nicholson presents a simple version of the 'classical dichotomy', the proposition that the general level of prices has no significance for the real economy. He makes it clear that this holds true only in the long run:

> A change in the level of general prices is the same thing as a change in the measure of values, and the mere change in the measure cannot in itself affect the relative value of things. The relative values depend on real causes, e.g. the quantity of labour and capital required to produce them, etc.; and these causes are not affected by the mode of measurement.
>
> At the same time it may be indicated that during the period of transition from one level to another there is often a temporary disturbance of relative prices, and thus of values. (p. 215)

This passage is closely followed by another which states a version of Say's law, that supply creates its own demand, seen by many as refuting the under-consumptionists. Yet the statement is not so dogmatic in this text as to rule out the possibility of an excess supply of goods at least for a time. It is not impossible that the ambiguities were intended:

An increase in the supply of commodities means indeed that those who make these things desire to spend this money when obtained, either in consumable things or in so-called intermediate goods, and thus exchange becomes barter and the extension of supply involves an extension of demand . . . It is no doubt true that there may be a disorganisation of the means of exchange, as in monetary and credit crises, and thus, relatively to the means of distribution by the agencies of trade, there may seem to be a general excess of supply or a deficiency of demand. In this sense overproduction may be very real; but not in the sense that more things of *all* kinds are produced than people in general desire to consume or are able to purchase. The disorganisation of markets through overproduction of some things or through the scarcity of money (or its credit representatives that will be accepted) is of frequent occurrence in modern times; but such disorganisation does not controvert the truth of these general propositions, but rather serves to illustrate the truth by contrast. (pp. 216–17)

Like all his contemporaries, Nicholson recognised that the quantity of money could not be measured or even defined:

In the course of monetary evolution coins took the place of ingots of merchandise; banknotes were issued to represent coins and were convertible into coins on demand; convertible notes suggested inconvertible notes that represent nothing but hopes of deferred payment; banks created by their credit the bank money that is circulated by means of cheques; and the cheque is itself the development of the bill of exchange which is still of the first importance in the settlement of international transactions.

It is practically impossible to give a satisfactory definition of money that will cover all these varieties of things that do the recognised work of money. It seems then best to adopt (though with a wider significance) the phrase of the late Professor Walker and to say: Money is that money does. (pp. 252–3)

This would seem to make the quantity theory inapplicable in practice. Nevertheless, Nicholson sets it out for his students as a logical proposition, holding under some simplifying conditions:

Suppose then that a market is set up under the following conditions: No exchanges are to be made without money passing from hand to

speculative writing about the causes of the business cycle, but this was not where reputations were being made. Indeed, some of those who were writing on these subjects were viewed with suspicion. Some of those now seen as precursors of Keynes were condemned as heretics in their day. In Britain, J.A. Hobson, who believed in 'under-consumption', lost his job as a lecturer as the price of his beliefs. His views gave support to the socialists, who taught that the market system was doomed.

It would be wrong to attribute to the neoclassical economists of this period the fully developed models of the economy produced by their disciples today. It would be anachronistic to call them 'monetarists', because they did not claim that the quantity of money could be measured or controlled. It would be misleading to suggest that they believed in rational expectations or continuous market equilibrium. These ideas have come as answers to questions which were not yet being asked.

A convenient way of illustrating the economics which was popular in the early years of the century is to quote from a textbook of the time. J.S. Nicholson, then Professor of Political Economy at the University of Edinburgh, was a prolific author, his major work being *The Principles of Political Economy*, in three volumes. The quotations which follow come from his shorter book, *The Elements of Political Economy*, intended for university students. It was first published in 1903, with a second edition in 1906.

Nicholson presents a simple version of the 'classical dichotomy', the proposition that the general level of prices has no significance for the real economy. He makes it clear that this holds true only in the long run:

> A change in the level of general prices is the same thing as a change in the measure of values, and the mere change in the measure cannot in itself affect the relative value of things. The relative values depend on real causes, e.g. the quantity of labour and capital required to produce them, etc.; and these causes are not affected by the mode of measurement.
>
> At the same time it may be indicated that during the period of transition from one level to another there is often a temporary disturbance of relative prices, and thus of values. (p. 215)

This passage is closely followed by another which states a version of Say's law, that supply creates its own demand, seen by many as refuting the under-consumptionists. Yet the statement is not so dogmatic in this text as to rule out the possibility of an excess supply of goods at least for a time. It is not impossible that the ambiguities were intended:

An increase in the supply of commodities means indeed that those who make these things desire to spend this money when obtained, either in consumable things or in so-called intermediate goods, and thus exchange becomes barter and the extension of supply involves an extension of demand . . . It is no doubt true that there may be a disorganisation of the means of exchange, as in monetary and credit crises, and thus, relatively to the means of distribution by the agencies of trade, there may seem to be a general excess of supply or a deficiency of demand. In this sense overproduction may be very real; but not in the sense that more things of *all* kinds are produced than people in general desire to consume or are able to purchase. The disorganisation of markets through overproduction of some things or through the scarcity of money (or its credit representatives that will be accepted) is of frequent occurrence in modern times; but such disorganisation does not controvert the truth of these general propositions, but rather serves to illustrate the truth by contrast. (pp. 216–17)

Like all his contemporaries, Nicholson recognised that the quantity of money could not be measured or even defined:

In the course of monetary evolution coins took the place of ingots of merchandise; banknotes were issued to represent coins and were convertible into coins on demand; convertible notes suggested inconvertible notes that represent nothing but hopes of deferred payment; banks created by their credit the bank money that is circulated by means of cheques; and the cheque is itself the development of the bill of exchange which is still of the first importance in the settlement of international transactions.

It is practically impossible to give a satisfactory definition of money that will cover all these varieties of things that do the recognised work of money. It seems then best to adopt (though with a wider significance) the phrase of the late Professor Walker and to say: Money is that money does. (pp. 252–3)

This would seem to make the quantity theory inapplicable in practice. Nevertheless, Nicholson sets it out for his students as a logical proposition, holding under some simplifying conditions:

Suppose then that a market is set up under the following conditions: No exchanges are to be made without money passing from hand to

hand at every transaction, thus excluding credit and barter. The money is to be considered as of no utility except for immediate exchanges; that is, there is no hoarding or reservation of money . . . Under these simple and fixed conditions, the value of the money will vary inversely with its quantity: in other words, the level of prices will depend on the quantity of money on the one side, and on the commodities to be exchanged on the other. Thus, if the money were increased tenfold (the commodities and the exchanges remaining the same), prices would rise tenfold; and similarly for a diminution of the money and a fall in prices. (pp. 261–2)

There is no mention in the book of the business or trade cycle, at least under that name. Instead there is an interesting passage on commercial crises, which seem to be closely related phenomena:

The term *commercial crisis* is generally used in an extended sense so as to include crises that are essentially monetary in their origin and principal effects . . . Essentially, then, a commercial crisis is a breakdown of credit, though it may be due ultimately to causes affecting the material production of wealth. The causes may be divided into two groups, first, those that lead to the inflation of credit and to overproduction or speculation; and secondly, those that precipitate the collapse . . .

All these influences may be illustrated in detail from the commercial history of the nineteenth century. And it seems probable, in spite of the improvements in the methods of banking and in the organisation of industry, that these causes will continue to operate. There is always the possibility of gigantic fraud or culpable ignorance, and the increasing delicacy of the industrial organisation involves new dangers. (pp. 309–10)

The theory expounded in this text seems to fit reasonably well with the facts of economic behaviour as it was at the time. The price level did not rise or fall substantially in any of the countries that observed the gold standard. It tended to rise gradually as the stock of gold rose, just as it had tended to fall gradually when the stock was not keeping pace with economic growth. The rise in output over the decades did not seem to be directly related to the rise in prices. If the money supply, however defined, was linked to the stock of gold, then the quantity theory and the long-run neutrality of money seemed to be at least approximately confirmed.

The movements of output and prices over the cycle, on the other hand, were clearly related to one another. It would have been difficult to maintain that money was neutral in the short run. But that was not what the theory said. It was, admittedly, unclear just how the relationship came about. Perhaps, as Fisher for example had suggested, producers mistook a general increase in prices for an increase in the price of their product relative to others, and thought that their market position had improved. He thought it would help if general price indices were better publicised.

The most important point to make is that the system did seem to be stable without the help of any management by governments or central banks. After the major recession of 1908, output recovered almost immediately to levels well above those of any previous year. Unemployment fell back more slowly, but within a few years it was no higher than it had often been before. Economies seemed to be able to right themselves. Perhaps 'enlightened' management could prevent recessions altogether; but at least one could claim that management was not essential. The classical long run, as far as one could tell, seemed to take a few years to arrive, rather than decades or longer. It was quite possible to be complacent, if that was one's inclination.

There were, as we have seen, suggestions that the system was getting less stable than it had been. Even the college textbook expressed some anxiety. Some writers thought that greater industrial concentration would make prices, and hence output, more predictable. Others thought that greater rigidity of prices, and especially of wages, would make adjustment more difficult to achieve. As we have seen, however, the prices which most visibly responded to the cycle were world prices of primary commodities. The producers would benefit if those prices were stabilised, but perhaps that would make the world economy as a whole less stable. It would be difficult to intervene helpfully in a system which noone could really claim to understand.

2 The First World War and after (1914–1925)

Conflict and disorder

The First World War, like most major wars before and since, was accompanied by major price inflation. This was not the result of deliberate acts of policy by the governments of the belligerent powers, but an inevitable consequence of the intensity and duration of the fighting. It occurred all over the world, not just in those countries which were actually engaged in the war.

Between 1914 and 1918, wholesale prices rose by 128 per cent in Britain, 105 per cent in Germany, 94 per cent in the United States, and by as much as 229 per cent in France. The increases in consumer prices were less in some cases: 103 per cent in Britain for example (Mitchell, 1998, tables H1 and H2). The sterling-based commodity price index compiled by *The Economist* rose by 117 per cent over the same period. As a rough approximation, therefore, prices were doubled during the war, with some considerable variation around that magnitude of increase for different indices and in different countries.

This was possible because the gold standard was, in effect, suspended for the duration of the war. Eichengreen (1995, p.) describes the wartime monetary regime like this:

> The preferred international monetary strategy of countries engaged in hostilities was to maintain the appearance of the gold standard even when forced to suspend the reality. The gold content of coins remained officially unchanged even where gold coins could no longer be obtained. Bullion exports were still officially permitted even when government officials placed insuperable bureaucratic obstacles in

Table 2.1 *Consumer Prices, 1913–1925, 1913 = 100*

	USA	UK	France	Germany
1913	100	100	100	100
1914	101	98	102	103
1915	102	120	120	129
1916	110	143	138	169
1917	129	172	162	252
1918	152	199	210	301
1919	174	210	264	413
1920	202	244	366	1016
1921	180	222	318	1337
1922	169	180	306	15,010
1923	172	170	342	n.a.
1924	172	172	390	n.a.
1925	177	172	414	n.a.

Source: Mitchell (1998).

their way. Exchange rates were pegged at levels rendered wholly unrealistic by persistent inflation.

One mechanism by which inflation spread from the belligerents to the world at large was through the export of gold to pay for munitions or other wartime necessities. This added to the liquidity of many neutral states, but it did not reduce the liquidity of the combatants, who simply allowed credit and cash to expand out of proportion to gold reserves. Taxes were raised, often substantially, and governments did all that they could to sell more of their debt, both at home and abroad. But this still left a great gap in the public finances, which could be bridged only by increasing the supply of money. This was accepted, even by conservative opinion; winning the war had to be the top priority.

Rates of interest appear to have taken virtually no account of this doubling of prices during the war. In Britain, the bank rate was raised briefly to the dramatic level of 10 per cent at the outbreak of war, but it was back down to a more normal 5 per cent within a matter of weeks. Taking 1914 to 1918 as a whole, it averaged about 5 per cent, not much up on the preceding decade. Over the same period, the yield on consols crept up a little, but was still only about 4.5 per cent at the end of the war.

The situation was similar elsewhere. In Germany, for example, the official discount rate was pegged at 5 per cent exactly, whilst the yield on high-grade bonds was only fractionally higher. In France, where the

boom and then a slump. Prices jumped up between 1918 and 1920,
ols were removed, but then they dropped very sharply back. In
he level of the consumer price index was the same in 1925 as it
n in 1917; it had risen by as much as 50 per cent and then fallen
ain in the period between. Similarly, in America, the 1925 price level
ut the same as that of 1919. Money wages rose and fell by com-
degrees. This was, emphatically, not a period of wage or price
Indeed such wage and price volatility had not been experienced in
untry before.

domestic product in Britain fell severely from 1919 to 1921. It
vith the transition from war to peace, when there was a sharp rein the labour supply and in hours worked, as women in particular
to domestic life. It was recognised that it must take a little time
cemen to find civilian jobs. But the continuing fall in output in 1921
cession of a more standard kind (Dow, 1998, p. 146). The bank
been raised to an average of 6.7 per cent in 1920, in response to
inflation continuing after the war. It may seem a modest increase
standards, but at the time it gave a very strong signal – possibly
ng. About the same time the government set about restoring bal-
its own finances, further reducing the disposable incomes of
ers.

st rates moderated again in the deflationary years of the early
but of course they could not adjust in full – real interest rates were
h in the years of price reductions, just as they had been very low in
s of rapid price increase. The bank rate came down from an aver-
6.7 per cent in 1920 to 3.5 per cent in 1923 – not much of an
odation. The yield on consols fell from 5.3 per cent to 4.3 per cent,
no accommodation at all. The figures for comparable rates in the
States are very much the same.

e mid-1920s one important difference had emerged between the
ns of the British and American economies. In 1921 the rate of un-
ment had been about the same in both countries, 11 or 12 per cent.
, however, it was down to around 2 or 3 per cent in America, but
igh as 8 per cent in Britain. This difference was to persist for the
he decade. The British economy faced much more serious problems
ural adjustment. They were due in part to the war, but also in part
r-term decline in some traditional industries. This difference of cir-
ce meant that perceptions of market economics were different as

25, despite this stubbornly high level of unemployment, Britain went
to gold, at the prewar parity with the dollar. This was what the

discount rate had been around 3 per cent for generations, it climbed up to
5 per cent in wartime – scarcely an adequate response to what was happening to the price level. In America short-term rates reached about 6 per
cent, with longs still lower at about 4.5 per cent (Homer and Sylla, 1991).

None of these financial markets was allowed to behave normally during the war, but it is striking nevertheless to observe the absence of inflation
adjustment. Perhaps investors really did believe that currencies would return at the end of the war to a normal relationship with gold. The
implication of that would be that wartime inflation would not merely halt,
but actually be reversed by a sharp fall. Perhaps they simply chose to save
and saw no way of safeguarding the real value of their assets. To those
considerations of individual advantage must be added patriotic sentiment
and a great deal of 'moral suasion' by public opinion, and by governments
selling their debt.

War, as always, called for great sacrifices, but also brought prosperity
to many businesses. This is reflected in the indices of gross domestic product for some countries in wartime. Taking 1913 as 100, total output at
constant prices in 1918 was down to 82 in Germany and to 64 in France,
so great was the destruction of productive resources and the dislocation
of the economy. But in Britain it was up to 113, and in America to 115.
Unemployment, which had been over 3 per cent in Britain before the war,
fell below 1 per cent. In America it was still over 8 per cent in 1915, but
three years later it was down to 1.4 per cent. In both Britain and America
real wages rose significantly during the war, as the excess demand for labour built up, despite the moderation practised by most trades unions.

All things considered, monetary control was remarkably well maintained
during the war itself. The scale of the conflict vastly exceeded anything that
had been anticipated before the event. No preparations had been made,
except for the accumulation of some gold reserves, which were thought of
as 'war chests' to pay for a brief campaign. These reserves were not actually spent. Yet neither side was prevented by a lack of finance from fighting
the war to the finish. The extreme hardship and the social unrest in
Europe at the end of the war were not the consequences of financial disorder. Markets were regulated and constrained as never before, with results
that were generally found to be satisfactory. Governments could count on
the cooperation of almost all citizens, and they took the powers they
thought necessary. Despite inflation, monetary order was preserved; it could
have been a great deal worse.

The breakdown of monetary and financial control came after the war
was over. In the years that followed, it would be right to point to either
inflation or deflation as causes of hardship and social upheaval in their own

right. The aftermath of the First World War saw some of the most catastrophic monetary instability ever known. In Germany, the rate of inflation, measured by consumer prices, was about 50 per cent in 1917, and again in 1919. It accelerated to over 100 per cent in 1920, but fell back a little in the next year. Perhaps this could be understood as a continuation and intensification of the wartime experience, enhanced by the social unrest and attempted revolution. What happened next was something different: inflation disappeared off any meaningful scale – the consumer price index for 1923 is quoted as 10,324 billion – and the currency became, for most purposes, worthless.

Interest rates, inevitably, lagged far behind – discount rates were a mere 39 per cent. The consequence was a serious disruption of the economy, although not such as to prevent the reconstruction work continuing. More importantly, the collapse of the currency wiped out the value of any savings that were held in assets of fixed nominal value. It was a cruel demonstration of the consequences of a complete loss of monetary control, and it left behind a sense of injustice and insecurity, which persisted for at least a generation ahead.

The hyperinflation in Germany can be blamed on two interacting causes. One was capital flight and the fall in the exchange rate. As always, the expectation of currency depreciation was self-fulfilling when it was not countered by a credible demonstration of resolve by the monetary authorities. This was a period of exceptional turbulence in the foreign exchange markets, circumstances of which neither central banks nor private operators had previous experience. There was nothing on which confidence could be built.

The other, more fundamental, cause was the inability of the German government to finance its expenditure. Following defeat and social unrest, the economy was not in good shape to cope with the demands of reconstruction. No political group was sufficiently confident of popular support to introduce the cuts in spending or the tax increases needed to balance the budget. The international credit of Germany was far from good, for political rather than economic reasons. Moreover, as usually happens in hyperinflation, the process itself made tax collection increasingly difficult. The delay between assessment and payment could virtually cancel the tax. The other factor, much stressed at the time, was the problem of meeting the demands for reparations, especially from the French. It certainly made the political task of winning support for tax rises more difficult – and it made it possible to blame the foreigners for the monetary collapse when it came.

From the end of 1923 a new German currency was introduced, with a

Table 2.2 *Indices of GDP, 1913–1925, 1913 =*

	USA	UK	F
1913	100.0	100.0	1
1914	92.3	101.0	
1915	94.9	109.1	
1916	108.0	111.5	
1917	105.3	112.5	
1918	114.8	113.2	
1919	115.8	100.9	
1920	114.7	94.8	
1921	112.1	87.1	
1922	118.3	91.6	
1923	133.9	94.5	1
1924	138.0	98.4	1
1925	141.2	103.2	1

Source: Maddison (1995).

value pegged to the dollar, and notionally b
remarkably easy to make a fresh start. Fisc
with the overhang of debt from the war r
economy expanded rapidly from 1923 to 192
bles were over.

The postwar years were also very difficult
the trauma of hyperinflation. There were sin
ership, and vast bills for the cost of reco
international debts outstanding, which the l
able to pay out of the reparations due to t
continued into the 1920s, although at a m
actually fell back in 1921. The prewar level o
1923.

At the end of the war, the French authori
vert to gold at the prewar value of the franc.
prices to fall to about one half of the level
early 1920s it was reluctantly accepted that
It was not even possible to restore the prew
or the pound, since wartime inflation, as
France than elsewhere. When the franc was
1926, a relatively low value was chosen, givi
petitive advantage in the following years.

In both the United States and the Unite

exchange markets had been expecting for some time, and it did not seem unrealistic in view of the relative price levels in the two countries. Wholesale prices, which were generally used at the time, showed British prices perhaps some 10 per cent above those in America – not a very wide margin by the standards of the time. The consumer price indices now available show Britain in 1925 at 175 compared with 100 in 1913, and America almost exactly the same at 172. But these calculations of purchasing power parity do not tell us what exchange rate between the pound and the dollar would have been consistent with full employment in both countries (Williamson, 1983).

It is interesting to compare the cyclical downturn in 1921 with the brief recession in 1908, which happened under the old gold standard. Both count as depressions in most countries according to the tables prepared by Mitchell (1927), although he records the downturn in Germany as over in 1921, just as the recessions in Britain and America really got under way. The fall in output in Britain was steeper in 1921 than that in 1908, but the reverse was true in America. Both recessions were of relatively short duration, and followed by good recoveries.

In one respect the behaviour of the world economy in the early 1920s was clearly very different from that of the prewar period. In the 1908 recession the *Economist* index of commodity prices fell back by 11 per cent; in 1921 the same index fell by 33 per cent, and that was followed by a further fall of 11 per cent in 1922. Changes of that magnitude were not a feature of the old regime. Such instability encouraged the resolve to restore the gold standard, as close as possible to its former guise, as soon as reasonably possible.

Mobilisation and economic management

According to Lionel Robbins (1976), in his history of political economy, 'it was the outbreak of the First World War in 1914 which constituted a watershed in the history of thought regarding the management of the stability of the economic system as a whole'. This view can be supported by reference to some writing of the time. In 1915, Denis Robertson published his study of the trade cycle, completed just as war broke out. He added the following passages in his preface:

> . . . Public opinion is likely to be in some ways more receptive now than ever before to a searching analysis of industrial problems, and less suspicious of drastic change. Necessity has destroyed many

shibboleths and torn down many veils. One of the most formidable obstacles to currency reform – the alleged impossibility of persuading the well-to-do Briton to live without clinking gold sovereigns in his pockets – vanished in a week-end. The sacred machine of high finance has been shown to be at once infinitely vulnerable, and far more amenable than its heirophants supposed to conscious manipulation and control. When the safety of the nation and no longer merely the welfare of millions of its citizens is at stake, that accurate knowledge of the real state of our resources for which this essay pleads has become a plain duty instead of an unthinkable impertinence . . .

The start of war is awakening men to a sense of the economic realities which, unless the nation and civilisation perish in the interval, may form the prelude to a less thoughtless and anarchic industrial age. (pp. iii, viii–ix)

Undoubtedly, wartime experience changed quite fundamentally perceptions of what the role of the state might be in the management of the economy. The mobilisation of manpower and productive resources was without precedent. Military expenditure as a share of national product peaked at 13 per cent in America, 38 per cent in Britain and 53 per cent in Germany (Mitchell, 1998; Maddison, 1995). Leaders of industry were given the task of planning production to meet the needs of the military. Small firms were encouraged to combine so as to increase their efficiency. The extensive legal powers taken by governments were used to replace the market mechanism. Leaders of organised labour were brought into the planning procedures and expected to co-operate in full. At the same time membership of trades unions increased sharply. All this was true, not just in countries like Germany, with traditions of state intervention in the economy, but also in countries like Britain, and even America, where public opinion normally supported the doctrine of laissez faire. Skidelsky (1998) describes the revolutionary changes as follows:

The First World War disclosed for the first time the techniques by which the economic and political life of a society might be effectively directed by the state. In the war economy, resources were allocated through state purchases and central planning rather than by markets and prices. Governments mobilised resources for the war effort by a combination of higher taxes, borrowing and inflation. They used businessmen and trade-union leaders as agents of wartime coordination and wage control and deliberately strengthened their organizations.

speculative writing about the causes of the business cycle, but this was not where reputations were being made. Indeed, some of those who were writing on these subjects were viewed with suspicion. Some of those now seen as precursors of Keynes were condemned as heretics in their day. In Britain, J.A. Hobson, who believed in 'under-consumption', lost his job as a lecturer as the price of his beliefs. His views gave support to the socialists, who taught that the market system was doomed.

It would be wrong to attribute to the neoclassical economists of this period the fully developed models of the economy produced by their disciples today. It would be anachronistic to call them 'monetarists', because they did not claim that the quantity of money could be measured or controlled. It would be misleading to suggest that they believed in rational expectations or continuous market equilibrium. These ideas have come as answers to questions which were not yet being asked.

A convenient way of illustrating the economics which was popular in the early years of the century is to quote from a textbook of the time. J.S. Nicholson, then Professor of Political Economy at the University of Edinburgh, was a prolific author, his major work being *The Principles of Political Economy*, in three volumes. The quotations which follow come from his shorter book, *The Elements of Political Economy*, intended for university students. It was first published in 1903, with a second edition in 1906.

Nicholson presents a simple version of the 'classical dichotomy', the proposition that the general level of prices has no significance for the real economy. He makes it clear that this holds true only in the long run:

> A change in the level of general prices is the same thing as a change in the measure of values, and the mere change in the measure cannot in itself affect the relative value of things. The relative values depend on real causes, e.g. the quantity of labour and capital required to produce them, etc.; and these causes are not affected by the mode of measurement.
>
> At the same time it may be indicated that during the period of transition from one level to another there is often a temporary disturbance of relative prices, and thus of values. (p. 215)

This passage is closely followed by another which states a version of Say's law, that supply creates its own demand, seen by many as refuting the under-consumptionists. Yet the statement is not so dogmatic in this text as to rule out the possibility of an excess supply of goods at least for a time. It is not impossible that the ambiguities were intended:

An increase in the supply of commodities means indeed that those who make these things desire to spend this money when obtained, either in consumable things or in so-called intermediate goods, and thus exchange becomes barter and the extension of supply involves an extension of demand . . . It is no doubt true that there may be a disorganisation of the means of exchange, as in monetary and credit crises, and thus, relatively to the means of distribution by the agencies of trade, there may seem to be a general excess of supply or a deficiency of demand. In this sense overproduction may be very real; but not in the sense that more things of *all* kinds are produced than people in general desire to consume or are able to purchase. The disorganisation of markets through overproduction of some things or through the scarcity of money (or its credit representatives that will be accepted) is of frequent occurrence in modern times; but such disorganisation does not controvert the truth of these general propositions, but rather serves to illustrate the truth by contrast. (pp. 216–17)

Like all his contemporaries, Nicholson recognised that the quantity of money could not be measured or even defined:

In the course of monetary evolution coins took the place of ingots of merchandise; banknotes were issued to represent coins and were convertible into coins on demand; convertible notes suggested inconvertible notes that represent nothing but hopes of deferred payment; banks created by their credit the bank money that is circulated by means of cheques; and the cheque is itself the development of the bill of exchange which is still of the first importance in the settlement of international transactions.

It is practically impossible to give a satisfactory definition of money that will cover all these varieties of things that do the recognised work of money. It seems then best to adopt (though with a wider significance) the phrase of the late Professor Walker and to say: Money is that money does. (pp. 252–3)

This would seem to make the quantity theory inapplicable in practice. Nevertheless, Nicholson sets it out for his students as a logical proposition, holding under some simplifying conditions:

Suppose then that a market is set up under the following conditions: No exchanges are to be made without money passing from hand to

hand at every transaction, thus excluding credit and barter. The money is to be considered as of no utility except for immediate exchanges; that is, there is no hoarding or reservation of money . . . Under these simple and fixed conditions, the value of the money will vary inversely with its quantity: in other words, the level of prices will depend on the quantity of money on the one side, and on the commodities to be exchanged on the other. Thus, if the money were increased tenfold (the commodities and the exchanges remaining the same), prices would rise tenfold; and similarly for a diminution of the money and a fall in prices. (pp. 261–2)

There is no mention in the book of the business or trade cycle, at least under that name. Instead there is an interesting passage on commercial crises, which seem to be closely related phenomena:

The term *commercial crisis* is generally used in an extended sense so as to include crises that are essentially monetary in their origin and principal effects . . . Essentially, then, a commercial crisis is a breakdown of credit, though it may be due ultimately to causes affecting the material production of wealth. The causes may be divided into two groups, first, those that lead to the inflation of credit and to overproduction or speculation; and secondly, those that precipitate the collapse . . .

All these influences may be illustrated in detail from the commercial history of the nineteenth century. And it seems probable, in spite of the improvements in the methods of banking and in the organisation of industry, that these causes will continue to operate. There is always the possibility of gigantic fraud or culpable ignorance, and the increasing delicacy of the industrial organisation involves new dangers. (pp. 309–10)

The theory expounded in this text seems to fit reasonably well with the facts of economic behaviour as it was at the time. The price level did not rise or fall substantially in any of the countries that observed the gold standard. It tended to rise gradually as the stock of gold rose, just as it had tended to fall gradually when the stock was not keeping pace with economic growth. The rise in output over the decades did not seem to be directly related to the rise in prices. If the money supply, however defined, was linked to the stock of gold, then the quantity theory and the long-run neutrality of money seemed to be at least approximately confirmed.

The movements of output and prices over the cycle, on the other hand, were clearly related to one another. It would have been difficult to maintain that money was neutral in the short run. But that was not what the theory said. It was, admittedly, unclear just how the relationship came about. Perhaps, as Fisher for example had suggested, producers mistook a general increase in prices for an increase in the price of their product relative to others, and thought that their market position had improved. He thought it would help if general price indices were better publicised.

The most important point to make is that the system did seem to be stable without the help of any management by governments or central banks. After the major recession of 1908, output recovered almost immediately to levels well above those of any previous year. Unemployment fell back more slowly, but within a few years it was no higher than it had often been before. Economies seemed to be able to right themselves. Perhaps 'enlightened' management could prevent recessions altogether; but at least one could claim that management was not essential. The classical long run, as far as one could tell, seemed to take a few years to arrive, rather than decades or longer. It was quite possible to be complacent, if that was one's inclination.

There were, as we have seen, suggestions that the system was getting less stable than it had been. Even the college textbook expressed some anxiety. Some writers thought that greater industrial concentration would make prices, and hence output, more predictable. Others thought that greater rigidity of prices, and especially of wages, would make adjustment more difficult to achieve. As we have seen, however, the prices which most visibly responded to the cycle were world prices of primary commodities. The producers would benefit if those prices were stabilised, but perhaps that would make the world economy as a whole less stable. It would be difficult to intervene helpfully in a system which noone could really claim to understand.

2   The First World War and after (1914–1925)

Conflict and disorder

The First World War, like most major wars before and since, was accompanied by major price inflation. This was not the result of deliberate acts of policy by the governments of the belligerent powers, but an inevitable consequence of the intensity and duration of the fighting. It occurred all over the world, not just in those countries which were actually engaged in the war.

Between 1914 and 1918, wholesale prices rose by 128 per cent in Britain, 105 per cent in Germany, 94 per cent in the United States, and by as much as 229 per cent in France. The increases in consumer prices were less in some cases: 103 per cent in Britain for example (Mitchell, 1998, tables H1 and H2). The sterling-based commodity price index compiled by *The Economist* rose by 117 per cent over the same period. As a rough approximation, therefore, prices were doubled during the war, with some considerable variation around that magnitude of increase for different indices and in different countries.

This was possible because the gold standard was, in effect, suspended for the duration of the war. Eichengreen (1995, p.) describes the wartime monetary regime like this:

> The preferred international monetary strategy of countries engaged in hostilities was to maintain the appearance of the gold standard even when forced to suspend the reality. The gold content of coins remained officially unchanged even where gold coins could no longer be obtained. Bullion exports were still officially permitted even when government officials placed insuperable bureaucratic obstacles in

Table 2.1 *Consumer Prices, 1913–1925, 1913 = 100*

	USA	UK	France	Germany
1913	100	100	100	100
1914	101	98	102	103
1915	102	120	120	129
1916	110	143	138	169
1917	129	172	162	252
1918	152	199	210	301
1919	174	210	264	413
1920	202	244	366	1016
1921	180	222	318	1337
1922	169	180	306	15,010
1923	172	170	342	n.a.
1924	172	172	390	n.a.
1925	177	172	414	n.a.

Source: Mitchell (1998).

their way. Exchange rates were pegged at levels rendered wholly unrealistic by persistent inflation.

One mechanism by which inflation spread from the belligerents to the world at large was through the export of gold to pay for munitions or other wartime necessities. This added to the liquidity of many neutral states, but it did not reduce the liquidity of the combatants, who simply allowed credit and cash to expand out of proportion to gold reserves. Taxes were raised, often substantially, and governments did all that they could to sell more of their debt, both at home and abroad. But this still left a great gap in the public finances, which could be bridged only by increasing the supply of money. This was accepted, even by conservative opinion; winning the war had to be the top priority.

Rates of interest appear to have taken virtually no account of this doubling of prices during the war. In Britain, the bank rate was raised briefly to the dramatic level of 10 per cent at the outbreak of war, but it was back down to a more normal 5 per cent within a matter of weeks. Taking 1914 to 1918 as a whole, it averaged about 5 per cent, not much up on the preceding decade. Over the same period, the yield on consols crept up a little, but was still only about 4.5 per cent at the end of the war.

The situation was similar elsewhere. In Germany, for example, the official discount rate was pegged at 5 per cent exactly, whilst the yield on high-grade bonds was only fractionally higher. In France, where the

discount rate had been around 3 per cent for generations, it climbed up to 5 per cent in wartime – scarcely an adequate response to what was happening to the price level. In America short-term rates reached about 6 per cent, with longs still lower at about 4.5 per cent (Homer and Sylla, 1991).

None of these financial markets was allowed to behave normally during the war, but it is striking nevertheless to observe the absence of inflation adjustment. Perhaps investors really did believe that currencies would return at the end of the war to a normal relationship with gold. The implication of that would be that wartime inflation would not merely halt, but actually be reversed by a sharp fall. Perhaps they simply chose to save and saw no way of safeguarding the real value of their assets. To those considerations of individual advantage must be added patriotic sentiment and a great deal of 'moral suasion' by public opinion, and by governments selling their debt.

War, as always, called for great sacrifices, but also brought prosperity to many businesses. This is reflected in the indices of gross domestic product for some countries in wartime. Taking 1913 as 100, total output at constant prices in 1918 was down to 82 in Germany and to 64 in France, so great was the destruction of productive resources and the dislocation of the economy. But in Britain it was up to 113, and in America to 115. Unemployment, which had been over 3 per cent in Britain before the war, fell below 1 per cent. In America it was still over 8 per cent in 1915, but three years later it was down to 1.4 per cent. In both Britain and America real wages rose significantly during the war, as the excess demand for labour built up, despite the moderation practised by most trades unions.

All things considered, monetary control was remarkably well maintained during the war itself. The scale of the conflict vastly exceeded anything that had been anticipated before the event. No preparations had been made, except for the accumulation of some gold reserves, which were thought of as 'war chests' to pay for a brief campaign. These reserves were not actually spent. Yet neither side was prevented by a lack of finance from fighting the war to the finish. The extreme hardship and the social unrest in Europe at the end of the war were not the consequences of financial disorder. Markets were regulated and constrained as never before, with results that were generally found to be satisfactory. Governments could count on the cooperation of almost all citizens, and they took the powers they thought necessary. Despite inflation, monetary order was preserved; it could have been a great deal worse.

The breakdown of monetary and financial control came after the war was over. In the years that followed, it would be right to point to either inflation or deflation as causes of hardship and social upheaval in their own right. The aftermath of the First World War saw some of the most cata-strophic monetary instability ever known. In Germany, the rate of inflation, measured by consumer prices, was about 50 per cent in 1917, and again in 1919. It accelerated to over 100 per cent in 1920, but fell back a little in the next year. Perhaps this could be understood as a continuation and in-tensification of the wartime experience, enhanced by the social unrest and attempted revolution. What happened next was something different: in-flation disappeared off any meaningful scale – the consumer price index for 1923 is quoted as 10,324 billion – and the currency became, for most purposes, worthless.

Interest rates, inevitably, lagged far behind – discount rates were a mere 39 per cent. The consequence was a serious disruption of the economy, al-though not such as to prevent the reconstruction work continuing. More importantly, the collapse of the currency wiped out the value of any sav-ings that were held in assets of fixed nominal value. It was a cruel demonstration of the consequences of a complete loss of monetary control, and it left behind a sense of injustice and insecurity, which persisted for at least a generation ahead.

The hyperinflation in Germany can be blamed on two interacting causes. One was capital flight and the fall in the exchange rate. As always, the expectation of currency depreciation was self-fulfilling when it was not countered by a credible demonstration of resolve by the monetary authori-ties. This was a period of exceptional turbulence in the foreign exchange markets, circumstances of which neither central banks nor private opera-tors had previous experience. There was nothing on which confidence could be built.

The other, more fundamental, cause was the inability of the German government to finance its expenditure. Following defeat and social unrest, the economy was not in good shape to cope with the demands of recon-struction. No political group was sufficiently confident of popular support to introduce the cuts in spending or the tax increases needed to balance the budget. The international credit of Germany was far from good, for po-litical rather than economic reasons. Moreover, as usually happens in hyperinflation, the process itself made tax collection increasingly difficult. The delay between assessment and payment could virtually cancel the tax. The other factor, much stressed at the time, was the problem of meeting the demands for reparations, especially from the French. It certainly made the political task of winning support for tax rises more difficult – and it made it possible to blame the foreigners for the monetary collapse when it came.

From the end of 1923 a new German currency was introduced, with a

Table 2.2 *Indices of GDP, 1913–1925, 1913 = 100*

	USA	UK	France	Germany	Japan
1913	100.0	100.0	100.0	100.0	100.0
1914	92.3	101.0	92.9	85.2	97.0
1915	94.9	109.1	91.0	80.9	106.0
1916	108.0	111.5	95.6	81.7	122.4
1917	105.3	112.5	81.0	81.8	126.5
1918	114.8	113.2	63.9	82.0	127.8
1919	115.8	100.9	75.3	72.3	140.9
1920	114.7	94.8	87.1	78.6	132.1
1921	112.1	87.1	83.5	87.5	146.6
1922	118.3	91.6	98.5	95.2	146.2
1923	133.9	94.5	103.6	79.1	146.3
1924	138.0	98.4	116.6	92.6	150.4
1925	141.2	103.2	117.1	103.0	156.6

Source: Maddison (1995).

value pegged to the dollar, and notionally backed by land. It then proved remarkably easy to make a fresh start. Fiscal order was quickly restored, with the overhang of debt from the war now virtually wiped out. The economy expanded rapidly from 1923 to 1925 and it appeared that its troubles were over.

The postwar years were also very difficult for France, although it escaped the trauma of hyperinflation. There were similar problems of political leadership, and vast bills for the cost of reconstruction. There were huge international debts outstanding, which the French thought they should be able to pay out of the reparations due to them from Germany. Inflation continued into the 1920s, although at a manageable pace; indeed prices actually fell back in 1921. The prewar level of output was not regained until 1923.

At the end of the war, the French authorities wished and intended to revert to gold at the prewar value of the franc. To do that would have required prices to fall to about one half of the level they had then reached. By the early 1920s it was reluctantly accepted that this ambition was unrealistic. It was not even possible to restore the prewar exchange rate to the dollar or the pound, since wartime inflation, as we have seen, went further in France than elsewhere. When the franc was eventually refixed, *de facto* in 1926, a relatively low value was chosen, giving French industry some competitive advantage in the following years.

In both the United States and the United Kingdom, there was first a postwar boom and then a slump. Prices jumped up between 1918 and 1920, as controls were removed, but then they dropped very sharply back. In Britain the level of the consumer price index was the same in 1925 as it had been in 1917; it had risen by as much as 50 per cent and then fallen back again in the period between. Similarly, in America, the 1925 price level was about the same as that of 1919. Money wages rose and fell by comparable degrees. This was, emphatically, not a period of wage or price rigidity. Indeed such wage and price volatility had not been experienced in either country before.

Gross domestic product in Britain fell severely from 1919 to 1921. It began with the transition from war to peace, when there was a sharp reduction in the labour supply and in hours worked, as women in particular reverted to domestic life. It was recognised that it must take a little time for servicemen to find civilian jobs. But the continuing fall in output in 1921 was a recession of a more standard kind (Dow, 1998, p. 146). The bank rate had been raised to an average of 6.7 per cent in 1920, in response to the rapid inflation continuing after the war. It may seem a modest increase by later standards, but at the time it gave a very strong signal – possibly too strong. About the same time the government set about restoring balance to its own finances, further reducing the disposable incomes of consumers.

Interest rates moderated again in the deflationary years of the early 1920s, but of course they could not adjust in full – real interest rates were very high in the years of price reductions, just as they had been very low in the years of rapid price increase. The bank rate came down from an average of 6.7 per cent in 1920 to 3.5 per cent in 1923 – not much of an accommodation. The yield on consols fell from 5.3 per cent to 4.3 per cent, almost no accommodation at all. The figures for comparable rates in the United States are very much the same.

By the mid-1920s one important difference had emerged between the conditions of the British and American economies. In 1921 the rate of unemployment had been about the same in both countries, 11 or 12 per cent. In 1923, however, it was down to around 2 or 3 per cent in America, but still as high as 8 per cent in Britain. This difference was to persist for the rest of the decade. The British economy faced much more serious problems of structural adjustment. They were due in part to the war, but also in part to longer-term decline in some traditional industries. This difference of circumstance meant that perceptions of market economics were different as well.

In 1925, despite this stubbornly high level of unemployment, Britain went back onto gold, at the prewar parity with the dollar. This was what the exchange markets had been expecting for some time, and it did not seem unrealistic in view of the relative price levels in the two countries. Wholesale prices, which were generally used at the time, showed British prices perhaps some 10 per cent above those in America – not a very wide margin by the standards of the time. The consumer price indices now available show Britain in 1925 at 175 compared with 100 in 1913, and America almost exactly the same at 172. But these calculations of purchasing power parity do not tell us what exchange rate between the pound and the dollar would have been consistent with full employment in both countries (Williamson, 1983).

It is interesting to compare the cyclical downturn in 1921 with the brief recession in 1908, which happened under the old gold standard. Both count as depressions in most countries according to the tables prepared by Mitchell (1927), although he records the downturn in Germany as over in 1921, just as the recessions in Britain and America really got under way. The fall in output in Britain was steeper in 1921 than that in 1908, but the reverse was true in America. Both recessions were of relatively short duration, and followed by good recoveries.

In one respect the behaviour of the world economy in the early 1920s was clearly very different from that of the prewar period. In the 1908 recession the *Economist* index of commodity prices fell back by 11 per cent; in 1921 the same index fell by 33 per cent, and that was followed by a further fall of 11 per cent in 1922. Changes of that magnitude were not a feature of the old regime. Such instability encouraged the resolve to restore the gold standard, as close as possible to its former guise, as soon as reasonably possible.

Mobilisation and economic management

According to Lionel Robbins (1976), in his history of political economy, 'it was the outbreak of the First World War in 1914 which constituted a watershed in the history of thought regarding the management of the stability of the economic system as a whole'. This view can be supported by reference to some writing of the time. In 1915, Denis Robertson published his study of the trade cycle, completed just as war broke out. He added the following passages in his preface:

> . . . Public opinion is likely to be in some ways more receptive now than ever before to a searching analysis of industrial problems, and less suspicious of drastic change. Necessity has destroyed many

shibboleths and torn down many veils. One of the most formidable obstacles to currency reform – the alleged impossibility of persuading the well-to-do Briton to live without clinking gold sovereigns in his pockets – vanished in a week-end. The sacred machine of high finance has been shown to be at once infinitely vulnerable, and far more amenable than its heirophants supposed to conscious manipulation and control. When the safety of the nation and no longer merely the welfare of millions of its citizens is at stake, that accurate knowledge of the real state of our resources for which this essay pleads has become a plain duty instead of an unthinkable impertinence . . .

The start of war is awakening men to a sense of the economic realities which, unless the nation and civilisation perish in the interval, may form the prelude to a less thoughtless and anarchic industrial age. (pp. iii, viii–ix)

Undoubtedly, wartime experience changed quite fundamentally perceptions of what the role of the state might be in the management of the economy. The mobilisation of manpower and productive resources was without precedent. Military expenditure as a share of national product peaked at 13 per cent in America, 38 per cent in Britain and 53 per cent in Germany (Mitchell, 1998; Maddison, 1995). Leaders of industry were given the task of planning production to meet the needs of the military. Small firms were encouraged to combine so as to increase their efficiency. The extensive legal powers taken by governments were used to replace the market mechanism. Leaders of organised labour were brought into the planning procedures and expected to co-operate in full. At the same time membership of trades unions increased sharply. All this was true, not just in countries like Germany, with traditions of state intervention in the economy, but also in countries like Britain, and even America, where public opinion normally supported the doctrine of laissez faire. Skidelsky (1998) describes the revolutionary changes as follows:

The First World War disclosed for the first time the techniques by which the economic and political life of a society might be effectively directed by the state. In the war economy, resources were allocated through state purchases and central planning rather than by markets and prices. Governments mobilised resources for the war effort by a combination of higher taxes, borrowing and inflation. They used businessmen and trade-union leaders as agents of wartime coordination and wage control and deliberately strengthened their organizations.

These expedients were to have a profound effect on subsequent peacetime practice. The idea that a government might plan its country's economic development took root. The notion that a community's resources, human and capital, could be freely commandeered by governments replaced the earlier liberal idea that individually owned resources might be made available to government only for certain limited purposes and under strict conditions. The corporatist or 'solidaristic' model of industrial relations replaced both the individual-contract model favoured by the Right and the class-struggle model of the Left.

A keen proponent of the free market might ask if it was not possible to use its presumed efficiency as a means of allocating scarce resources even in wartime. Why were mercenary armies not recruited, as they had been often in the past? Why were firms not encouraged to compete as suppliers of uniforms, or indeed of armaments for the services? Was so much compulsion really necessary? These are fundamental questions that clearly need answering if it is true that wartime practice had such a profound effect on policy for the rest of the twentieth century. They do not seem to have been asked often, at the time or since.

Two kinds of answer might be given. The first would be that the reactions of markets were thought to be too slow or unreliable. Given the urgency of the situation, no risks could be taken. By the time that information about the government's military strategy and resource needs had been translated into relative price changes, and individuals and firms had decided how to react, the war would be over, and lost. That would have one kind of implication for peacetime practice. Perhaps the need for economic restructuring or technical progress was sometimes too urgent to be left for private initiative to meet.

The second kind of answer may be just as significant. In wartime the market solution to the problems of resource allocation would often be viewed as grossly unfair. When some citizens were dying for their country, it was not morally acceptable that others should profit from the situation. The war effort required, and also enhanced, patriotism, solidarity and community spirit. Some would say that the same virtues were needed in other contexts as well. They are not virtues that are fostered by a market economy.

Once the war was over the natural inclination was to revert to the ways of thinking which had characterised the previous regime. The war was not seen as a 'watershed' by those responsible for policy at the time. There was little reason to change the arrangements which seemed to have worked well in the past. The enlargement of government for the duration of the war was seen as just a temporary aberration, to be reversed as soon as possible. Just as normal democracy should be resumed in ancient Rome, once the need for a dictatorship was over, so the markets for economic resources and for finance should be reopened, once the need for planning had gone.

That was essentially what happened in America, and even in Britain, after the war. Elsewhere the political system was transformed, and the old regime was never re-established. The revolution in Russia is to be seen as a consequence of defeat in war. The Bolsheviks who seized power did not have a ready-made economic model for the allocation of resources. They took over, and adapted, the methods of wartime, drawing especially, it is said, on the German experience. Eventually, after much experimentation and failure, they developed a more complex and sophisticated planning system of their own.

After the war, political opinions polarised, with growing support for a radical right, as well as for a radical left. The former can be seen as a reaction to the latter. But the perceptions of political economy at both extremes tended to converge. On the right as well as the left, the experience of wartime controls was taken as a precedent, and thought to be the basis for a planned economy, involving partnerships with big business and with any sympathetic trades unionists. This was the philosophy of the fascists, who came to power in Italy in the 1920s, and whose effect on the efficiency of government was much applauded at the time.

Everywhere, the experience of prolonged fighting tended to strengthen the political awareness of the mass of the population. The 'ruling classes' could no longer be certain of setting the whole agenda of politics. In Britain, for example, a Labour government took office briefly in the 1920s. But what is most striking about that episode in the present context is how little effect it had on economic or financial policy. The representatives of the workers did not have alternative policies in these areas; they wished rather to be accepted as responsible stewards of the nation's finance. At this stage, democratic socialists did not regard fiscal or monetary policies as important to the achievement of their distinctive political objectives.

There was, nevertheless, a debate getting under way amongst economists about the nature of the postwar monetary regime. The sentiments expressed in the quotation from Denis Robertson were being echoed by others. Perhaps the right solution was not just to put the clock back. In a book written at the present time, it is particularly appropriate to include the following passage from Paul Einzig, written in 1935:

> The student of financial history in the year 2000 or thereabouts who tries to gather information about our period from books by ortho-

dox economists will learn some strange things. He will be struck by
the contrast between the divine wisdom and angelic goodness of the
rulers of the world before the war, and the amazing stupidity or dia-
bolical wickedness, or both, of those who were responsible for the
destinies of mankind after 1914 . . .

. . . Should the student of the year 2000 derive his information
from radical literature, he will get a totally different picture. He will
be told that whatever evil consequences the war had, it certainly had
one compensating advantage. It released mankind from the bond-
age of orthodox financial principles . . .

. . . If our student in the year 2000 is endowed with a certain
amount of common sense, he will doubtless realise that the truth lies
somewhere between the two extremes . . . The financial revolution
since the war was characterised by a high degree of fatality which
is not realised even by our own generation. How can we expect future generations to understand it properly? Though, perhaps, they
will be in a better position to realise it, after the violent controversies which are at present raging have died down, and when it
becomes possible to regard developments with dispassionate eyes."
(pp. 13–14)

It is not in fact so easy, even now, to regard the interwar period with such
dispassionate eyes. The debate goes on, and strong feelings are still aroused.
It is part of a bigger controversy about the role of the state and the role of
the market, about the nature of community and the freedom of the individual. That is the subject matter of much of this book. If however, we
concentrate specifically on the phase of that debate reached in the 1920s,
then one of the most significant issues concerned the rights and wrongs of
currency, and hence price, inflation. Was it essential for governments to
prevent the recurrence of inflation? Should the inflation that had already
occurred actually be reversed?

In a fully rational neoclassical economy, anticipated inflation would be
a trivial annoyance, requiring the recalculation of nominal magnitudes, and
little more than that. Interest rates on all financial instruments would adjust to compensate in full for all general price increases that were
anticipated. Only those holding a few notes and coins in their purses or wal-
lets would lose out in real terms from inflation. Anticipated inflation in this
model would have no effects on output or on employment, or on the share
of wages in national income. There would be no point in a government
encouraging inflation, as it would achieve so little by it.

The debate about the rights and wrongs of inflation must begin from the assumption that inflation is *not* anticipated, and that interest rates do not rise to compensate. That, as we have seen, was the case during and after the First World War. The massive gains and losses which resulted from inflation, and indeed from deflation as well, were essentially arbitrary in their incidence. The gainers from inflation were those who had issued debt, especially governments, but also those households or businesses who had borrowed to invest in real property. The main losers were the so-called 'rentiers', who had accumulated assets of nominal value, which they had thought would be safe.

At one time inflation was seen as a sort of 'act of God', the consequence of warfare or other natural disasters which no-one could be expected to foresee, and which noone could in fact prevent. It was not then a political issue. By the 1920s, however, attitudes were changing, and governments were being held responsible for much more than they had been in the past. It was recognised that inflation was something which governments should be able to control, so if it got out of hand, then it was the government which took the blame. Moreover, it was also being recognised that governments could, if they wished, bring about a little inflation deliberately. It could be a matter of political choice. It was something by which elections could be fought and won.

In the 1920s Keynes had not yet fully developed his distinctive theories of macroeconomics, but he had already set out his position on the political economy of monetary policy. He believed that the First World War had made monetary policy an established fact. Governments were responsible for money and prices, whether they wanted to be or not. This is how he put it in the *Tract*, published in 1923:

> The Individualistic Capitalism of today, precisely because it entrusts saving to the individual investor and production to the individual employer, *presumes* a stable measuring rod of value, and cannot be efficient – perhaps cannot survive – without one.
>
> For these grave causes we must free ourselves from the deep distrust which exists against allowing the regulation of the standard of value to be the subject of *deliberate decision*. We can no longer afford to leave it in the category of which the distinguishing characteristics are possessed in different degree by the weather, the birth rate, and the Constitution – matters which are settled by natural causes, or are the resultant of the separate action of many individuals acting independently, or require a Revolution to change them. (p. 40)

The war has effected a great change. Gold itself has become a 'man-

aged' currency. The West, as well as the East, has learnt to hoard gold, but the motives of the United States are not those of India. Now that most countries have abandoned the gold standard, the supply of the metal would, if the chief user of it restricted its holdings to its real needs, prove largely redundant. The United States has not been able to let gold fall to its 'natural ' value, because it could not face the resulting depreciation of its standard. It has been driven, therefore, to the costly policy of burying in the vaults of Washington what the miners of the Rand have laboriously brought to the surface. (p. 167)

Advocates of the ancient standard do not observe how remote it now is from the spirit and requirement of the age. A regulated non-metallic standard has slipped in unnoticed. *It exists.* (p. 173)

The quest for peace and stability

Whilst many countries were, in their domestic policies, trying to restore prewar conditions, in international relations the hope was for something new, and better. Instead of conflict between nations, there was to be peaceful cooperation; disputes would be resolved by law or by open diplomacy. The League of Nations would protect the weak, and discipline the strong. The world would be orderly, and people would feel secure.

The treaties which followed the war dismantled several old empires and created many new states. The victors took advantage of the occasion to redraw boundaries at the expense of the vanquished. Smaller-scale conflicts continued, and populations were displaced. In the first half of the 1920s international relations were continuously under strain, characterised by bitter resentments, distrust and fear.

Yet agreement on the major issues outstanding in Europe was at last achieved by diplomacy, at Locarno in 1925. It seemed that a new era of peace and cooperation could begin. A recent history describes it thus (Keylor, 1996):

> The Locarno agreement was universally hailed as an almost miraculous resolution of the conflict between the two powers on the Rhine that had unsettled Western Europe since the end of the war . . . Almost as important as the actual text of the treaty was the atmosphere of cordiality that pervaded the meetings that produced it. German, French, and British officials dined together, exchanged pleasantries during festive boat cruises on Lake Maggiore, and gave every

indication that the acrimony of the past had been buried in a universal enthusiasm for détente. (p. 117)

It was indeed a major achievement, demonstrating that the search for reconciliation was not always in vain. There was good reason for hope, at the time.

This was the context in which the attempt was made to reorder international relations after the war. At first all was chaos and confusion, but gradually new patterns emerged. As each country put its own affairs in order, each was more able and willing to help the others. With the benefit of hindsight we may now want to tell a story in which the breakdown of the new order created after the war was inevitable, but that was not how it was experienced at the time. At the time it looked as if nations were gradually becoming more willing to cooperate in financial, as in other, affairs. It looked as if the worst problems of postwar adjustment were solved, and that prosperity was gradually being restored. We now know that this was not to be a lasting success, but it was a real success all the same.

The history of international economic relations in this period is commonly told as the prelude to the tragedies of the 1930s. For example, Peter Temin (1996), in explaining the Great Depression, describes the First World War as the impulse or shock and the revived gold standard regime as the 'propagating structure'. The thesis of Eichengreen's (1995) major study is similar: the gold standard produced order before the war, but chaos after it, because the war had changed everything:

> The explanation for the contrast lies in the disintegration during and after World War I of the political and economic foundations of the prewar gold standard system. The dual bases of the prewar system were the credibility of the official commitment to gold and international cooperation . . . Both the credibility and the cooperation were eroded by the economic and political consequences of the Great War. The decline in credibility rendered cooperation all the more vital. When it was not forthcoming, economic crisis was inevitable.

A contrary view, also worth consideration, is that the shock of the war and its aftermath had been successfully absorbed by the mid-1920s and that the main causes of the Great Depression are to be found elsewhere.

The war produced not one shock wave but many. Four propositions have been distinguished as to how lasting damage was caused to the world economy (Feinstein et al., 1997, p. 14). It created structural imbalances; it destroyed British hegemony; it precluded international cooperation and it undermined the ideological basis of the monetary system. I shall consider each of these briefly in turn. Then a fifth proposition about the effect of the war will be identified – one which seems at least as plausible as the other four.

Undoubtedly the war brought about profound changes in patterns of international trade, or at least served to accelerate changes which were taking place already. The devastation of much of Europe, and the diversion of resources to the war effort, provided the opportunity for output growth in the rest of the world, especially in the United States and Japan. The United States became the main trading partner of Latin America, and Japan of nearby Asian countries. The balance of economic power, in that sense, shifted quite abruptly, albeit in the direction in which it was moving already.

The disruption to trade also encouraged protectionism. Indeed the new small national economies of Europe would have found it impossible at first to compete in a free market. They had lost their main market in the East as the Soviet Union retreated into isolation. Some countries drew the lesson from wartime shortages that political independence required economic autarky. But even the United States, the strongest and most secure economy in the world, did not favour free trade, as the Fordney–McCumber Tariff of 1922 demonstrated (Keylor, 1996, p. 94). Having gained such a commercial advantage during the war, American producers were not prepared to let it go.

Before the war the major European countries had surpluses on current account which they lent back to the rest of the world to help finance economic development. After the war they were often in deficit themselves. The American economy, which had inherited the surplus position, was it-self developing, and seeking to attract capital rather than export it. Japan also became a net importer of capital after the earthquake of 1923.

The belligerent European Allies were obliged to liquidate overseas assets and to borrow vast sums from one another or from America. The official international debts left over from the war were linked to the problem of reparations. If Germany could pay France, perhaps France could pay Britain, and then Britain could pay America. But, for many years, Germany could not hope to earn an export surplus with which to settle its obligations. The other countries did little to help the revival of German industry, because they wanted to retain their commercial advantage.

Yet, we may ask, were not all these problems solvable? Were they not, in good part, solved? The Dawes Plan to modify the reparations schedule was accepted at the London Conference of 1924. In effect this agreement enrolled private capital. Investment firms in America would finance the reparations payments, and hence support reconstruction in both Germany and France. The financiers lent to Germany, which could then pay France, and the Allies could then resume service of their debts to the United States Treasury. It was a very large scale recycling operation of just the kind needed to underpin the new structure of the world economy. Perhaps it would have been even better to write off more debts and more of the reparations, or to settle them by transferring the ownership of existing assets. But getting private capital circulating in the right direction was a great achievement all the same.

It is no doubt true that the war, or rather the cost of it, took away any claim that Britain had to hegemony in the world economy. Keynes, writing in 1923, recognised that the Bank of England on its own could not 'manage' the world monetary system; it needed to work closely with the Federal Reserve System:

> We have reached a stage in the evolution of money when a 'managed' currency is inevitable, but we have not yet reached the point when the management can be entrusted to a single authority. The best we can do, therefore, is to have *two* managed currencies, sterling and dollars, with as close a collaboration between the aims and methods of the managements. (Keynes, 1923, p. 204)

This passage from Keynes, and indeed any talk of hegemony, presumes that the system has to be run by someone; it cannot be left to run itself. Yet it was the self-regulating and automatic character of the prewar regime that was perhaps its real strength. Those who sought to rebuild the gold standard as far as possible to the original design did not do this for the benefit of Britain, nor in recognition of any unique British role. They did not want a supranational controller at all, and the old regime did not in fact require one. To talk of hegemony in this context is out of place: it is a concept belonging to power politics, not to the shared traditions of central banking and monetary control.

There was in fact some evidence of a willingness to cooperate over international finance, or at least to confer, under the auspices of the League of Nations. A report on *Currencies after the War*, compiled by the Secretariat (League of Nations, 1920), denied any intention 'to suggest the lines upon which future policies should be framed'; yet it concluded with the following words:

> It is perhaps by international cooperation alone that we can hope to stay the breakdown of currency and credit which over large

areas is rapidly developing into a disaster of the first magnitude. (p. xiii)

Conferences were held in Brussels in 1920 and in Genoa 1922. According to Eichengreen (1995, p. 153):

> Britain and other countries saw these parleys as an opportunity to erect a formal framework for international monetary cooperation. The financial difficulties of the first decade of the twentieth century had taught them that their fortunes were linked. Wartime experience provided a further illustration of the advantages of international financial cooperation. Rather than trusting that collective management of international monetary affairs could be organized on an ad hoc basis, European leaders sought to negotiate an agreement that would regularize cooperative responses to international monetary problems. Their efforts came to naught.

Certainly the more ambitious plans to establish a new world currency or an international central bank were rejected. The Americans in particular, reluctant participants in such discussions, were against the creation of more supranational authorities of any kind. But if one does not expect too much from conferences, one could respond that the efforts were not altogether in vain. It was agreed that there was a world shortage of gold. To economise on its use most countries should hold reserves of foreign currencies which were linked to gold, rather than the precious metal itself. Central banks were encouraged to coordinate their operations in exchange markets and to keep closely in touch at 'working level'. That was progress of a sort, perhaps the most that could be expected.

The fourth of the legacies of the war identified above was the way in which it changed ideas of what was normal in economic life. More was expected of governments once they had shown how their powers could be extended to meet a national emergency. This was changing quite profoundly the political context in which monetary policy was conducted in some countries. But the countries did not all think alike. In some cases the experience of war seemed only to reinforce the determination to restrict government power to the bare minimum. The effect was to add to uncertainty, and to the difficulty of reaching international agreements. There were now issues of doctrine at stake as well as narrow national self-interest.

The fifth, and perhaps most significant, change following from the war was in the behaviour of world financial markets. During and after the war there were many occasions of panic when capital fled from one country or currency – to escape depreciation, default or just high rates of taxation. The movement of funds became much more volatile. Banks and individual investors had to take a view on future exchange rate movements, something that they rarely did before the war. Vast profits and losses could be made from guessing whether the French franc, for example, would be refixed to the dollar, when and at what rate. Once the authorities had taken it on themselves to decide what an exchange rate should be, they might be expected to change their mind some time. Policy had to be conducted with the purpose of affecting market sentiment. Sometimes market expectations would be self-fulfilling; sometimes speculation would be destabilising. This would change profoundly the way in which policy was set.

However successful the restoration of the old gold standard might be, it would take some time for speculation to die down. Perhaps, had there been a decade or two of experience similar to that of the prewar period, confidence would have been fully restored. It would certainly have taken some time, even in the most favourable of circumstances. We cannot be sure. The restored system did not, in the event, survive long enough for us to know. It was indeed partly the speculation itself which destroyed it.

The interpretation of instability

In 1923, Alfred Marshall published his long-delayed volume on *Money, Credit and Commerce*. In the Preface he recalled the motto, *Natura non facit saltum* (Nature does not jump), attached to his previous work, the *Principles of Economics*, first published in 1890. He believed that economic change was gradual, and that economic science made progress slowly but continuously, refining the old doctrines, but not displacing them. He did not say whether he still believed that in 1923. Certainly his new publication did not introduce any startling innovations. It took very little notice of the momentous events of the First World War and the years that came after.

One of the few references to recent history is to be found in a footnote to the chapter on exchange markets. It reads (p. 140):

> War is apt to disturb violently the values of currencies even though they have been firmly based on gold or silver, or both. For under the stress of a great war, even a strong and resolute Government is likely to issue inconvertible paper currencies in such quantities, as to reduce its value greatly. In this connection reference may be made to a note on 'The Mark Exchange' in *A Revision of the Treaty*, by J. M. Keynes, C.B., 1922.

Keynes returned the compliment by citing Marshall's new book when he published his own *Tract on Monetary Reform*. In his exposition of the standard quantity theory of money, he explains how adjustment of the price level tends to equate the real value of the money supply to the demand to hold it. 'The matter cannot be summed up better than in the words of Dr. Marshall'. But this was just a preliminary to Keynes' severe criticism of those by whom this standard theory was misapplied. The passage, containing one of his most celebrated aphorisms, is worth quoting in full (Keynes, 1923, p. 80):

> If, after the American Civil War, the American dollar had been stabilised and defined by law at 10 per cent below its present value, it would be safe to assume that n (the quantity of money) and p (the price level) would now be just 10 per cent greater than they actually are and that the present values of k, r and k' (velocity of circulation and reserve ratios) would be entirely unaffected. But this *long run* is a misleading guide to current affairs. *In the long run* we are all dead. Economists set themselves too easy, too useless a task if in tempestuous seasons they can only tell us that when the storm is long past the ocean is flat again.

The main point that Keynes was making in the *Tract* was that nation states should take responsibility for stabilising the price level, instead of leaving this for the market, and the gold standard mechanisms, to secure. That was to suggest a radical change in policy regime, but at this stage in his writing it was not supported by any great innovation in economic theory. Keynes, in the *Tract*, did not question the existence of a classical equilibrium, merely developing the familiar distinction between the long run and the short. He just displayed some impatience with the time it might take for the classical conditions to be fulfilled. That was not surprising, given the conditions of the time in which he wrote.

Between 1920 and 1922, the price level in Britain, on the figures that Keynes was using, had fallen by a third. Over the same period, the money supply (narrowly defined) had fallen by just 14 per cent. Clearly the instability of prices could not be adequately explained by a very simple application of the quantity theory. We now know that movements in the money supply, used in this rather primitive fashion, would fail to explain movements in prices throughout the 1920s, either in Britain or in America. It was not just a matter of waiting for a more normal relationship to be reestablished: the price level remained well below prediction.

The *Tract* also includes a more thorough empirical study of the relationship between exchange rates and prices in the postwar years. Keynes shows that the Purchasing Power Parity theory, which he associates with Gustav Cassel, 'has worked passably well'. That is to say that prices in many countries, even prices of non-traded goods, had kept roughly in line with one another after conversion into a common currency. But, with exchange rates free to find their own levels in the market, causation could be running either way. If exchange rates were fixed again, it might not be so easy for relative prices to adjust. Keynes did not believe that prices, or money wages, were sufficiently flexible for the purpose; he therefore opposed the refixing of sterling at its prewar parity to the dollar.

Subsequent opinion has generally held that Keynes was right. It is interesting, therefore, to find the contrary view argued by Cassel not long after the event. He felt that British opinion made too much of the difficulties created by the exchange rates set in 1925. The degree of overvaluation was slight, and should have been easy to correct. The Swedes had coped better:

> When finally, in April 1925, Mr. Churchill, as Chancellor of the Exchequer, restored the pound sterling to its old gold parity, the necessary deflation was not yet completed, and a somewhat uncomfortable process of adjustment was forced upon the country. Strong opposition was raised to the measure, particularly on the part of British industry. This opposition was very much strengthened by the support of Mr. Keynes, who led a vigorous campaign against a return to the gold standard. No doubt the opposition stressed the difficulties of the adjustment required, sometimes with exaggeration
>
> ... These figures [for price indexes in the three countries] certainly do not give the impression that Great Britain had greater difficulties than Sweden in carrying through the necessary adjustment of her price-level. As for the rigidity of British wages, it must be remembered that the Trade Union movement in Sweden is at least as strong as that in Great Britain. (Cassel, 1936, pp. 36–7 and 38–9)

Wages in fact seem to have been remarkably 'flexible' in the 1920s. This was true in Britain and America, as elsewhere. In some industries, for example coal mining, wages were actually linked by agreement with the prices at which the product could be sold. No doubt wage cuts were always unwelcome, but that did not mean that they were not made. Consumer prices were also falling, very rapidly at times. What we call 'nominal rigidity' came later on.

The problem of the 1920s was not too little price flexibility, but too much. Around 1920, central banks decided that policy had been too slack; the time had come to impose some discipline again. The level of short-term interest rates (around 7 per cent in both Britain and America) was set very high in comparison with previous experience. Quite what this was intended to achieve is hard to say. There was fear of lapsing into hyperinflation, well enough justified, as Germany was to demonstrate. In fact what followed, in both Britain and America, was very sharp deflation, induced principally by the collapse of commodity markets.

There was nothing new in the fact that commodity prices responded to a tightening of monetary conditions. That was one way that the prewar gold standard itself had operated. The new factor in the postwar situation was profound uncertainty as to the equilibrium towards which commodity and other prices would tend. That depended on application of the quantity theory in a new setting, and interpretation of institutional changes brought about by the war. What now was the equilibrium ratio of gold reserves to the money supply? What now was the velocity of circulation? Even if those questions could be answered, there was still the problem of anticipating decisions about the conduct of policy to be taken in the future. Some people continued to expect that the prewar price level would be re-established. On that basis, the sterling commodity price index was some 150 per cent overvalued in 1920. Others expected political instability to spread round the world, undermining all attempts at monetary control. There was no floor to the market that anyone could trust.

Classical economics requires that agents can make rational calculations of the risks that they run. They may not know what the future will bring, but at least they can guess at the distribution of probabilities. Frank Knight, in his 1921 study, *Risk, Uncertainty and Profit*, drew attention to the unreality of this assumption. He wrote: 'Uncertainty must be taken in a sense radically distinct from the familiar notion of Risk, from which it has never been properly separated'. This was the basis for a new theory of the firm. Perhaps it reflected the increased uncertainty of the period in which it was written.

The implications of radical uncertainty are especially profound for macroeconomics. It will result in instability in asset markets, since there is no secure basis for stabilising speculation based on an understanding of the 'fundamentals'. There is plenty of evidence that this was happening in the 1920s. Potentially the instability that is caused by uncertainty can spread from financial markets to the level of production itself. Firms have to base production decisions on guesses as to the size of the market, at conditions of boom or slump, and what a 'normal' level of national output would be.

In the 1920s the level of output seemed to follow the sort of pattern familiar from previous cycles; there was less instability in real variables than in the price level. But in a very uncertain world, this could no longer be guaranteed.

One definition of economic equilibrium is that prior views about the distribution of expectations should not systematically prove wrong. After a period like 1914–25, it must take time for the new lessons to be learnt before that condition can be restored. Mistakes must be made, because it is only through experience that knowledge accumulates. Those mistakes cause further disruption, which further delays the return of stability. In the meantime the market system is unusually vulnerable to shocks. Taking an optimistic view, in the framework of classical theory, it might well take a decade or two before the system could settle down completely again after a disturbance on the scale of the First World War.

Such was a reasonable hope in the late 1920s. Economic behaviour had changed as a result of the war. But the main change was the consequence of increased uncertainty, especially uncertainty about the system of monetary control. If all went well, and conditions were calm, then the uncertainty would be reduced, and in consequence the changes that had occurred in behaviour would themselves eventually be reversed. It was not unreasonable to hope that something like the prewar regime could be restored. The main mechanisms, involving interest rates, capital flows and commodity prices were still in working order. They might not work well at first: central banks might accidentally send a stronger signal than they intended; private investors might need the prompting of national governments to get capital flowing in the right directions; commodity prices might over-correct. Yet, as time went by, such difficulties should be overcome. In the long run, it might indeed be true that the storm would pass and the ocean would be flat again.

The trouble was that people were not prepared to wait. There was another possibility which people found increasingly attractive. The state, which had proved its competence in war, could run the peacetime economy as well. If the price level was falling too fast, as it surely was in the early 1920s, then the government should step in to stabilise it. Quite how that was to be done was not made very clear. Perhaps it involved manipulation of interest rates, exchange rates or the reserve base of the banks. But, whether explicit or not, these ideas were in the air. That made it more difficult for the old regime to regain credibility. People had to believe that there was no alternative – when in fact an attractive alternative was being proposed. It takes faith to calm a storm.

It may be thought that the gold standard was already outdated by institutional and behavioural change when the attempt was made to revive it after the war. There is little evidence to support that view. What had happened was different from that. The gold standard had been left behind by political change. It was no longer in accord with the ambitions and responsibilities assumed by the nation state. That was the direction in which faith was being transferred. The economic instability reflected the uncertainty resulting from this process of transition. In political terms it was impossible to put the clock back; hence it ultimately proved impossible in economic terms as well.

3   Crisis and depression (1925–1939)

Failure of the market system

In the early 1930s, unemployment rose to over 15 per cent in Britain, to about 25 per cent in America, and higher still in Germany (Mitchell, 1998). This was not just a short-lived recession, or a brief set-back to economic expansion. In America, unemployment was over 15 per cent for eight years out of ten. Indices of gross national product show a collapse of output levels at the end of the 1920s, continuing for several years, and followed by a slow and hesitant recovery. The 1929 level of output was not regained until 1934 in Britain, 1936 in Germany, 1939 in France and the United States. This disastrous economic performance was accompanied by financial turmoil, severe individual hardship, political extremism and international tension. It changed fundamentally the way in which economic policy was formulated and conducted in subsequent decades.

The economic and financial disorder of the 1920s could be attributed to events external to the market economy, most notably to the war and its political consequences. No such direct explanation is readily available for the crisis and depression of the 1930s. It seemed at the time, and still seems today, to have resulted from the failures of the market system itself. The mechanism of the market appeared to be faulty. Or one might say that the 'invisible hand' that guided the economy had become weak and clumsy. One could rely on it no longer.

Even now it is neither simple nor uncontroversial to identify the causes of the Great Depression. 'The episode of monetary disorder that began in 1930 and continued through the decade . . . is almost too much for mortal mind to assimilate, let alone explain', as one historian of the period has put it (Timberlake, 1978, p. 274). At the time there were some who saw it as

Table 3.1 *Consumer prices, 1925–1939, 1929 = 100*

	USA	UK	France	Germany	Japan
1925	102	107	69	91	120
1926	103	105	90	92	110
1927	101	102	94	96	103
1928	100	101	94	99	101
1929	100	100	100	100	100
1930	97	96	101	96	86
1931	89	90	97	88	75
1932	80	88	88	78	76
1933	76	85	85	77	80
1934	78	86	82	79	82
1935	80	87	75	80	84
1936	81	90	80	81	88
1937	84	94	101	81	96
1938	82	95	115	82	110
1939	81	96	122	82	123

Source: Mitchell (1998).

the price which had to be paid for the excesses and euphoria of the 1920s, as the 'bust' which inevitably follows a boom. But, from the much longer perspective of the present day, that seems to provide only a partial explanation. At best, it may explain why output and employment turned down at the start of the 1930s; it can scarcely be adequate as an explanation of the scale or the duration of the depression which followed.

As we have seen, by the mid- to late 1920s, the economic problems of the war and its aftermath seemed largely to have been solved. The process of reconstruction was well under way. Prices were relatively stable: rising moderately in France and Germany, falling gradually in Britain and America. Output growth in Britain was adequate to keep unemployment constant, admittedly at a relatively high level. In Germany output was growing very fast, although again this was accompanied by high levels of unemployment. In America, and also in France, growth was rapid and sustained, under conditions of full employment.

These were, for many people, good years, years of prosperity and relative stability. They were not untroubled years – as the General Strike in Britain made very clear – but it was not unreasonable at the time to be optimistic about the future. The economic system seemed to have righted itself and regained its equilibrium. There were, no doubt, plenty of problems remaining under the surface as legacies of the war: this has been called 'The Era of Illusions' (Keylor, 1996). Yet the prosperity was not an

Table 3.2 *Indices of GDP, 1925–1939, 1913 = 100*

	USA	UK	France	Germany	Japan
1925	141.2	103.2	117.1	103.0	156.6
1926	150.4	99.4	120.2	98.8	158.0
1927	151.9	107.4	117.7	117.2	160.3
1928	153.6	108.7	125.9	119.9	173.4
1929	163.0	111.9	134.4	121.3	178.8
1930	148.5	111.1	130.5	113.9	165.8
1931	137.1	105.4	122.7	102.3	167.2
1932	119.0	106.2	114.7	92.8	181.2
1933	116.5	109.3	122.9	102.5	199.0
1934	125.5	116.5	121,7	110.4	199.4
1935	135.1	121.0	118.6	120.4	204.9
1936	154.3	126.5	123.1	133.0	219.8
1937	160.9	130.9	130.2	141.0	230.3
1938	154.5	132.5	129.7	151.9	245.7
1939	166.8	133.8	139.0	166.2	284.4

Source: Maddison (1995).

illusion, and the remaining problems might well have been solved.

The image of the 1920s as a period of excessive exuberance is derived most of all from the behaviour of the American stock market. The story of wild speculation and absurd credulity is well told by J.K. Galbraith (1954), who clearly enjoyed describing the spectacle of human greed rushing head-long to destruction. But one looks in vain for indicators of more general overheating or inflationary pressure. No doubt a stock market correction was necessary and inevitable, but that does not begin to provide an ad-equate explanation of the character of the next ten years.

There is another school of thought which blames the Great Depression on errors of monetary policy. During the stock market boom the monetary authorities faced something of a dilemma. They would have liked to raise interest rates to stem what they recognised as speculative excess; but they did not want to hold back the growth of industrial activity which they saw as being soundly based. They tried, without much success, to persuade the commercial banks to be more discriminating in their lending. With the rates on call money lent to speculators sometimes as high as 20 per cent, there was not much more that could be done to stem or divert the tide. A mod-est tightening of policy was one factor precipitating the market crash, but the bubble would have burst soon enough anyway.

Once the recession in America took hold short-term interest rates did fall significantly. Prime commercial paper paid around 6 per cent in 1929,

Table 3.3 *Financial indicators, USA and UK, 1925–1939*

	USA			UK		
	Share prices 1920=100[(a)]	Treasury bill rate %	Govt bond yield %	Share prices 1920=100[(b)]	Treasury bill rate %	Consols yield %
1924	113		4.1	96	3.4	4.4
1925	140		3.9	105	4.1	4.4
1926	158		3.7	111	4.5	4.6
1927	193		3.3	116	4.3	4.6
1928	251		3.3	136	4.1	4.5
1929	327		3.6	131	5.3	4.6
1930	264		3.3	105	2.5	4.5
1931	172	1.4	3.3	85	3.6	4.4
1932	87	0.9	3.7	81	1.5	3.7
1933	112	0.5	3.3	96	0.6	3.3
1934	124	0.3	3.1	120	0.8	3.1
1935	133	0.1	2.8	131	0.5	2.9
1936	187	0.1	2.7	151	0.6	2.9
1937	184	0.5	2.7	141	0.6	3.3
1938	136	0.1	2.6	116	1.3	3.4
1939	152	0.0	2.4	111	1.0	3.7

Source: Liesner (1989).
Notes: (a) 1924–35, Standard and Poor; linked to 1935–9, Dow Jones; (b) Industrial Ordinary SP Index.

little more than 2.5 per cent in 1931. But the effect on longer-term rates was, to start with, almost imperceptible. It would be difficult to argue that the depression was caused by the actions of the monetary authorities, either in encouraging excessive growth in activity in the late 1920s, or in bringing about the subsequent recession. The fact is that they did very little. It is, naturally, much easier to say that the authorities were responsible for the depression because of their *inactivity*. That is a quite different kind of explanation, and it is the one most often put forward.

The best-known exposition of this view is in the now classic study by Friedman and Schwartz (1963). They suggest that the Federal Reserve System had the power and the knowledge to prevent the reduction in the money supply which they see as the cause of the fall in output:

> The monetary collapse was not the inevitable consequence of other forces, but rather a largely independent factor which exerted a powerful influence on the course of events. The failure of the Federal Reserve System to prevent the collapse reflected not the impotence

Table 3.4 *Unemployment, 1925–1939, per cent*

	USA	UK[a]	Germany
1925	3.2	7.9	6.7
1926	1.8	8.8	18.0
1927	3.3	6.8	8.8
1928	4.2	7.5	8.4
1929	3.2	7.3	13.1/4.3
1930	8.7	11.2	15.3
1931	15.9	15.1	23.3
1932	23.6	15.6	30.1
1933	24.9	14.1	26.3
1934	21.7	11.9	14.9
1935	20.1	11.0	11.6
1936	16.9	9.4	8.3
1937	14.3	7.8	4.6
1938	19.0	9.3	2.1
1939	17.2	5.8	n.a.

Source: Mitchell (1998).
Note: (a) Great Britain only.

> of monetary policy but rather the particular policies followed by the
> monetary authorities and, in smaller degree, the particular monetary
> arrangements in existence.

This is not so much a statement about causation, as an attribution of responsibility. The authorities might have reacted differently, and better, but it remains unclear why the crisis occurred at all.

It may be wrong to focus attention too much on one country. Although it was particularly severe in America, the depression was world-wide. It is not often that the turning points of output in many countries coincide as closely as they did in 1929. When they are synchronised it is usually because of some identifiable common cause. The usual explanation is that the financial disturbances in America, both the boom and the bust, were transmitted almost instantaneously round the world through the movement of capital. Money was attracted to New York by the prospect of easy gains, thus starving other centres of liquidity or working capital. The flow of short-term capital into America was offset to a degree by a longer-term outflow, but this did not last for long. When the break in confidence came, it caused American investors to repatriate whatever funds they could secure.

It is also true that the rest of the world benefited from the prosperity of America in the 1920s as a market for exports, and the collapse of that market in the 1930s obviously contributed to recession elsewhere. But that, on its own, is not enough to explain the extent of the fall in output, particularly in Germany. No doubt the troubles of each country added to the troubles of the rest, but in few if any countries could one say that all of their troubles came from abroad. Similar crises hit different countries at the same time, perhaps by chance. The cumulative effect, particularly on business confidence, was all the greater for that.

Initially the downturn was not much different from other business cycles. There might have been a recovery in 1931 or 1932, according to the normal pattern, much studied at the time. The most recent precedent was the recession of the early 1920s which was over after a couple of years. It was reasonable to expect the same to happen again, but the outcome was very different. The crisis intensified and changed its nature. There followed several waves of bank failures, in America and also in Germany. Instead of recovering, business confidence was destroyed.

The American banks had survived the stock market crisis well, although their attempt to stabilise the market had been a conspicuous failure. They were much more at risk in the subsequent recession as their customers suffered from falling prices, output and profitability. Being small and decentralised the American banks were particularly at risk. There was, of course, nothing new about bank failures in America during a recession, as the 1907 episode illustrates very well. Indeed the Federal Reserve System had been set up in the hope of providing greater support. In the event it proved even less effective than the informal arrangements which had previously been organised by the big commercial banks themselves. Once the panic took hold there was little that could be done to arrest it.

In Europe, the weakness of the commercial banks and the risk of exchange rate changes interacted. The gold standard had been restored, but it was still fragile. If foreign deposits were withdrawn both individual banks and also the national currency could be in jeopardy. It is a situation which has become very familiar in later periods. Neither better banking supervision nor an exchange rate guarantee on its own will suffice to build confidence; both are essential. Moreover, any attempt that a central bank might make to support the banking system could be seen as potentially inflationary – therefore increasing pressure in the exchange markets.

Germany was particularly exposed to these doubts, because it had a recent history of hyperinflation, because of its remaining obligations to pay reparations and because its banks held the equity of companies hit by the recession. The event which precipitated the European banking and exchange crisis was the failure of the Austrian Kreditanstalt, in 1931, but it spread almost immediately to the German banks as well. The political risk created by the growth of extreme nationalism was an added complication, both as a reason for market suspicion and as an obstacle to inter-governmental cooperation. The rest of the story of the demise of the gold standard, including the fall of the pound, is told below (p. 81).

Before the mid-point of the decade one could begin to speak of a recovery. The *Economist* index of world commodity prices in sterling, which had fallen by 40 per cent since 1929, turned up in 1933; consumer prices in America and Britain reached their lowest levels in that same year – about the same as in 1917 and in 1916 respectively. Thus, the postwar inflation had been completely reversed in both those countries. Now that all this 'excess' had been 'purged away', it was widely believed that a 'sound' recovery of output would at last be possible.

The upturn in output began in Britain in 1932, helped by the depreciation of sterling and the stability of the banking system. In Germany it came in 1933, thanks to a number of special measures, some introduced before and some after the Nazis came to power. America had to wait for an annual increase in output until 1934, after Roosevelt had introduced the first elements of his New Deal. In France the recovery of 1933 proved to be a false dawn, and a sustained increase did not come until as late as 1936.

The figures for unemployment tell a similar story. In Britain the series peaked in 1932, although it remained at a high level throughout the decade. In Germany unemployment began to fall in 1933, and full employment was restored by 1938, thanks to the introduction of a controlled economy. In the United States the highest level was in 1933, but the fall from that level was hardly perceptible, for at least another two years. In France the turning point was delayed until the output recovery in 1936. Almost everywhere it was the same experience of hope disappointed and deferred. When some indications of economic revival did appear, they commonly coincided with rearmament and the fear of another great war.

The causes of the recovery are almost as difficult to identify as the causes of the depression itself. Was this a spontaneous move back towards a full-employment equilibrium? Was it the result of specific expansionary policy measures? Or did it require a change of regime, a whole new way of thinking about the objectives and conduct of economic policy? We can begin to answer those questions by looking at the actual movements of interest rates. These could have an essential role to play in restoring equilibrium, either as a market response or as a deliberate act of monetary policy. But it is possible to doubt whether interest rate movements on their own can do enough to correct an imbalance between supply and demand as severe as that registered in the middle years of the 1930s.

In America short-term interest rates fell, in the latter half of the decade, to below 1 per cent. They could fall no further. In this respect, as much was done as was technically possible to stimulate recovery. In fact money was pouring in from abroad, fleeing from the political crisis approaching in Europe. The narrow money supply (M1) increased by about 40 per cent in three years (Liesner, 1989). The increase in the dollar value of the gold reserves made monetary expansion possible; indeed the authorities felt obliged to increase the reserve requirements of commercial banks.

But if monetary expansion is to stimulate investment in the conventional way then it must result in a fall in long-term as well as short-term interest rates. In the early years of the 1930s the yield on US government securities actually rose, from about 3.3 per cent in 1930 to about 3.7 per cent in 1932. This was despite the recession and despite a fall in the price level. Thereafter yields did fall, but neither very far nor very fast: at the end of the decade they were around 2.3 per cent. A gap opened up between the short rates, which the authorities could control or influence directly, and the long rates, which depended rather on market expectations and beliefs. We cannot be sure what expectations of inflation were in the minds of investors, to what degree they anticipated the outbreak of another war. It is reasonable to deduce, however, that for one reason or another they did not expect the very low level of short rates to continue for very long.

In Britain the bank rate was reduced as low as 2 per cent after sterling went off gold and was decoupled from the dollar in 1931. The fall in sterling, initially by 24 per cent, was in itself expansionary, but later reversed. The banking system remained intact and the money supply increased in real terms. One could say that the stance of monetary policy was very expansionary, compared with any previous time in the century. The yield on consols was high at about 4.6 per cent when the recession began, and it remained high until after sterling broke away from the dollar. Thereafter, as in America, there was a gradual reduction, but nothing at all dramatic. In 1935 the yield dipped below 3 per cent, an average rate for the year not seen since 1909. It went no lower than that, and by the end of the 1930s it was inching up again.

One might conclude that monetary conditions played some part in the recovery in America and in Britain: at least they did not perversely hinder it. But one must add that clearly they did not do enough, whether one interprets that as a failure of the monetary authorities, or as a failure of the market system itself. The recovery was far more rapid and far more complete in Germany where the authorities broke all the rules of the orthodox policy tradition and did not rely on market forces.

Towards the end of the 1930s the economic condition of all the major democracies remained deeply worrying. In 1938 America suffered another recessionary year: unemployment rose again, as high as 19 per cent. It was not a good advertisement for free-market capitalism, even if real wages for some were rising very fast. The New Deal had not proved altogether successful, and the administration was being held responsible for its shortcomings.

In France there was a problem of a different kind. The long battle to save the gold standard had finally been lost. The fear of renewed inflation, which had inspired that fight, was proving to have been well founded. Consumer prices rose by 26 per cent in 1937, a further 14 per cent in the following year. This was not the result of overheating: output was still below its 1929 level and unemployment had scarcely begun to fall. The dangers inherent in an adjustable exchange rate and an unbalanced budget were all too real. The opposition in Europe to 'unorthodox' policies of the kind being advocated by more 'radical' economists was not based on purely imaginary dangers.

By contrast, all seemed well with the German economy, now that it had adopted economic control and regulation. Output in 1939 was up by nearly 80 per cent compared with the low point in 1932 – an average increase of about 8.5 per cent a year. Unemployment was recorded at just 0.9 per cent. Inflation was about 1 per cent a year, or less. As the prospect of war drew closer, this record was regarded not only with envy, but with apprehension as well.

New deals

The theory of government changed under the stress of events. It was simply not possible, in the twentieth century, for politicians dependent on popular support to stand aside when faced by economic breakdown and disaster. They had to be seen to take action. They could, for example, announce a programme of public works, a direct and easily understood response, creating jobs so as to fight unemployment. They had to do that, even if the received wisdom of the time was that such measures would do little, if any, good.

It became clear, however, during the 1930s, that much more than such gestures was required. A new political philosophy evolved which expected government to take responsibility for directing the economy, to an extent never before attempted in a peacetime democracy. It was a matter, as a League of Nations (1944, p. 231) report on *International Currency Experience* would later explain, of 'will, and knowledge, and power'. The will came from popular pressure; the knowledge (perhaps) came from advances in economics; the power came from new legislation and new governmental institutions. The experience of economic planning in wartime provided a precedent, but it was hoped that control could be made effective without the same interference with personal liberty.

In 1936 the Brookings Institution in Washington published a report on the economic situation. It said that the power of government was, for the first time in history, being 'extensively invoked to stem the tide of depression and to stimulate recovery'. It offered an overview of recent events worldwide, observing that:

> In every important country in the world the current depression has been marked by vigorous effort on the part of government to influence or control the course of business. In part because of a growing belief that the government may be used as a sort of balance wheel in the economic system but more, perhaps, because of sheer desperation, the powers of government have recently been utilised in ways that are wholly incompatible with the economic and political philosophy of the nineteenth century. (Moulton, 1936, p. 103)

In fact, the methods and degrees of intervention varied considerably from one country to another, according to their different traditions and experiences. Countries which had suffered from runaway inflation in the 1920s took a very different view of the responsibilities of government from those where unemployment was a chronic problem. The threat of revolution was perceived to be present everywhere, but to a much greater or lesser degree. Some countries moved to accommodate socialism, others to eradicate it. Political opinions hardened and polarised, with economic policy as one of the most contentious issues.

The free-market libertarian tradition was especially strong in the United States. After many decades of rapid growth in productivity and in prosperity, both attributed to enterprise and competition, there was a great reluctance to let government interfere at all. Yet it was in America that the depression hit hardest. The resulting dilemma is well illustrated in the views expressed by Alvin Hansen (1932), before his conversion to Keynesianism.

He did not regard the market economy as robust. It was a 'complicated system easily thrown out of equilibrium'. But he saw instability as the necessary price of progress. Stabilisation would increase the power of cartels and trades unions. Higher levels of wages would be achieved in the absence of recessions; hence, in the end, structural unemployment would rise even as cyclical unemployment was reduced. Technical advance would slow down if there were no booms to stimulate it. The trend he saw as being towards greater 'social control' and he feared that it would lead to a planned economy. He was concerned by the apparent attraction of that alternative:

> It is contended, not without a show of reason, that a planned economy is more efficient than a competitive one. While capitalism is floundering in perhaps the worst depression in history, Russian communism is working at top speed with no serious unemployment problem. (Hansen, 1932, p. 361)

Later on, after reading Keynes' *General Theory*, Hansen was to be an advocate of demand management, seeing in that the best hope of avoiding the need to follow the Russian, or indeed the German, model. By the late 1930s there was a new conventional wisdom in America. The chairman of the Federal Reserve Board could write (in a book of essays dedicated to Irving Fisher) that:

> The very continuance of our individualistic profit system in economic life and our democracy in political life depends on measures being taken to lessen the booms and depressions from which we have suffered in the past. (Eccles, 1937)

The measures which comprised Roosevelt's New Deal covered far more than mere demand management. He offered relief, recovery and reform. He introduced social security in America, imitating schemes which had operated in Europe since before the war. He strengthened the position of trades unions, actively encouraging the growth of real wages. Some of his most radical legislation was overturned by the Supreme Court, indicating the limitations on the powers of the executive under the American constitution. He spent a great deal of money on public works, for example on the Grand Coulee dam, and he established the Reconstruction Finance Corporation to lend aggressively in a way that the commercial banks would, or could, not.

The standing of the Federal Reserve System had been much diminished by its failure to prevent or correct the depression, and even more by its failure in its more basic task of supporting the banking system. Much of the New Deal passed it by. In the late 1930s it lost its pre-eminence with respect to economic, and even monetary, affairs. The balance of power within the System had shifted away from the New York Fed., which was close to the markets, towards the headquarters in Washington, under the eye of Congress. The most important changes in legislation, for example the Banking Act of 1935, and the introduction of deposit insurance, were the initiatives of politicians, not of bankers. Monetary policy, when it was not just a matter of boring technical detail, was more and more coming under political control.

There were divergent views as to how monetary policy should be formulated. The old idea that the Federal Reserve System should respond to the needs of trade was discredited, and the constraints of convertibility had been removed. Instead, some argued that policy should aim at price stability, others for targeting employment or national income. Equally there were those who believed that the best objective was to stabilise the growth of the money supply.

Another contribution to the Irving Fisher *Festschrift* argued that the financial system may be dynamically unstable, so that any small perturbation can readily become explosive. The author, J.W. Angell, therefore favoured what might now be called 'fine tuning':

> Monetary policy should be planned and operated not only to deal with acute booms and collapses after they have occurred, but also to counteract as far as possible the less extreme fluctuation in which booms and collapse presumably originate, while at the same time securing continuously a reasonably full utilisation of the existing factors and techniques of production. (Angell, 1937, p. 53)

This may sound like a Keynesian prescription, but it is in fact an anticipation of Friedmanian monetarism. Angell goes on to argue for control of the money supply, even suggesting, in a footnote, that this would best be secured directly by setting a 100 per cent reserve requirement. Political instincts in America favoured rules as against discretion, even in the era of the New Deal.

The debate in Britain was on rather different lines. Keynes, as we have seen (pp. 12–13 above), believed that control of aggregate national income by means of monetary and fiscal policies was consistent with a free-market system – indeed, necessary for its continued viability; detailed planning was not required. This view did not go unchallenged. G.D.H. Cole (1935, p. 115), for example, maintained that expansionary monetary policy on its own would not work. It would result in inflation as the monopolists took advantage of the extra demand to increase their prices and their profits. There had to be a more comprehensive system of economic planning. Paul Einzig expressed a similar view:

> It is essential that the authorities who control the creation of purchasing power should also control production and distribution. This

is the point that is usually overlooked by would-be currency reformers. They think that by simply jiggling with currency all the world's troubles can be brought to an end, without having to change for that purpose the fundamental economic structure of the community. (Einzig, 1935, p. 90)

That reads like an attack on Keynes. Yet, on some occasions, Keynes' own position was not entirely clear, especially on the question of trade policy. He wrote about the state 'taking an ever greater responsibility for directly organising investment'. This could just mean a few public works to mitigate a recession, or it could mean a programme of road-building like that being undertaken in Germany. It could even mean the state taking responsibility for investment by industry. Some of his allies were rather more explicit. Kaldor (1938), for example, said that policy must have multiple objectives in order to maintain full employment; and multiple objectives require multiple instruments. It was never quite clear where demand management ended and economic planning began.

The ambitions of the Keynesians ran well ahead of their real influence in Britain in the 1930s. Policy in practice was more often driven by events than by ideas. The currency was driven off gold by market pressure, not set free by deliberate choice. Thereafter interest rates were reduced cautiously, as the exchange markets permitted. Fiscal policy remained cautious too, until the priority of rearmament dictated otherwise. The Treasury remained unconvinced that it held the key to economic recovery. The most significant change of economic strategy was the introduction of discrimination in trade policy. There was no New Deal in Britain. There was however a gradual shift of opinion in favour of policy activism which led to the formation of a new consensus during and after the Second World War.

The reaction to the depression in France was to build a wall round the economy, adding quotas to tariffs, and subsidising unprofitable production. As the franc remained on the gold standard long after sterling and even the dollar had left it, prices of French products became increasingly out of line with those of their competitors. Yet the French remained strongly antagonistic to devaluation, preferring austerity and self-reliance.

The political situation became unstable, with risks to democracy from the extreme right as well as the extreme left. In 1936 the Popular Front formed a government supported by the communists as well as the Democratic Socialists. The measures that it took were certainly unorthodox, but not of the kind usually associated with Keynesianism. Wages were increased to stimulate consumer demand and hours were cut to reduce the excess supply of labour. Political as well as economic fears resulted in a flight of

private capital. At first the pressure to devalue the franc was resisted, but ultimately it proved unavoidable. The sequel, as we have seen, was inflation rather than real growth. After the dissolution of the Popular Front, a more conservative regime was proposed, but it hardly had time to influence the French economy before the outbreak of war.

The growing popularity of the Nazis in Germany in the early 1930s is often attributed to the rise in unemployment. According to Eric Hobsbawm (1995, p. 130), 'it was patently the Great Slump which turned Hitler from a phenomenon of the political fringe into the potential, and eventually the actual, master of the country'. A full explanation would have to account of the political as well as the economic disasters which Germany had endured, but clearly the prospect of an alternative to the free market was part of the attraction of the extreme right in the 1930s. The interwar period as a whole shows that economic depression is neither necessary nor sufficient as a cause of dictatorship, but it weakened the foundations of democracy everywhere, and in Germany they gave way.

Germany was another country reluctant to leave the gold standard. The convertibility of the Reichsmark was suspended in 1931 as a result of the banking crisis and capital flight. As unemployment rose the removal of an external constraint might have been the signal for expansionary measures, but initially nothing of the kind was attempted. On the contrary the Emergency Decree of Bruning increased taxes and cut wages. With tax revenues depressed by the recession the German government was, quite simply, running out of money. It needed to borrow but could not do so, either at home or abroad. Its powers had been limited by law and by treaty, following the experience of hyperinflation and the lengthy negotiations over reparations. Even so, at the very bottom of the slump, some relief measures were introduced before the Nazis came to power.

Under the Four-Year Plan, the reduction in unemployment was given top priority (Guillebaud, 1939; Borschart, 1991). A method was found for the central bank to finance public spending. Capital work programmes were introduced on a large scale, notably house building and the construction of motorways. Women were encouraged to withdraw from the labour force and hours of work were cut. Employers were persuaded to recruit more labour than they saw need for by means of political pressure. Output rose and unemployment fell, but the problem of the balance of payments remained. In 1934, devaluation was an option, but it was rejected. Instead exchange control was tightened, and import controls were introduced. The plan was, for strategic as well as economic reasons, to aim at the maximum degree of self-sufficiency. From 1935 onwards, a major stimulus to activity came from rearmament.

In such a tightly controlled economy, monetary policy was of no great significance. Inflation was suppressed by wage and price controls. The banks acquired a growing mountain of public debt, but this presented no threat to monetary stability as long as they had no real choice in the matter. Similarly, individuals accumulated bank deposits, but had no real opportunity to spend them.

A professor of political economy from Berlin was another of the contributors to the Irving Fisher *Festschrift* of 1937. His paper was entitled, 'Germany's present currency system' (Schumacher, 1937). He described how the move from the gold standard to a managed currency had been forced on Germany by the fear of inflation and the shortage of reserves. 'No country takes this course voluntarily', he maintained. When the adjustment mechanism breaks down, however, it becomes the duty of the state to 'regulate the regulative system', that is to provide, in place of the currency flow, its own means of achieving international monetary equilibrium.

Having introduced exchange control to protect its reserves, it was necessary for the state to determine the priority in using scarce receipts of foreign exchange. The result was 'the great compulsory organisation which Germany was compelled to build up in order to preserve her existence'. He thought that other countries would come to view all this 'with sympathetic admiration'! He recognised that the system of controls was like a wartime economy, although he said that it was 'more systematic and better organised'. He looked forward to the day when it would be possible to return to some form of gold standard and do away with the restrictive measures that were required by the current emergency.

Events in Japan followed a broadly similar pattern. The Irving Fisher volume also includes a contribution from an ex-governor of the Bank of Japan (Fukai, 1937). He tells how the return to gold after the war was delayed until 1930, first by the earthquake in 1923 and then by the financial panic of 1927. Japan faced the downturn in the American economy with an overvalued exchange rate. The linkage to gold lasted little more than a year.

In 1931 the Bank of Japan wanted to stimulate economic recovery. But 'the spirit of the people was at a low ebb', and the action was therefore ineffective. The ex-governor reflected: 'the experience has shown that it is after all well-nigh impossible to control the trend of economic forces by monetary means'. Instead the government began to borrow heavily from the Bank of Japan, primarily to finance the war in Manchuria, but also to stimulate the economy. In a controlled economy it was possible, but perhaps superfluous, to bring about a substantial fall in the rate of interest.

All these national variations have in common some increase in the power of the state to regulate or control the economy. This was in accord with the mood of the times. The successive chapters which describe the 1930s in the history of the 'short twentieth century' by Hobsbawm (1995), are called 'Into the economic abyss' and 'The fall of liberalism'. He offers four conditions which are needed to make representative democracy viable, one of which is sufficient economic wealth and prosperity. Elected politicians are good at sharing out dividends amongst their supporters, not so good at demanding sacrifices. But the problems of liberalism in the 1930s were more fundamental than that. It looked as if liberalism itself, that is to say the philosophy of limited government, was to blame for the poverty and hardship which people were expected to endure. The countries that had abandoned liberalism were prospering, whilst those that had retained it were not. It looked as if the nineteenth-century model of government was outdated, incompatible with a modern economy. For those who valued freedom and democracy, the hope was still that governments would need only limited or temporary powers to make the market work properly. That issue was still in doubt when the Second World War began.

Striking off the fetters

The international gold standard, as revived in the 1930s, was not quite the same as the prewar institution. Gold did not circulate freely as a means of payment; instead it was mainly held in the reserves of central banks. The quantity of gold had not increased in line with inflation and the real growth of the world economy, and it was feared that there would be a world shortage of the metal. But the replacement of gold coins with paper notes should have been sufficient to remove the scarcity. The difficulty was, rather, that the gold was unevenly distributed, with too high a proportion in America and in France.

Most countries did not hold much gold in their reserves, making do with foreign currency deposits instead. The theory was that sterling or dollar deposits were 'as good as gold', with the added advantage of paying interest to the holders. There was however a potential instability in the 'gold exchange' system, since countries with, for example, sterling deposits in their reserves would want to convert them into gold if the exchange rate were ever in doubt. It also implied that the total of international reserves available to the system depended on the balance of payments of the countries whose currencies were commonly held by foreign central banks.

Peter Fearon (1979) includes in his list of causes of the Great Slump what he calls 'ambivalence' over the gold standard. He mentions the growing belief that the gold exchange standard was just a temporary expedient, to be replaced by a true gold standard at the first opportunity. This encouraged some countries to accumulate gold in anticipation. More fundamentally there was uncertainty as to how far it was an automatic, rather than a managed, system. Increasingly central banks took a view as to how they would respond to balance of payments surpluses and deficits, looking at the condition of their domestic economies as well as the needs of international equilibrium. It was not easy to predict how they would behave.

Adjustment was no more symmetrical than it had been prewar. Countries with balance of payments deficits, or with persistent weakness in their currencies in the market, had little choice but to take action to contract domestic demand. Surplus countries, or those with currencies that were strong, did not face the same pressure to take action to increase demand. They might prefer to accumulate reserves, whilst preventing an increase in their domestic liquidity by selling bonds to 'sterilise' or 'mop up' the inflow of capital from abroad.

Kindleberger blames the instability of the interwar monetary system, and indeed the Great Depression, on a lack of leadership. What was needed was one country that could help the rest out of their difficulties by providing a reliable market for their goods, and access to capital whenever they needed it. The system was not automatic, neither was it symmetrical; what it needed was a public-spirited surplus country to take responsibility for the rest. He later wrote:

> The world economic system was unstable unless some country stabilized it, as Britain had done in the nineteenth century and up to 1913. In 1929, the British couldn't, and the United States wouldn't. When every country turned to protect its national interest, the world public interest went down the drain, and with it the private interests of all. (Kindleberger, 1973, p. 292)

No doubt, in writing this, he had in mind the role to be played by America after the Second World War. But it remains possible that a more automatic system could have worked in the interwar years, as arguably it did before the First World War.

The most serious weakness of the revived system was the instability of private capital. The experience of wartime and postwar inflation had changed the psychology of markets. The confidence which sustained the prewar system would take many years to rebuild. Without that confidence no conceivable quantity of reserves would suffice.

Barry Eichengreen makes a connection between the erosion of confidence and the need for international cooperation:

A shadow was cast over the credibility of the commitment to gold . . .The markets, rather than minimizing the need for government intervention, subjected the authorities' stated commitment to early and repeated test. Those tests underscored the need for international cooperation. (Eichengreen, 1995, pp. 391–2)

The need for cooperation was also clear to contemporary commentators and policymakers. The Bank for International Settlements was set up to facilitate payments and to encourage the exchange of ideas between central banks. Keynes, in his *Treatise on Money*, originally published in 1934, visualised a much more active role for the institution. At this stage he was a supporter of the gold standard, but he had not abandoned his idea for a managed system. He looked to the creation of a supranational authority which would set world interest rates and thus stabilise the price of a commodity basket. He recognised that the BIS had a long way to go before it could fulfil that ideal. But he wrote, 'we may hope, nevertheless, that we have there the nucleus out of which a supranational bank for monetary management may be eventually evolved' (Keynes, 1934, p. 363).

As the world recession took hold, events actually moved rapidly in the opposite direction. The willingness to adjust domestic monetary policy in the interests of international harmony was weak even in the 1920s; as the political pressure to do something about unemployment built up, it became more and more difficult to preserve even the appearance of international cooperation. The purpose of tariffs might be presented as the raising of revenue, but popular support for them came from those who saw the need to protect markets, and more especially to protect jobs, if need be at the expense of other countries. Similar arguments were behind calls for exchange controls and currency devaluation. Once the markets understood that the gold standard was unpopular, they quite rightly questioned its durability. Once market confidence was lost the system was quickly destroyed.

The crucial event was the fall of the pound in 1931. Once the pressure built up following the crisis in Germany, it would have taken a vast commitment of support from other countries, chiefly America and France, to save sterling from the run. The pound was vulnerable because of doubts about the repayment of loans made to Germany to prop up the Reichsmark. But, more fundamentally, its weakness reflected the state of the British economy, with high unemployment and a balance of payments deficit. Moreover the countries which used sterling for their reserves were also in difficulties because of the depressed state of commodity markets. There was also great uncertainty, not to say suspicion, about the intentions of the Labour government and the union movement on which it depended for support.

Attention focused on the British fiscal deficit. Unemployment insurance benefits were proving very expensive, a complication which would not have arisen in a comparable situation in the nineteenth century. Somewhere in the back of people's minds was a fear of inflation, or perhaps of punitive taxation of the rich. It was, as it would often be again, a test of the loyalty of the left in power. What mattered to them more, financial stability or social solidarity? A symbolic sacrifice was required: unemployment benefit should be cut, not just to save money, but also to demonstrate resolve. It took the formation of a National Government to secure support for an emergency budget, including a cut of 10 per cent in both unemployment benefit rates and public sector pay.

It was not enough. Opposition to the cuts was so vigorously expressed that it was doubtful if they could be implemented. Protest action in the Royal Navy was seen as particularly disquieting. The run on the pound resumed, and there was nothing more that could be done to stop it. There was no question in Britain of propping up the currency with exchange controls; that would destroy the business of the City of London. An Act of Parliament suspended the convertibility of sterling into gold. The exchange rate against the dollar fell by more than 20 per cent. It was a dramatic failure of financial policy, with profound consequences for the world monetary system as well as the British economy.

At the time, the fall of the pound came as a relief to Britain and it came to be seen as a victory for common sense, rather than a humiliating defeat. This perception of events was well conveyed by the historian A.J.P. Taylor, writing in the mid-1960s.

> The value of the pound fell by more than a quarter on the foreign exchange. Otherwise nothing happened. Englishmen had been using paper money for seventeen years. They had forgotten the gold sovereign, and their paper pound seemed to them just as valuable as it had been before. This anti-climax took everyone by surprise. Passfield spoke for all his late colleagues when he complained: 'Nobody told us we could do this'. The ministers of the National government could have said the same. The 'mutiny' at Invergordon provoked a common-sense solution which politicians and economists had been incapable of discovering for themselves. A few days before, a managed currency had seemed as wicked as family planning.

Now, like contraception, it became a commonplace. This was the end of an age. (Taylor, 1965, p. 297)

The problem with this interpretation was that there was nothing very satisfactory to put in the place of gold. It was indeed the end of an age for the international monetary system, followed by a period of competitive devaluations and a retreat into bilateral clearing. For Britain it brought relief for the moment, but the underlying dilemma remained to be resolved. The same conflict between objectives would arise again and again in subsequent periods. The drama of 1931 was to be repeated, almost blow for blow, in nearly every one of the remaining decades of the century, one such episode following close on the publication of Taylor's book.

In the 1930s international relations deteriorated progressively. Germany became increasingly bellicose and uncooperative. The League of Nations demonstrated its ineffectiveness. Some at least of the instability of financial markets was due to the justified fears of approaching conflict. But even countries that shared the same political philosophy, and faced the same threats, could not work together in financial affairs. The World Economic Conference in London in 1933 was, in the words of Eichengreen, 'a complete and utter failure'.

Initially, after the fall of sterling, America as well as France wanted Britain to go back onto gold. They wanted to give the old regime another try. Britain had no wish to repeat the experiment. There was, indeed, no going back, now that the fragility of the system had been so convincingly demonstrated. Instead the Americans chose to go off gold themselves, in the hope that this would help overcome their domestic crisis. This left just a small group of countries, led by France, trying to play according to the old rules of the game.

The experience with floating exchange rates in the late 1930s was not a happy one (League of Nations, 1944). The uncertainty over currency values was thought to inhibit trade. Transactions in the forward market to eliminate currency risks were expensive. Changes in exchange rates in one year might be reversed in the next. This was seen as unnecessary disruption, requiring shifts of resources from one industry to another and back again. It was believed that exchange rates were driven more by short-term speculation than by the economic fundamentals of trade and longer-term capital flows.

Exchange rates did not in fact float freely. Many countries had exchange controls, which in some countries at least were effective. Most countries intervened in the markets in an attempt to stabilise, or to manage, their currencies. There was no expectation that private capital would smooth out perturbations, on the contrary it was seen as the main source of the problem. Few people would have said then that the market knew best. But the markets could not be ignored. Even with floating exchange rates there was still an international dimension to monetary policy. The constraints, or 'fetters', were loosened but not really struck off.

In 1936, as we have seen, the French finally accepted that they could not preserve the gold standard on their own. They feared, however, that a depreciation of the franc would set off a round of competitive devaluations. They preferred therefore to devalue as part of an international agreement. It was perhaps the germ of the idea of 'fixed, but adjustable' exchange rates. The result was the Tripartite Agreement with America and Britain, an example of limited but real international negotiation. For a few countries this might have led to the invention of a cooperative regime, although opinions were still very different as to what the nature of that regime should be. In the event reform had to wait until after another world war.

The attempt to revive the gold standard, which looked so promising in the late 1920s, ended in tears. It is clear enough that the Great Depression was largely responsible for that failure. A more interesting and controversial thesis is that the attempt to revive the gold standard was itself the cause of the Great Depression. This view is expressed with great clarity by Eichengreen, although it is by no means unique to him. It is argued that the policy measures needed to preserve the gold standard helped to precipitate the downturn, both in America and in Germany. It is also maintained that the constraints of the gold standard prevented national monetary authorities from taking the action necessary to bring about recovery. In support of this thesis it can be shown that the countries which were the first to be released from their 'golden fetters' were the first to begin their recovery. It is conceded, however, that the 'ethos' of the gold standard remained influential even after its demise.

Implicit in this account of causation must be some assumption about the alternative regime which might have been put in place after the First World War. There might, for example, have been a general move to national regimes of economic planning. They could have developed out of the experience of economic management during the war. This was what happened in Russia, and eventually in Germany and Japan. These regimes did indeed prove to be relatively immune to the effects of the depression, either avoiding it altogether, or achieving a complete recovery. The same might conceivably have happened in Britain or even in America. But this does not seem to be what the proponents of the thesis have in mind.

Neither does it seem that the natural counter-factual case is a regime of freely floating exchange rates. From the concluding chapter of *Golden*

Fetters it appears that the preferred alternative would be a regime of international cooperation and management, with common objectives and 'a common conceptual framework'. Eichengreen concludes that, 'these are all matters that, in principle, are within the control of societies and their governments. Between the wars they were allowed to elude control, with catastrophic consequences' (Eichengreen, 1995, p. 399). This is not far from the approach to policy developed by Keynes and others in the interwar years themselves.

This thesis is not the only way of attributing causation. Another view, related but different, would be that no amount of international cooperation can substitute for public confidence in a regime. The Great Depression occurred because the gold standard could no longer give the underpinning to the stability of the world economy that it provided before the First World War. There were banking crises in America and Germany at the same time in the early 1930s, for different largely domestic reasons. Confidence worldwide tumbled. At this crucial moment it was unclear whether the public should put its trust in the market system or in government action. The regime was not as clearly defined as it once had been. People felt that they could put their trust in neither the old conventions nor in the state – and so the economy collapsed. On this view the reason for the Great Depression was not that the wrong regime was chosen after the First World War. The problem was that there was no credible regime in place at all.

The origins of macroeconomics

In 1933 Ragnar Frisch published a paper called, 'Propagation problems and impulse problems in dynamic economics'. It was, as the title suggests, a formal analysis of economic behaviour over the business cycle, using analogies from the physical sciences. It made the important distinction between 'micro-dynamic analysis' of particular markets and 'macro-dynamic analysis', which 'tries to give an account of the fluctuations of the whole economic system taken in its entirety'. It explained those fluctuations in terms both of the shocks which impinge on the system and of the characteristic response of the system. Economics becomes a kind of engineering, describing behaviour by means of mathematical equations. Although there would need to be literally millions of such equations to describe the economy in detail, it is maintained that its essential properties can be summarised by perhaps half a dozen or so relationships. A new method of doing economics was being developed.

Frisch belonged to a Scandinavian tradition, derived from Cassel and

Wicksell, which originated independently of the Keynesian school in Britain and America. Writing in the 1960s, Klein argued that 'The Keynesian system, as a mathematical model, could have come into being without Keynes, as a natural outgrowth of the economic discussions of the 1930s' (Klein, 1966, p. 224). He cites the works of Frisch, Ohlin and Kalecki. The aim of this new kind of economics was to describe the behaviour of output and prices from year to year, not just in some theoretical long-run equilibrium. Perhaps for that reason it sought to establish empirical laws based on actual observations rather than on the rational foundations of classical theory. In the 1930s, it was, of course, especially concerned to understand the causes of events like the Great Depression and to suggest how policy might correct or prevent them.

The progress of empirical macroeconomics required the collection of aggregate economic data. Statistics on industrial output, prices and employment existed even in the nineteenth century; financial variables like interest rates and exchange rates were easy enough to document. In the interwar years the concepts of national income accounting were developed, and one could for the first time speak unambiguously about such concepts as aggregate consumption or investment, which played a central part in the new approach to macroeconomic theory. By 1939, the League of Nations had estimates of national income for twenty-six countries in all (Hobsbawm, 1995, p. 109).These data series were all very short, but that did not stop the new breed of econometricians using them to test the new ideas of their colleagues.

How did this new economics relate to the old kind? Did it extend and amplify classical economics? Or did it replace it? It was to this question that Keynes' *General Theory* was principally addressed. The question was crucial to the debate going on around the role of government policy in the management of the economy. If the system was self-stabilising, as the old theory implied, then there was no need for management at all: it was best left to the rational decision-making of individuals, who in seeking their own self interest would in effect serve the interest of all. If, on the other hand, the economy was more like a physical system, operating blindly according to its own laws of motion, then there was every reason to hope that its performance could be improved by deliberate and intelligent control. Added urgency was given to the debate because the economy was so obviously malfunctioning at the time.

Keynes saw himself as making a major and fundamental advance in economic theory, rather like the invention of non-Euclidean geometry, or perhaps like Einstein's general theory of relativity. He thought that classical economics was at best misleading, relevant only to the special case of

full employment. He was not, on this occasion, writing a tract for the times
– his new insights claimed to be of general application. He wanted to apply his general theory to the urgent problems posed by the depression, and
to propose a cure. But his main task in this book was to change, quite fundamentally, the way in which professional economists thought, and also,
as a consequence of that, to change public opinion.

He claimed that classical economics just assumed away the whole problem of involuntary unemployment. It was wrong, he said, in assuming that
a fall in money wages would restore full employment, wrong in assuming
that the rate of interest would adjust to maintain equality between planned
savings and planned investment in aggregate, most fundamentally wrong
in assuming that a decision to produce and to sell was always linked to a
decision to buy and to consume or invest.

It could be said, against Keynes, that classical economics, even in his day,
had answers to each one of these criticisms. The answer in every case is
that the price level will fall if necessary so as to clear the market for money.
If the supply of money is fixed then a fall in all prices will increase the demand for goods and services. This will stimulate the demand for labour. If
savings are being hoarded in money instead of being invested, the disequilibrium will be resolved in the same way. If producers do not want to
consume or invest as much as they can sell, then again the prices of goods
and services must fall until they do.

This was, and still is, the standard theory of general equilibrium. Keynes,
on occasion, recognised it, even in the *General Theory* itself. One particularly clear example is in chapter 19, when he describes the effect on
unemployment of a fall in money wages. He clearly identifies one way, although not the only way, in which general deflation could be equilibrating:

> The reduction in the wages-bill, accompanied by some reduction in
> prices and in money-incomes generally, will diminish the need for
> cash for income and business purposes; and it will therefore reduce
> *pro tanto* the schedule of liquidity-preference for the community as
> a whole. *Cet. par.* this will reduce the rate of interest and thus prove
> favourable to investment. (Keynes, 1936, p. 263)

In this passage at least, Keynes concedes that his opponents had a logical
argument to present in defence of their position. He was not so much gen-
eralising the accepted theory as identifying situations in which it might not
be applicable.

In much of his argument, Keynes treated money wages as fixed. He sim-
plified the situation greatly by suggesting that the supply of labour was

perfectly elastic up to the point of full employment, so that more labour could always be employed without any increase in wages. Above that point, in contrast, there was no elasticity at all, so that an addition to the demand for labour would simply bid wages up higher. He wrote as if all wages were settled by collective bargaining. He also forgot, or chose to ignore, the effect of demand on the prices of goods and services themselves, as if the profit mark-up on costs never varied. In this his own theory clearly lacked generality.

Keynes did not think that making wages more flexible would help to avoid, or correct, persistent unemployment. A fall in money wages would reduce consumer demand; a fall in the price level, if it was expected to continue, would increase real interest rates and deter fixed investment. Even if the real value of the money supply did increase, these other effects would dominate in the short to medium term, and the level of unemployment could go on rising. So, wage flexibility could make the employment problem worse. (See Flemming, 1987, for a more recent version of this argument.)

There was nothing new in the suggestion that wages and prices might be 'sticky'. Keynes was much more original in his treatment of interest rates. Even if the price level did fall, he argued, the rate of interest might remain too high to equate saving and investment at a full-employment level of output. Long-term interest rates depend on expectations. Even if the economy became very liquid indeed, thanks to a fall in prices or an increase in the money supply, interest rates might not come down below the level regarded as the norm. Moreover, investment decisions depend on expectations as well, on the expected value of the increment to output at the margin. Again, that expectation could be so low that no feasible reduction in the cost of capital could make investment appear sufficiently attractive.

One might claim that Keynes generalised the classical theory to cover the case in which expectations were not rationally determined. He certainly showed how vulnerable the concept of equilibrium is to the loss of that assumption. If expectations are fixed and unchanging, then they determine the feasible level of output, which will not, in general, be such as to secure full employment. What really matters is confidence, the so-called 'fundamentals' never have a chance to influence the outcome.

Yet Keynes did not develop a theory to explain expectations themselves. They are erratic, unreliable and not really governed by reason at all. They are even referred to as 'animal spirits', the complete negation of all that classical economics assumes. Presumably the next stage in the development of economic theory should have been to psychoanalyse economic man! The conclusion instead was that policymakers, who are tacitly assumed to be very rational indeed, should take control of the system and guide it to a more satisfactory equilibrium.

Keynes did not believe that classical theory was applicable even to the nineteenth century. He thought that full employment was seldom achieved. There were regular cycles in output, but they were around a level determined by the prevailing expectations, a rate typically too low to provide jobs for all. His theory of output was intended to explain its long-run tendency, not its short-run fluctuations. Demand deficiency was a chronic problem, avoided only in exceptional circumstances. The heretical writers who worried about 'under-consumption' had seen something that their more orthodox contemporaries had missed. Nations commonly competed for overseas markets, not just for profit but also for jobs. Despite what economic theory told them to the contrary, practical men had always recognised that the best hope of maintaining employment at home was to win markets for their products overseas.

The situation in the twentieth century, according to Keynes, was even worse than it had been in the nineteenth. There was no longer the same optimism, the same opportunity to introduce new products and to win new markets. The outlook was for secular stagnation and ever higher levels of unemployment. Keynes talked about building pyramids or cathedrals to make work for people to do. There were going to be fewer and fewer profitable investment projects which the private sector would want to undertake. Instead the state would have to invent projects of its own, not just to smooth out a cycle, but to prevent investment from falling too low all the time. The alternative, which many Keynesians found very attractive, was to redistribute income from the rich to the poor. Not only was that more equitable, it would also solve the problem of demand, since the poor would have a lower propensity to save.

Subsequent history has shown that this pessimistic view of demand, and particularly of private investment, was totally wrong. Fifty years after the General Theory the capital stock was growing as fast as ever and living standards were still rising with no sign of satiation in sight. Keynes' argument that the state would have to take over investment was supported by a mistaken view of economic development, a false generalisation from the special circumstances of a particular decade. In retrospect the depression of the 1930s looks much more like an enlarged fluctuation, a phenomenon of the business cycle but on an unusually large scale. The defence of Keynesian policies would now have to be made in terms of stabilisation rather than of promoting long-term growth.

The General Theory had many interpreters, right from the time of its first publication. Different readers read it differently because of its many ambiguities and possible inconsistencies. The presentation of Keynesianism which became standard in the textbooks was invented by Hicks (1937). He constructed an even more general theory, of which both Keynes and the classics were special cases. At one extreme the level of output was fixed, at a full employment equilibrium; at the other extreme the rate of interest was fixed by convention or by expectations. In general both variables would be determined simultaneously. This exposition certainly helped to introduce the new discipline of macroeconomics to many generations of academic economists. Its practical usefulness has never been so certain.

Meade (1936) apparently addressed a rather different audience. There were those who questioned whether the market system could ever secure full employment. He took it as self-evident that the market on its own would fail, but he maintained that it could be 'made to function successfully' by means of demand management. It was simply a matter of ensuring that sufficient purchasing power was available to pay for the appropriate level of production. It was a matter of arithmetic. Classical economics and the price mechanism hardly rate a mention at all. This was the form in which Keynesianism came to be adopted by policymakers rather than academic economists. One had to estimate what demand would be forthcoming on existing policies, compare that with productive potential and then adjust fiscal or monetary policy to make up the difference. It makes plain a new function of government which in the *General Theory* is never quite explicitly described.

Keynes was, in the first instance, a monetary economist. In the *General Theory* he was concerned to integrate monetary theory with the new study of aggregate income and expenditure flows. At an earlier stage in his life he had been an advocate of active monetary management, as against the rules of the old gold standard. But, by the mid-1930s, he had become doubtful of the effectiveness of any monetary policy at all. That was one of the main messages of the book – to argue against the position which he had once held himself. His followers took the process of revision a stage further: monetary policy ceased to be of much significance at all. In America, Lerner (1944) argued that fiscal policy was the instrument of macroeconomic control. The authorities could turn on or off the flows of expenditure, by adjusting the flows of income and of borrowing. The availability of finance was important, and it could be controlled by the issue of government debt. But the stock of money was an unimportant consequence of the actions which the authorities had taken, just a residual item in the accounts. This was a far cry from the teaching of the *Tract* or the *Treatise* which Keynes had written in earlier years.

Ever since the 1930s, economists have been divided into two opposing camps. There are those who start from the rational behaviour of individuals and go on to construct a theory of general equilibrium on that foundation. In the other camp are those who start from the observation of events at a national or world level and seek to explain them by any means they can, in terms of institutional behaviour, crowd psychology, natural propensities or just common sense.

Both methods aim to achieve understanding which is of general application. The split became serious at the time of the Great Depression, because of the stark contrast between two very different interpretations of particular events, but neither is content to be a special theory of that one historical period: there are contrasting views of the events of all later decades as well. One might question, however, whether such generality can ever be attained in this field. Macroeconomics may be fundamentally different in different historical periods, and under different policy regimes.

Perhaps the economics appropriate to the 1930s was not the same as that appropriate to earlier times. Alvin Hansen (1932), in his pre-Keynesian phase, contrasted the happy balance of the world economy before the first world war with the troubles of his own days. He emphasised how complex the productive process had become; he thought that, as a result, it was more prone to maladjustment. He noted, in America at the start of the 1930s, how the free action of the market was being impeded:

> It is not necessary to labor the point that we are living in an era of increasing social control . . . Unregulated capitalism is being superseded by regulated, organized and controlled capitalism . . . Control of certain aspects of economic life, while at the same time other fields remain quite unregulated, may throw the whole machinery out of gear and cause violent disturbances in the economic system . . . The tension and strain placed upon the internal price structure, in consequence of a general fall in prices, is increased in the measure that institutional arrangements and governmental regulation prevent, or render difficult, the adjustments without which a new equilibrium in the entire price system cannot be reached. Social control tends to put society in a straightjacket. This might not be so bad in a static world, but it is very painful in a dynamic one, particularly one subject to violent price fluctuations.

Hansen seems to be suggesting that institutional change, particularly the growth of trades union power and price setting by large producers, rendered obsolete the classical economics based on perfect competition. As he says, it is particularly difficult to understand an economy in which some sectors are competitive, and others are not. The monetary regime appropriate to a flexible market could clearly come to grief in a new world where adjustment was reluctant, lop-sided and slow. That might be one reason why Keynesian theory and policy were right for their own times, but not for all.

Another institutional development which changed economic behaviour was the growth of speculation in financial markets, the 'beauty contest' so vividly described in the *General Theory*. Hicks suggested that this could be a case of the market system undermining its own institutional foundations. At one time it had been too expensive to transfer funds from one asset to another in pursuit of short-term gains. These transaction costs helped to stabilise the system, making it less dependent on volatile market sentiments. Competition between intermediaries had reduced these costs, whilst the spirit of capitalism had made men more eager in the pursuit of profit. 'In doing these things, capitalism is its own worst enemy, for it imperils the stability without which it breaks down' (Hicks, 1935). Again one can see how a different kind of macroeconomics might have become necessary as a result of differences between one period and the next.

In these respects, as in others, the 1930s were a time of transition. The economy was getting more rigid, but in fact wages and prices did still fall. The problem seemed to be that the economy did not respond as it should have done to the fall in prices. Interest rates were not altogether unresponsive: short rates went very low indeed, and long rates followed a little of the way. Eventually there was a recovery in some kinds of private investment, particularly in housing. The statistics for the period do not paint quite the same picture as contemporary economists do.

Nevertheless they were right to suggest that the market mechanism was seizing up. That mechanism had always been dependent on a general belief in its efficacy. Now people were looking to the state to provide security, to make the system work. This destroyed the old belief that the economy was, as it were, a separate order of creation, removed from mundane politics, guided by a providential invisible hand. But the state was not yet able to discharge the new responsibility assigned to it. The new regime was not yet in place. It was a kind of inter-regnum, when the old faith was discarded, but nothing had yet quite taken its place.

4 The Second World War and after (1939–1950)

Repeating history?

The Second World War was, in many respects, a repeat of the First. Certainly its economic consequences were similar in kind. As before, the market system was suspended, or else heavily regulated, in all the main belligerent countries. Again, there was a great surge of demand, producing both full employment and inflation. Again there was a vast increase in government debt and in liquidity. Again there was widespread destruction and devastation.

At the outset it was expected that new military technology would ensure a much briefer conflict, in which initial preparations would be decisive. By 1942, however, it was clear that this would be another test of stamina and endurance, in which the ability to produce armaments and to feed the population would be amongst the main determining factors. By 1944, the Allies were producing about three times as much combat equipment as the Axis powers (Millward, 1987).

On the outbreak of war, commodity prices rose sharply, as the markets anticipated inflation and shortages. The *Economist* sterling price index rose by 30 per cent in 1940 and by a further 10 per cent in 1941. As usual, it was the prices of raw materials, rather than of finished goods, that responded more promptly to the changed economic outlook. But in the early years of the war price inflation was quite general in most of the countries involved (Brown, 1955).

Between 1939 and 1942, consumer prices rose by 17 per cent in the United States, by 27 per cent in Britain, and by 21 per cent in Japan; the increase was only 8–9 per cent in Germany, whilst in France it was as much as 68 per cent. The differences in these figures partly result from relative

Table 4.1 *Rates of consumer price inflation, 1939–1950, per cent*

	USA	UK	France	Germany	Japan
1939	–1.0	1.1	6.1	0.0	12.0
1940	1.0	16.7	18.9	3.7	16.1
1941	5.0	8.0	17.2	2.4	1.5
1942	10.5	0.8	20.6	2.3	3.0
1943	6.0	–0.8	23.9	1.1	5.9
1944	1.6	1.7	22.4	2.2	11.8
1945	2.4	0.8	48.2	n.a.	14.3
1946	8.6	0.0	52.5	10.3	513.1
1947	14.4	0.0	48.5	6.7	113.4
1948	7.5	8.1	59.4	15.0	83.4
1949	–1.2	2.6	12.7	7.6	31.8
1950	1.2	2.5	9.9	–7.1	– 6.9

Source: Mitchell (1998).

dependence on world markets for imported raw materials and food. From 1941 in Britain, and from 1942 in America, a combination of controls and subsidies proved very effective in suppressing inflation – at least inflation as measured by the cost of living index. By contrast, inflation continued briskly in France throughout the occupation.

Statistics of total output do not have quite the same meaning in times of war as in times of peace. Nevertheless the contrast between the figures for the United States and the other major industrial powers is certainly worth noting. In 1943, in the middle of the war, the level of gross domestic product compared with 1939 was down by 44 per cent in France, up by 5 per cent in Japan and by 11 per cent in Germany; in Britain it was up 26 per cent, but in the USA it was up by as much as 83 per cent, a phenomenal recovery from the depression.

In America the war achieved what the New Deal could not. The economy boomed as never before or since. Unemployment fell from nearly 15 per cent in 1940 to under 2 per cent in 1943. Everything that had been said about the structural weakness of the American economy or about the low productivity of the workforce was proved spectacularly wrong. All that had been lacking in the 1930s, it now appeared, was a sufficient stimulus to demand. Where the market had failed for so many years, wartime planning and regulation worked exceedingly well.

In wartime one cannot look at interest rates as an indicator of economic conditions. In the United States, throughout this great boom, short-term interest rates were under 1 per cent. In Britain, after a brief increase in 1939,

Table 4.2 Indices of GDP, 1939–1950, 1913 = 100

	USA	UK	France	Germany	Japan
1939	166.8	133.8	139.0	166.2	284.4
1940	179.7	147.2	114.7	167.4	292.7
1941	212.4	160.6	90.7	178.0	296.7
1942	254.9	164.6	81.3	180.4	295.1
1943	305.6	168.2	77.2	184.0	299.3
1944	331.2	161.6	65.2	188.7	286.4
1945	317.9	154.5	70.7	134.2	143.2
1946	252.3	147.8	107.5	79.7	155.6
1947	248.5	145.6	116.5	89.5	168.0
1948	257.9	150.2	125.0	106.0	139.0
1949	258.9	155.8	142.0	123.5	205.9
1950	281.4	160.8	152.6	147.5	227.1

Source: Maddison (1995).

the bank rate was held at 2 per cent. Similarly in France the discount rate was held at a historical low, despite accelerating inflation. Longer-term rates were also managed by the authorities and bore little relation to the supply and demand for capital. Yields on government stock were similar to those to be had in the First World War: in Britain, for example, this was a 3 per cent war.

Meanwhile, almost everywhere, financial liquidity was building up. Although taxes were increased as never before, the finance of wartime expenditure could not all be covered in that way. The German authorities managed to finance much of their spending at the expense of the countries they occupied, and that resulted in excess money creation as well as overt inflation. In the countries where inflation was suppressed, consumers often chose to save rather than to spend, for patriotic reasons or simply because the goods they wanted to purchase were not obtainable. One legacy of the war, therefore, was a mass of accumulated spending power ready to be used at the first opportunity.

When price controls were lifted in the USA in 1946 the consumer price index rose abruptly, setting off an inflationary spiral. A similar, but more modest, increase followed in Britain two years later. This was in line with experience immediately after the previous war, and caused little alarm. What was being remembered with more trepidation was that the postwar inflation from 1918 to 1920 had been quickly followed by a sharp deflation, by recession and rising unemployment. That was what many economists were expecting to happen at the end of the 1940s.

There was, indeed, a pause in the growth of the American economy in

1949, with unemployment rising to 5.9 per cent in that year. This gave some relief from inflation, but at the time it was viewed with considerable concern. A report published by the United Nations at that time drew attention to this situation and called for a determined policy response. The shadow of the 1930s just briefly fell on the late 1940s. The report said that 'Uncertainty can be removed only if governments can assure the world that they are in a position to deal with a recession if it occurs' (United Nations, 1949, p. 9).

In practice, American economic policy lacked clarity and direction in the postwar years. It was far from certain that measures could or would be taken to stabilise demand. Interest rates remained very low, as a matter of policy to ease the burden of the national debt. Truman asked a hostile Congress to give him greater powers to combat inflation, raising fears of renewed controls and regulations. All he was given were renewed powers to regulate consumer credit. When the boom slowed itself down, little was done to prevent a recession, but in fact very little was needed.

The next year saw the beginning of the Korean War boom. It is hard to say what would have happened to the world economy without the onset of the Cold War. It was the mounting tension between the USA and the USSR which kept military spending at a high level. America also made financial assistance available to strengthen recovery in Europe and in the Far East. This was not just disinterested benevolence; it was also fear of a communist takeover. Nothing like that had happened after the First World War. One could say that the Cold War was accompanied by a kind of 'cool' inflation, persistent but never getting altogether out of hand. But that outcome was not foreseen by many when the Korean War rekindled the flames.

Britain faced some special national problems in the transition from war to peace after the Second World War, as after the First. There was an urgent need to increase exports, to service the debts incurred in war and to make up for the loss of productive capacity at home. Partly for this reason much more comprehensive controls remained in place in Britain than in America. Even so, it is doubtful if output and employment could have been so well maintained without the benefit of Marshall Aid. The fact that some parts of the economy remained on an almost wartime regime may help to explain how price inflation remained relatively low, despite a very low level of unemployment.

Interest rates in Britain were actually reduced after the war, as a deliberate policy move. Bank rate stayed at 2 per cent, but the yield on Treasury bills was brought down from 1 to ½ per cent. More significantly, a determined campaign was mounted to reduce long-term rates from about 3 to about 2½ per cent. The main aim was not to influence the pressure of demand in the economy, or indeed to weaken the exchange rate; the intention was simply to reduce the cost of servicing the national debt, with perhaps a more remote hope of redistributing income to the workers and away from the idle rich. The policy of 'cheap money' was not a success; the authorities at this time were not in a position to dictate terms to the bond markets. By 1948 yields on consols were significantly above 3 per cent again. At the time few economists made a connection between this stance of monetary policy and the low level of unemployment or the persistence of inflation. In retrospect one cannot be so sure. A relaxed policy may have been necessary, even if not sufficient, as a cause of the postwar recovery.

The problems of the European continent were a great deal more serious. France, in 1944, after the Liberation, was not far from political anarchy. For the next four years there was no government with sufficient authority and popular support to mount an effective resistance to inflation. On the contrary, wages were increased to win support from the unions, interest rates were held at a low level, whilst much of the banking system was nationalised to ensure that it would provide adequate funds for reconstruction. Proposals for a monetary reform, on the pattern that had been successful in Belgium, were rejected. This was partly a matter of economic doctrine, but also an acknowledgement that no reform would be acceptable to the far left or to the farmers (Sherwin, 1956). From 1946 to 1948 inflation was in the region of 50 per cent; it inspired enough fear to change the priorities of the electorate.

A stabilisation programme was introduced in 1948, despite threats of violence from both left and right. Credit controls, which had been in place for several years, were severely tightened, whilst the access of commercial banks to central bank funds was limited. The exchange rate was lowered, but then fixed. Freeing wages from political control removed one recurrent source of inflationary pressure. The result was a period of slowdown in output and a much reduced increase in prices. It had taken a long time to bring the wartime inflation to a halt, but perhaps the politics of the time made a quicker cure too costly.

For the German economy a painful medicine was essential, and it fell to the occupying powers to administer it. For more than three years after VE Day nothing could be done because of disagreements between the Allies. The price freeze and the rationing system remained in place, but in fact the old reichsmark was unusable for most transactions. Firms kept production going, using barter exchange, whilst retail transactions were conducted in cigarettes. Industrial production stagnated; gross domestic product in 1946 and 1947 is estimated at roughly half the prewar level.

When it became clear that no agreement could be reached with the Russians, the Western powers went ahead with a currency reform in their three zones. Each of the *Länder* was given its own central bank, as an expression of the principle of decentralisation. Then, in 1948, a central bank for the whole of West Germany, the Bank Deutscher Länder was established. It was made independent of government, setting a precedent for its successor the Bundesbank, but initially it was answerable to the Allied Bank Commission.

It was the task of the new central bank to issue and manage the new currency, the Deutschmark, although the new banknotes had been secretly printed in America. The currency reform meant the cancellation of official debts and, for many people, the destruction overnight of a lifetime's savings. The mountain of excess liquidity left in the economy by the methods of war finance was simply eliminated. Wages, rents and pensions were converted as one-for-one, but most bank balances as one-for-ten – and even then half of the new balances were blocked. It was manifestly unfair and caused much complaint. In the recent official history of the Deutschmark it is recognised that such a drastic move was possible only because the Allies took responsibility for it:

> It would have been impossible for a democratically elected German government to agree on a project for currency reform so radical, a factor on which its success heavily depended. (Buckheim, 1999)

It was Erhard, however, who decided to abolish price control immediately. In doing this he had to overcome the opposition of the Americans, as well as a general strike. Initially the success of the reform was in doubt, as prices began to rise again in terms of the new currency. Unemployment was high, thanks partly to the inflow of refugees from the east. But the currency reform, and the prospect of greater political stability, encouraged a rapid recovery of output. Goods which had been hoarded were again offered for sale. Marshall Aid was helping to pay for the necessary imports. In 1949 the Deutschmark, in common with other European currencies, was devalued against the dollar; the prospect then opened up of export-led growth. The style of economic management typical of West Germany was set at an early stage. Even in 1950 we see the Americans urging the German authorities to expand domestic demand, and we see them responding with great reluctance.

This story has a parallel in Japan (Cohen, 1960). This was another devastated economy rescued by American aid, and rebuilt according to a model designed by the Americans. The consumer price index rose six-fold in 1946, and doubled again in 1947. An attempt at a currency reform in 1946 was a complete failure. Thereafter the Bank of Japan financed reconstruction by adding to the already excessive liquidity left over from the war. It was not until 1949 that an effective stabilisation plan could be introduced. It was named the Dodge Plan after its American author.

The policy mix was not the same as in Germany or France. Fixing the exchange rate was an important element; wage and price control was imposed. The fiscal budget was brought into surplus, with an explicit and limited amount of American aid.

Credit was rationed. There was no currency reform: the yen, which had been 15 to the dollar in 1945, was fixed at 360 – an inconveniently low denomination which was to be a lasting reminder of the chaos out of which the new and highly successful Japanese economy emerged.

Essentially the Dodge Plan was just an abrupt tightening of monetary and fiscal policy, introduced at a time when the inflationary forces may, in any case, have been beginning to abate. It caused output to stand still and unemployment to rise, and in doing so it halted the inflation of prices. As in West Germany the instructions of a foreign power enabled the national government to overcome domestic political obstacles. One Japanese economist has written:

> There is no doubt that the Dodge monetary contraction policy was best fitted to serve the purpose, to stop the galloping tendency of inflation, and without this mighty measure prescribed from outside, no political power from within could have been expected to arise to overcome inflation. (Shinjo, 1962, p. 157)

At the end of the 1940s it was becoming evident that the history of the previous postwar period was not going to be repeated. The politics were very different as well as the economics. Instead of withdrawing into relative isolation, the Americans were playing an active, often a dominant, part in reconstruction and stabilisation. Meanwhile much of Europe was going through a period of profound social and political change, which would transform its economic performance. Indeed, those changes were so profound that the lessons of the first half of the century provided a most unreliable guide to the way in which those economies would behave in the second.

'Never again'

Paul Samuelson published the first edition of his best-selling college textbook *Economics* in 1948. In the closing section he describes what he calls 'the crisis of capitalism'; he surveys the world from an American viewpoint and wonders what future there is for the market system which his book has described. This is what he sees:

> After World War I, democratic governments were set up all over Europe. By 1927 the future of the capitalistic way of life appeared serene and assured. After World War II, the outlook is radically changed. Socialist governments are in power in England, in France, in all of Scandinavia, in all the Balkans and eastern Europe. Russia with its communistic government appears to be on the march. Fascism lingers on in Spain. In our own hemisphere, dictatorships are to be found in numerous countries of Latin America . . .
>
> Only the United States remains as an island of capitalism in our increasingly totalitarian and collectivised world. Even here, the scene is drastically changed in the direction of strengthened powers of government over economic activities. The capitalistic way of life is on trial. Not only must it perform adequately – more than that, it is required to perform superlatively. A decade of unemployment here at home would have disastrous repercussions upon our prestige abroad, to say nothing of the internal political unrest that a slump would involve. (Samuelson, 1948, p. 584)

Clearly Samuelson exaggerates the extent to which European countries had abandoned the free market. America was not really alone in the way that he describes; in later editions of his book, he rewrote this passage. Nevertheless what he was observing in the late 1940s was a change of regime, that is of the way in which the role of government was perceived, its powers and its responsibilities. Having once again taken comprehensive authority over the economy in wartime, many governments were unwilling, or unable, to lay it down when the battle was over. In some countries it seemed as if the management of the economy by government was to continue indefinitely. The record of market failure in the interwar years had affected public opinion profoundly. 'Never again' would it be trusted – or so it seemed at the time (Hennesey, 1993).

The Labour government in Britain nationalised the railways, the coal mines and much else; it reformed social security and established the National Health Service. This was what was meant by 'socialism', not the replacement of the market system by a command economy, or the public ownership of all productive capital. But in the 1940s it was not yet clear how far the changes would go, how the mixed economy would work once the postwar emergency was over. Government direction was accepted for a transitional period, but it remained to be seen how long that period would be, and what it was a transition towards.

In 1947 Cripps became Chancellor of the Exchequer but retained his title of Minister for Economic Affairs. The economic planning staff was transferred to the Treasury. This small reorganisation within government was actually very significant (Dow, 1964). It marked the elevation of fiscal policy over direct control as the preferred method of economic management. This was not to be a planned economy as many socialists had hoped; it was to be a regulated market economy with social security and redistributive taxes, with full employment guaranteed by demand management. This combination was now enjoying bipartisan support.

The situation in France in the 1940s was different. Effective government and political consensus were notably lacking. Yet one of the most successful innovations in postwar economic policy was made at that time. The first French Plan was made public in 1947. At first it was regarded with great suspicion, not least by industry which feared the consequences of nationalisation. It was largely indicative in form, but there was some power behind it. The nationalised banking system used the Plan as a basis for the allocation of scarce capital. The Plan survived many changes of government and came to be a focus for cooperation across a wide range of political opinion and economic interest (Gildea, 1997).

Paul Samuelson implied in his *tour d'horizon* that the state was everywhere supplanting the market in the 1940s. He did not mention that West Germany was moving decisively in the opposite direction (Kettenacher, 1997). Having renounced economic planning as practised by the National Socialists, the new regime put its faith in a 'social market economy'. This was not quite capitalism as practised in America, but neither was it the managed economy of the United Kingdom or the planned economy of France. It drew on the teachings of famous exiles such as Hayek, as well as the ordo-liberals of the Freiburg school. It recognised a need for social security and respected the rights of trades unions. But, most importantly, it required all executive action by government to be under the rule of law. It therefore regarded Keynesian discretionary policies with particular suspicion. This was to prove another highly successful species of the genus of 'mixed economies' (van der Wee, 1987, ch.7).

In America there was no decisive change of regime after the Second World War. Most of the special powers of government taken to wage war were promptly handed back to Congress or to the market system. Perhaps the most significant event of the late 1940s was the passing of the Taft-Hartley Act of 1947, restricting once more the rights of trades unions, despite President Truman's attempt to veto it. The philosophy of the New Deal was now in retreat.

There was, however, a sense in which the war was not over for America, and therefore the wish to return to normal times was frustrated. International tension prevented the eclipse of government. In the passage quoted from Samuelson there is feeling of approaching conflict, or at the least of dangerous competition and national rivalry. The Cold War preserved a leading role for government in the economy. Military programmes required planning, however uncongenial that might be; and American business had to plan too if it was to fulfil all those military contracts. The defence of 'capitalism' required that the market system should be seen to work better than communist or socialist planning. That meant that there must be no more deep recessions or periods of mass unemployment; and that, as Samuelson himself must have seen, somewhat ironically meant that government had to underwrite the stability of a system which it did not wish to control.

The trend to big government did not go unchallenged. It was during the war, when state control was most pervasive, and when opinion increasingly favoured its retention in peacetime, that Hayek (1944) published his most effective defence of the free market. He compared the trend of public opinion in Britain with that which had brought the Nazis to power in Germany:

> There exists now in this country certainly the same determination that the organisation of the nation we have achieved for purposes of defence shall be retained for purposes of creation. There is the same contempt for nineteenth-century liberalism, the same spurious 'realism' and even cynicism, the same fatalistic acceptance of 'inevitable trends'. At least nine out of every ten of the lessons which our most vociferous reformers are so anxious we should learn from this war are precisely the lessons which the Germans did learn from the last war and which have done much to produce the Nazi system.

He found the changes in the role of government which had already taken place in the 1930s totally unacceptable. 'We have progressively abandoned the freedom in economic affairs without which personal and political freedom has never existed in the past.' This was a very strong argument at the time. The only alternatives to the free market on offer were dictatorships of left or right. Those who believed in government intervention to stabilise the economy had to explain how this would be compatible with democracy and free choice. That was why William Beveridge, when he wrote about postwar strategy, called his book *Full Employment in a Free Society*.

The experiences of the 1930s were too recent and too painful to ignore. Hayek wrote as if unemployment might be tolerable if it was inflicted by an impersonal market and not by the deliberate choice of some economic supremo. In fact the prospect of mass unemployment was no longer found tolerable however it might be caused. Everywhere the same lesson was learned, not from the war but from the years that preceded it: the state could not avoid responsibility for maintaining a high level of employment.

The United Nations, which replaced the failed League at the end of the war, included a commitment to full employment in Articles 55 and 56 of its charter (United Nations, 1949, p. 9). That objective was said to be consistent with all manner of social and economic organisation. It was no doubt consistent with communism, but it was also declared to be consistent with capitalism. It was claimed, in a report written from a Keynesian perspective, that the policies required 'do not involve any change in the economic institutions of private enterprise countries'. That was far from obvious at the time.

In the United States the postwar aim of full employment was expressed in statements made during the war. After the war was over, the Employment Act of 1946 was inspired by Keynesians, but as finally drafted it fell short of a commitment to full employment. A Council of Economic Advisers was set up to monitor the performance of the economy, particularly keeping an eye on the labour market. The President presented a report to Congress each year and this did much to ensure that the principle of demand management was not altogether forgotten. There was nothing in this, however, to which a Hayekian could take violent dislike. The debate over full employment as a policy aim was more significant in Britain.

Beveridge (1944) argued that the threat of unemployment could not be countered purely by the reform of social security. People needed jobs as well as incomes:

> Idleness is not the same as want, but a separate evil which men do not escape by having an income. They must also have the chance of rendering useful service and of feeling that they are doing so.

He also wrote:

> A person who has difficulty in buying the labour that he wants suffers inconvenience or reduction in profits. A person who cannot sell his labour is in effect told that he is no use. The first difficulty causes annoyance or loss. The other is a personal catastrophe.

Economic policy had found a new role, a new mission, concerned not just with material prosperity, but with the well-being of individuals and of communities. Noone should be excluded from participation in the economic life of society. The sense of social solidarity was especially strong in a nation at war. Far more was being expected from economic policy than ever before.

The sentiments expressed by Beveridge were supported across the political divide. The result was a commitment by the wartime coalition government in the White Paper on Employment Policy of 1944:

> The Government accept as one of their primary aims and responsibilities the maintenance of a high and stable level of employment after the war.

As in America, the actual words 'full employment' were avoided, but that was in fact the aim, especially of the Labour government which came to office after the postwar election.

It remained unclear, however, what policy actions this commitment actually implied. At one extreme it would mean that the same instruments would be used as before the war – interest rates, public works, perhaps tariffs – but with more skill and determination. At the other extreme it meant a command economy, as in wartime. The crucial question was the control of wages. Was full employment possible without inflation?

Beveridge was clear that he wanted something more than just the balance of supply and demand in the labour market. He wanted to create a sellers' market for labour, in which there would be more vacancies than workers unemployed. He recognised the risks involved, but was willing to rely on the goodwill and cooperation of unions and employers to avoid any excessive increase in pay. That was how the economy was being run during the war. He wrote:

> The degree of liberty . . . which can be left to agencies independent of the State, without imperilling the policy of full employment, depends on the responsibility and public spirit with which those liberties are exercised. There is no reason to doubt that that responsibility and public spirit will be forthcoming. (Beveridge, 1944)

Others were prepared to accept that the maintenance of full employment called for wide powers to be retained by government. A report by a group of Oxford economists concluded that:

> Wage bargaining in full employment is, in fact, a political problem, and will be settled on the political plane. (Burchardt, 1944)

For the efficient allocation of resources:

> the reserves of idle labour which exist in unemployment will be replaced by planning. (Worswick, 1944)

For that very reason, others rejected full employment as an objective. It would imply either persistent inflation or else a threat to personal liberty. Lionel Robbins (1954), for example, said that the moderation of wage claims could not be taken for granted in normal times. To eliminate unemployment would require wages to be controlled. It would also restrict mobility between industries and reduce international competitiveness. A little unemployment was not unacceptable, provided that its duration was short. He thought that any kind of employment guarantee would tempt the unions to raise wages. Instead the government should define its objectives in terms of price stability and external balance.

Those who sought to maintain full employment did not see monetary policy as a useful means to that end. It was believed that fiscal policy was a more effective instrument for expanding demand, whilst monetary restraint might be appropriate for contracting it. The asymmetry was captured in the image of trying to push on a string. As ever, it was the inflation 'hawks' who wanted to resurrect monetary policy after the war, whilst the unemployment 'doves' were content to leave it in limbo.

To the extent that monetary policy was active at all in the 1940s, in the major industrial countries, it was firmly under the control of governments. The Banque de France and the Bank of England were both nationalised after the war. In France the most important decisions concerned the allocation of credit. They were taken by the National Credit Council which was chaired by the Minister of Finance; the governor of the central bank was in a clearly subordinate role as vice chairman. In Britain the Act of 1946 gave the Treasury power to issue instructions to the Bank of England; the Bank could also issue instructions to the commercial banks, but only with the agreement of the Treasury. These powers were never actually used, but they nevertheless determined the character of relationships.

Even in America the Federal Reserve System in this period did not enjoy much independence in practice. In wartime it had been altogether subordinate to government, and this remained essentially the position for the rest of the decade. But a debate was going on behind the scenes. As the threat of recession abated, and as concern about inflation increased, the old ideas about central banking and sound finance were being heard again. Monetary policy was not redundant after all.

Bretton Woods and American hegemony

The international monetary system established after the Second World War was the result of negotiation, careful analysis of previous experience and deliberate choice. That cannot be said of the gold standard either before or after the First World War; neither can it be said of the world monetary system as it was to emerge from the chaos of the 1970s. The history of the Bretton Woods system shows that it is possible, sometimes at least, to design the interaction of sovereign states, to write a constitution to govern their relationships. It is possible for such a human artefact to survive and, in some respects, to work well, for two decades or more.

Circumstances were undoubtedly favourable for such deliberate choice at the time when this new era began. The initial planning, started about 1942, really involved only two countries, America and Britain. They had been the most important centres of international finance since the nineteenth century, so at any time their views would have carried weight. Although they had failed to coordinate their policies in the past, they did share some common understanding of the nature and scope of economic policy – their views were different, but not irreconcilably so. However, the most important point was that other countries, especially Germany and France, which might have supported a quite different approach, were in no position to argue their case.

The new constitution was, therefore, essentially Anglo-Saxon in style. Even so, there was plenty of disagreement to be resolved. The US and the UK were in very different financial positions as the war drew to a close, and their interests were sometimes diametrically opposed. For the foreseeable future, the dollar would necessarily be strong, and the pound weak. Britain would be struggling to pay for essential imports, whilst American trade would be in comfortable surplus. Much of British industrial capacity was behind the times, whilst America led the world in many sectors of production and in the introduction of new technology. Britain desperately needed American help to win the war, and to rebuild thereafter. Any bargaining was bound to be one-sided.

There were also differences in the domestic policy aims of these two main protagonists. As we have seen, the Americans intended to move back to what was essentially a free market system, modified only by some of the ideas behind the New Deal. Corresponding to this, they wanted an international system with relatively free trade and currency convertibility. They would not have wanted to see all tariffs and protection abolished, but they did want to get rid of bilateral trade deals and preferential trading systems. They were against exchange controls on principle. They were especially unhappy about the development of the sterling area and Commonwealth preference in the 1930s. Some members of the administration might agree that Europe could not face a free market system for some years, but it was not so easy to convince Congress on that point.

The British position was largely devised and also presented by Keynes himself. Domestic stability of output and employment was the top priority. International obligations should not be such as to obstruct that aim. If America were again to fall into a depression, it must be possible for the rest of the world to escape infection. The world economy should be managed as well as it could be, but if that management failed then national governments should be free to find their own solutions to their national problems. Seen in that light, free trade and convertibility were less important. Access to international credit was essential, so that countries did not need to suffer recessions in order to keep their trade in balance. The freedom to adjust exchange rates was particularly important to those in Britain who blamed their interwar traumas on the overvaluation of sterling in 1925.

A League of Nations (1944) report on the interwar years gives us the background to these debates. It was written from a distinctly Keynesian point of view. It suggested that any new international system should be built on the common acceptance of the need for stable employment. It contrasted this with the aim of exchange rate stability which it said was the common objective of countries which adopted the gold standard. It said that the only true equilibrium was one in which all countries were at a position of full employment. Persistent unemployment in any one country should be interpreted as a sign that its currency was overvalued. It was not necessary for trade actually to be out of balance.

The concept of 'fundamental disequilibrium', as the justification for realignment is explicit in this report:

> The general interest may call for an occasional revision of currency values so as to eliminate as far as possible any chronic and structural disparity between price levels and exchange rates in different countries.

The need arises because wages and prices are rigid – there is no suggestion that they should be made more flexible. If currency values are not appropriate then there will be 'fundamental and persistent disequilibrium'. No more precise definition is offered. The action to be taken is a matter for international agreement, since the general interest is involved. Countries should not simply change their exchange rates unilaterally.

Before the Bretton Woods conference was called there were originally two plans (described in detail in van Dormael, 1978): the American White plan and the British Keynes plan. They were similar in most respects: both envisaged a fixed but adjustable exchange rate regime and a new unit of account, fixed, more or less firmly, to gold – White had the Unitas and Keynes had Bancor. The White plan had a Fund from which loans could be made, whilst Keynes had a Clearing Union to settle payments between central banks, with the possibility of overdrafts on the British model. The difference in terminology indicated a difference in emphasis: the Americans attached more importance to the re-establishment of an international capital market in which the private sector could participate as well as official institutions.

The Articles of the International Monetary Fund, as they were agreed after the conference, were determined by what Congress would accept. One concession made to the British position was the so-called 'scarce currency clause'. This was supposed to reduce the asymmetry between the positions of borrowers and lenders. It was obviously aimed in the first instance at the risk of an American refusal to cooperate. It was not forgotten that America had gone on accumulating reserves during the interwar period when the rest of the world was desperate to rebuild them. If such selfish behaviour was repeated after Bretton Woods then the IMF could, in theory at least, apply some sanctions. In practice it was clear that the Fund would find it very difficult to take any action which displeased its largest shareholder. The fact that its headquarters were to be in Washington was a sign of where the power was located.

Agreement at Bretton Woods left much still to be settled. How soon, for example, would convertibility be restored? The Americans wanted to make progress almost straight away. In 1947 Britain was pressing for a loan to replace the grants by which America had financed British expenditure during the war. Convertibility of sterling was made a condition before any funds would be provided, despite British advice that it would be impossible to comply. In the event the experiment failed in a matter of weeks as everyone in the world who was short of dollars rushed to buy them in exchange for sterling. It would be more than a decade before the arrangements for general multilateral clearing envisaged at Bretton Woods could actually come into force.

The degree of exchange rate flexibility was another question which had to be settled by experience. The initial par values of IMF members were set by their own monetary authorities, as a matter of policy and judgement – there was no market in which their viability could be tested. Even supposing that they were appropriate at the outset, they were quickly overtaken by the very different rates of inflation in various countries in the late 1940s.

Many countries at this stage preferred to keep their exchange rates high, simply to reduce the cost of essential imports. Their exports were limited by industrial capacity, not by price competition. But as the years passed the anomalies got worse, and the US Treasury thought the time was ripe for a general realignment.

With exchange controls in place, governments might have thought that they could set their rates at any level they chose. In fact it was not as simple as that. The controls leaked, and speculative pressure could build up, for example through distortion to the timing of trade flows and the payments for them, known as 'leading and lagging'. Sterling, in particular, came under increasing pressure – reflecting the problems of the 'outside' sterling area countries, as well as the British economy itself.

A reasonably orderly devaluation was achieved in 1949. The pound was marked down by 30 per cent, along with most of the other sterling area currencies. France devalued by 22 per cent and Germany by 20. The main effect therefore was to increase the value of the dollar relative to most other currencies. At the time the extent of the changes seemed if anything excessive. Certainly the speculative pressure was removed, and the prospects for European exports began to look very good. The onset of the Korean War did much to solve the problem of the US surplus, at least for the next few years.

The extent to which funds would in practice be available to ease balance of payments adjustment was another question unresolved in the 1940s. One view of how the system ought to work was articulated in a report prepared, not for the IMF, but for the United Nations (1949). Its authors included Kaldor, the ultra-Keynesian. It recommended that all countries should publish clear and quantified objectives for employment, with a view to promoting stability and confidence. More than that, they should also pre-announce the measures that they would take to increase demand if their targets were not met – for example reductions in income tax or general sales tax. (No such automatic response was thought appropriate in the case of incipient inflation.)

The report went on to describe how countries should plan their economies in collaboration with each other. Targets for exports and imports should be set and compared across countries to see if they were mutually compatible. A country which could not sell sufficient exports to its trading partners should not, for that reason, contract domestic demand in order to reduce its imports. On the contrary, it should *expand* domestic demand so as to maintain the level of output and employment. The governments of countries that foresaw a balance of payments surplus could buy imports of raw materials to hold in stock.

The most provocative recommendation in the report was that the finance of balance of payments deficits should be automatic. Countries with surpluses should not be allowed to accumulate reserves. Instead any excess of receipts over payments should be lent straight back to the IMF, which would then lend them on to the countries that were in deficit. This would ensure that no country was prevented from maintaining full employment by a constraint on its external account. If it ever happened that funds were not made available to a country in deficit then it might suspend convertibility, or resort to bilateral trading. In no case should it be obliged to abandon its objective of full employment.

The report shows what arrangements would have had to be put in place if full employment really was to be guaranteed. It was an attempt, after the event, to describe what would have had to be done by the rest of the world in the 1930s in order to offset the international effects of the American depression. Fortunately that situation was not in fact repeated. But the measures in the report were the necessary counterpart of the domestic policies contemplated by many followers of Keynes. They were, of course, quite different from the measures actually put into place.

Prospective surplus countries had no intention of providing unlimited and unconditional funding to those which ran deficits. The German position is summed up by Ropke (1960) in a critique he wrote of the UN report. He described the arrangements proposed for IMF lending, and commented:

> This means that the more extravagant the economic policy of a country is, the more it will be entitled to refill its depleted reserves at the expense of the more responsible countries.

What actually happened was very different from the recommendation of the UN report, but it did involve a very substantial transfer of funds from the United States to the countries of Europe (including Germany). In 1947, as a result of the deteriorating economic and political situation in Europe, the Americans provided Marshall Aid. It was very generous, but it was not automatic or unconditional. Indeed, the availability of this aid, and the terms on which it was granted, had a profound effect on the domestic policies of some European countries. Perhaps Britain and France, for example, would in any case have backed away from the more extreme versions of the planned economy by the end of the 1940s. Certainly American influence was pushing them in the direction of a freer market.

Marshall Aid also required European countries to coordinate their plans for economic recovery amongst themselves. This was the original purpose of the Organisation for European Economic Cooperation (the OEEC), which later on became the Organisation for Economic Cooperation and Development (the OECD). This body did something which, at this stage, the IMF could not. It provided an effective framework, and technical support, for practical discussions of policy between officials. It was located in Paris and, perhaps for that reason, escaped complete domination by the Anglo-Saxons. Since the countries of eastern Europe were never members, it also escaped the worst of the ideological rhetoric which plagued the debates in the UN Economic Commission for Europe in Geneva.

There are those who maintain that a stable international monetary regime requires that one country should exercise hegemony. They will want to point to the years immediately following the Second World War as an example of a successful regime brought about by the dominant influence of the United States. The system was to be orderly, unlike that of the 1930s; but it was to be managed, unlike that of the 1920s. It was to be managed principally by the American Treasury, although other countries could be expected to gain more influence as they regained economic strength. It was doubtful from the very start how well it would function if American leadership became less effective, or if others began to challenge it. Management without hegemony was indeed to prove problematic.

The existence of an international regime of this character had implications for domestic policy everywhere. Considerable divergences were tolerated, but the hope remained in many minds that all the various systems would one day converge on something close to the American model. However, the American model itself had first to demonstrate its superiority. It had, after all, failed dismally in the tests of the 1930s. Memories of that failure were still present, despite the phenomenal success of the American economy in war. By the end of the 1940s another development was shaping attitudes. As the contest with the Soviet Union became explicit, it became an article of faith in America that the free market was a better system than state control. Those who needed the protection of the United States armed forces could not afford, whatever their mental reservations, to diverge too far from that fundamental belief.

The new economics

During the 1940s Keynesian economics became the new orthodoxy in Britain and increasingly in America as well. In the best-selling college textbook of Paul Samuelson, the multiplier, the marginal efficiency of capital, liquidity preference and the rigidity of wages simply replace the classical theory of general equilibrium. Students are not even encouraged to study the ideas which were current before 1936. The part of the book which describes them begins with this dismissive aside:

> This and the next section on the inadequacies of the quantity theory of money and prices may be skipped by readers not interested in the relationship between modern and older viewpoints. (Samuelson, 1948, p. 292)

Nowhere is the theoretical basis for the long-run neutrality of money clearly set out. It is tacitly assumed that the economy is characterised by what Irving Fisher had called 'money illusion'. It is asserted that changes in the money supply have effects on real variables, so that neither output nor the velocity of circulation of the money stock can be regarded as given, even in the long run. Hence it is possible to double the money supply without ever doubling prices. The quantity theory is not worth studying because it is either irrelevant or wrong.

In the second edition of the same textbook, the quantity theory has actually been relegated to an appendix. There is, however, a highly significant footnote to that appendix, which reads:

> For those interested in the refinements of economic theory it can be said that recent discussions have greatly reduced the area of disagreement between the different theories. (Samuelson, 1951, p. 355)

This is followed by a reference to the work of Pigou (1941), who had indeed published a book which showed how the *General Theory* need not be inconsistent with the quantity theory in the long run. His point was that consumers would be likely to spend more out of any given income if they had accumulated savings on which they could draw. Thus the quantity of money, and other liquid assets, could have a direct effect on spending, and hence on prices. Keynes had, in any case, admitted that the quantity of money could influence spending indirectly though its effect on interest rates. Both effects, direct and indirect, would continue to operate until the price level had risen sufficiently to reduce the real value of the money supply to the level which the public wished to hold.

The main concern of Keynesians was not with such 'refinements', but with the development of a new method of interpreting, and perhaps predicting, the behaviour of national output and income. During the war the national income accounts were found to be useful as a framework for deciding what resources were available for government to spend. After the war the same calculation was made to estimate what resources were available for export. But the format could also be used to estimate what the level of output would be for any given level of government spending and taxation; in other words it could be a tool of demand management.

In this new context, causation was seen as running from expenditure decisions (for example the investment plans of the private sector) to output (for example of machine tools) to incomes (and especially wages and salaries) and hence back to expenditure (especially on consumer goods). All the elements in this model were measured in real terms, the level of wages and prices being treated as invariant. The assumption was that at each stage in the circular flow there was some small delay in response, making it possible for a well-informed observer to anticipate events by a few months, or perhaps even a year or two. This very simple way of viewing the economy is sometimes called 'hydraulic Keynesianism', because it concentrates exclusively on flows, of income and of expenditure.

Keynes died in 1946; there followed what has been described as the struggle for the apostolic succession (Harris, 1947). His writings contain enough ambiguity to be claimed as support for very different economic and political views. Some 'Keynesians' were in favour of economic planning, others of an active monetary policy – confusion over the meaning of the word was to persist for decades. But one thing that all his followers did have in common was a disbelief in the self-righting properties of the market system.

It is sometimes difficult to distinguish the elements of economic theory or observation from the elements of political philosophy or commitment. One has, for example, to distinguish between the assertion that wages are in fact inflexible and the feeling that it is unreasonable to require them ever to fall. Equally, one must distinguish the proposition that the level of unemployment has no equilibrium, from the political or moral conviction that the level of unemployment is often too high. Some of the converts to the new economics were impressed by its ability to explain the events of the 1930s; others were perhaps attracted more by its implicit values, by ideals of social solidarity reinforced by the shared hardships of the war.

Keynesian economics, variously understood, became the new conventional wisdom in Britain and in some influential circles in America. Economists and policymakers on the continent of Europe did not follow the same lines of thought. To be radical in France or Germany was usually to be Marxian in outlook. This meant offering a quite different analysis of the problems that beset market economies. There was some fruitful hybridisation between Marx and Keynes, often breaking all links with the methods of classical theory.

There were also those on the Continent who regarded Keynes as a dangerous heretic. They saw in his policy proposals the thin end of a wedge which would open the way to a planned, and hence a dictatorial, economy. This was the position of Jacques Rueff (1947), of the Banque de France, when he came to the defence of his compatriot, Say, against the attack on Say's law in the *General Theory*. Significantly, he begins with the assumption that the money supply consists of gold coins – appropriate enough for the period in which the law was formulated, and not quite as irrelevant to twentieth-century France as it would seem to the British postwar disciples of Keynes. The hoarding of gold was a familiar problem in France. It caused deficient demand for consumer goods, but, Rueff maintained, it substituted a demand for newly produced gold. Thus demand in total was not deficient, the problem was rather its structure. Resources had to be transferred from one industry to another, and there might indeed be some structural unemployment in the process.

Rueff said that a similar analysis could be applied to a modern banking system. Excess demand for money to hoard in the form of bank deposits could also be understood as an indirect demand for goods and services. Corresponding to the deposits created to satisfy the demand for money were bank loans, which might finance new investment. He also noted that an increase in the propensity to hoard would result in a fall in the level of prices. Thus, by one means or another, the classical assumption that supply creates demand was valid even in the circumstances of a depression: it just took time for all the structural adjustments to be made. He added that Keynes' preferred remedy – public works – also required labour to shift from one industry to another. In effect he is rejecting the concept of aggregate demand and the whole macroeconomic apparatus built upon it. In France the new planning framework took account of the structure of output and employment, not just the total of activity. Similarly the new methods of credit control determined the direction, not just the magnitude, of its increase.

Noone, observing the effects of monetary reform in Germany, or monetary restraint in France, could easily dismiss the old idea that financial conditions determine price behaviour. In more extreme conditions that relationship was more obvious, as even the proponents of the new economics had to admit. One could question whether the growth of the money supply caused the increase in prices, or vice versa. But it was difficult to avoid the conclusion that stopping the growth of the money supply, if it could be done, was enough to ensure that inflation ended too. This demonstration does not seem to have had much effect on opinion in Britain and America. In fact a rather different 'experiment of nature' was being conducted in those countries at the same time.

Although it does not seem to have been much noticed at the time, the behaviour of market economies in the late 1940s was generating new data very relevant to the disputes between the new economics and the old. The war itself added little to knowledge, as the market system was not free to operate. Noone doubted that a world war would secure full employment, and that it would result in inflation, either open or suppressed. The interesting question was what happened next. Would demand fall away as the stimulus of military spending was withdrawn? Would the level of employment revert to that of the 1930s?

The war left most economies awash with excess liquidity – perilously so in Germany, Japan and France, but abundantly so also in Britain and America. In 1947, the money supply (M1) was up by 115 per cent in Britain and by 167 per cent in America, in real terms adjusting for consumer prices. Any other measure of liquidity or disposable financial wealth would tell a similar story. Classical economics would forecast continuing demand for goods and services, and continuing price inflation until the real value of the liquid wealth was reduced to a more normal relationship with real incomes. A purely 'hydraulic' version of Keynesianism would ignore any such influence from asset stocks.

At the end of the 1940s it appeared that the classical prediction was being proved wrong. Output growth slowed down and inflation almost stopped. There was talk of another recession, reminiscent of that of the 1920s. But classical economics is never very precise in the time scale of its predictions. Looking a little further ahead, the theory might seem to have been vindicated. The recession never really took hold. Output recovered and the rise in unemployment in America was halted at about 6 per cent, far below the prewar level. There followed a few years of worldwide expansion and price inflation, with commodity prices in the lead. Was this the delayed consequence of monetary expansion during the Second World War? Or was it the result of contemporaneous military expenditure renewed during the conflict in Korea? As so often, alas, the evidence was not conclusive.

Even if the quantity theory was out of fashion, the new economics did not neglect the study of inflation. Indeed the actual process was being studied in close detail (see, for example, Brown, 1955). A distinction was made between prices which respond directly to demand, principally those of raw materials and foods, and those which are based on a competitive or conventional mark-up over costs. In the industrialised countries, most prices are of the latter kind. This implied that, in those countries, inflation is mainly a phenomenon of the labour market. The crucial issue is how wages will respond to the demand for labour. As another departure from the classical model, that market is regarded as very imperfectly competitive, dominated by the monopoly power of the trades unions. Its behaviour depends on collective bargaining strategies, rather than the forces of market supply and demand.

It was becoming standard in wage negotiations to assume that workers should be compensated in full for the increase in the cost of living since their last settlement date. Together with cost-plus pricing, this created a spiral of inflation, which could be set off by even a small disturbance. The speed of the spiral would depend on the frequency of wage increases, typically once a year, and the time it took for firms to reset their selling prices. The lags in adjustment made it possible to forecast inflation with some success a few months ahead.

If inflation became really fast, however, the lag in adjustment would itself be curtailed. There seemed to be no brakes on the price level at all. Monetary policy at this time was generally described as neutral. This meant that the quantity of money was intended to grow in line with incomes and that interest rates were intended to remain unchanged. In an open economy the exchange rate could provide an alternative anchor, but the philosophy of Bretton Woods was that exchange rates which got out of line with relative price levels should be adjusted to remove the 'fundamental disequilibrium'.

It was in the 1940s that the prediction could first be made with confidence that the trend of the price level will always be upward. After the First World War there was a common expectation that the price level would fall back to its prewar level, and that was indeed what happened in a few countries by the 1930s. Friedman and Schwartz (1963, ch. 10) suggest that a similar expectation influenced behaviour in America during the Second World War. If so, that expectation was proved quite wrong. During and after that war the level of prices, as opposed to their rates of change, ceased to be a matter of any significance to policymakers, or indeed to anyone else. There was no longer any suggestion that what went up should later come down. This attitude had been forced on governments and central banks in many countries at a much earlier date; now it was true of America and Britain as well.

The observation that prices almost always go up, but at speeds which vary from year to year, could be explained by the model of the ratchet. When demand is strong prices rise; when demand is weak they do not fall. This model did not apply to commodity prices, but it did seem to fit wages very well, and perhaps the prices of manufactured goods. It is already implicit in the treatment of wages in the *General Theory*, since they are assumed to respond to demand only when employment is full. The implication must be that price stability can be preserved, over a period of many years, only if full employment *never* occurs, even at the top of the economic cycle.

There was great reluctance even to slow down inflation by allowing demand to weaken and unemployment to rise. The hope rather, especially in
Britain, was that trades unions would exercise restraint in their wage claims
so as to make the maintenance of full employment possible. Beveridge believed in 'responsibility and public spirit'. These are not words very familiar
in economic theory; this does not mean however that they are unknown in
the real world.

During the war no-one could realistically describe the setting of wages
as motivated solely by economic self-interest. There was a sense of common purpose, backed up by the threat of sanctions against those who tried
to break ranks. That was how people actually behaved at the time, not just
an ideal to which only utopians would aspire. After the war was over, the
appeal of patriotism might be felt with less force, but the incentive to find
a cooperative solution to the 'game' of wage bargaining was actually
strengthened. During the war it was safe to assume that full employment
would be maintained whatever the rate of inflation; after the war it was
not. By agreeing to moderate their claims, the big unions acting together
could have a powerful influence on inflation, and hence make it easier for
government to keep up the pressure of demand.

Such was the new economics, as it developed from the experience of the
1930s and the practice of the war years. It is a theme of this study that accepted economic theory can have an influence on subsequent economic
behaviour. Belief in the stability of the market contributed to the resilience
of economic activity in the days of the gold standard. The new economics
may have contributed to the downfall of the old regime in the 1930s; it was
to be the foundation of the new regime that replaced it. The new economics disbelieved in the stability of the market system, but it substituted for
that a belief in the efficacy of government policy.

The new article of belief was that governments could reliably achieve and
maintain full employment. They have the technical knowledge to do the
job. The new economics gives them the right formula to use. To accept that
proposition required a tremendous leap of faith. The claim to new knowledge was altogether untested; the new theories were only a decade or so
old and still in the process of refinement. It is easy to see why the claim
was accepted that the market on its own would not work well – recent
experience amply confirmed that. It did not follow from that claim, however, that government intervention could put things right. Yet that
proposition was generally accepted – and the fact that it was accepted
changed the way that the economy behaved.

Some governments themselves accepted the new theories which attributed so much power to them. If they really had the knowledge to ensure

full employment, then they could hardly refuse to make use of it. A serious lapse from full employment would be regarded as the fault of governments; it would all the more risk political instability. When governments pledged themselves to achieve employment objectives, at the end of the war, that commitment was credible, because it was in their own interests to keep it.

A popular faith in economic stability is itself a powerful, perhaps an indispensable, stabilising force. A government with a fully credible commitment to a fixed exchange rate will never need to intervene in the market. In a rather similar fashion, a government with a fully credible commitment to full employment may not need to manage demand very actively at all. It may need only to stand ready and able to inject extra demand into the economy should it be needed. So long as the instruments of policy do not need to be used at all energetically, then their real effectiveness will never be put to the test.

In his review of economic policy in Britain at this time, Booth points out, quite correctly, that most of the policy proposals put forward by Keynes were never in fact adopted. There was, for example, little active counter-cyclical variation in either fiscal or monetary policy. He writes:

> The inescapable conclusion is that, although Keynesian *analysis* was embedded at the centre of the policymaking machine, most of the elements of the Keynesian proposals were discarded. (Booth, 1989, p. 175)

But if the analysis really was accepted, not just by policymakers but by the public at large, then perhaps there was less need for the policy action to be taken.

5   The golden age (1950–1965)

A success story

If the aim of economic policy is to combine stability with growth, then the 1950s and early 1960s must be the high point of success in the twentieth century. After a careful review of statistics for seven major countries over more than a hundred years, Michael Bordo concluded:

> The Bretton Woods regime exhibited the best overall macro perform-ance of any regime. (Bordo and Eichengreen, 1993, p. 27)

This judgement is based on comparisons of the level and constancy of inflation, output growth, real interest rates and real exchange rates. The paper does not even mention the remarkably low level of unemployment in almost all countries for the whole of the 'golden age'. That can only re-inforce its conclusion.

Contemporaries were aware that they lived in good times. Christopher Dow (1964), for example, in his study of the British economy wrote:

> In terms of its fundamental aim – the desire so to manage the economy as to prevent the heavy unemployment that accompanied the prewar trade cycle – modern economic policy has clearly been a success.

He went on to point out some less welcome developments, in particular the persistence of inflation, but he left the reader in no doubt as to his favourable overall judgement on the outturn. The British Prime Minister summed it up in the famous words, 'You've never had it so good'.

Table 5.1 *Consumer price inflation, 1950–1965, per cent*

	USA	UK	France	Germany	Japan
1950	1.2	2.5	9.9	−7.1	−6.9
1951	7.6	9.9	16.7	8.7	16.5
1952	2.2	9.0	12.1	2.0	4.8
1953	1.1	3.1	−2.0	−2.0	6.7
1954	0.5	2.0	0.0	0.0	6.4
1955	−0.5	3.9	1.0	2.0	−1.1
1956	1.6	3.8	3.0	7.8	0.4
1957	3.6	3.6	4.8	−2.7	3.1
1958	2.5	2.6	14.7	1.9	−0.3
1959	1.0	0.9	6.4	0.9	0.9
1960	1.4	0.8	3.8	1.8	3.7
1961	1.0	3.4	2.9	1.8	5.3
1962	1.4	4.1	4.9	3.5	6.8
1963	0.9	2.3	4.7	2.5	7.5
1964	1.4	3.1	3.2	2.5	3.8
1965	1.8	4.4	4.3	3.2	7.7

Source: Mitchell (1998).

Taking 1950 as the base year, the level of gross domestic product in 1965 was as follows: 152 in the UK, 178 in the USA, 207 in France, 277 in West Germany, and a phenomenal 365 in Japan. Before the event, noone seems to have predicted growth rates remotely like that. Before the war the expectation was of secular stagnation – a prospect which alarmed Keynes in particular. Even in retrospect it is not easy to explain what happened. Clearly, the initial years of the 1950s were still part of the postwar recovery, but that explains only a small part of the phenomenon. The expansion of trade, which contributed to growth, can be seen as making up for the ground lost in the 1930s. Similarly, the increase in the capital stock can be explained as making up for investment opportunities missed in the depression and in wartime. Japan, and to a lesser extent the countries of Europe, were catching up with techniques of production developed earlier in the United States. Even so, one is left marvelling at the speed of progress, and uncertain that a complete explanation has been found.

Earlier in the century, fears were expressed that economic stabilisation and 'social control' were not compatible with enterprise and growth. The 1950s and 1960s saw the development of mixed economies, with governments playing a major, sometimes a dominant, part in the allocation of resources. They were also years of relative stability in output and inflation,

Table 5.2 *Growth rate of GDP, 1950–1965, per cent*

	USA	UK	France	Germany	Japan
1950	8.7	3.3	7.5	19.4	10.3
1951	9.8	3.0	6.2	9.8	12.5
1952	4.3	−0.2	2.7	9.2	11.6
1953	3.7	3.9	2.9	8.8	7.4
1954	−0.7	4.1	4.9	7.7	5.7
1955	5.6	3.6	5.7	12.0	8.6
1956	2.0	1.2	5.1	7.6	7.5
1957	1.9	1.6	6.0	5.9	7.3
1958	−0.5	−0.2	2.5	4.3	5.8
1959	5.5	4.0	2.9	7.8	9.1
1960	2.0	5.8	7.0	8.7	13.1
1961	2.5	3.3	5.5	4.5	12.0
1962	6.1	1.0	6.7	4.6	8.9
1963	4.4	3.8	5.4	2.8	8.5
1964	6.0	5.3	6.5	6.7	11.7
1965	6.3	2.6	4.8	5.4	5.8

Source: Maddison (1995).

due in part it seems to demand management using both fiscal and monetary policies. This did not seem to get in the way of innovation and economic progress in any way. Neither did it require the sacrifice of individual liberty and human rights; it was not in fact the 'road to serfdom'.

It is an open question however to what extent the growth rates of this period can actually be scored as achievements of government policy. At the time it was widely believed that the deliberate expansion of demand, and official fostering of investment, both made important contributions. We may note for example one comment by a Japanese economist, seeking to understand the remarkable record of the previous decade:

> Postwar growth cannot be fully understood without first considering the nature and characteristics of the fiscal and monetary policies adopted by the government. (Tachi, 1966)

He emphasised particularly the low level of interest rates and the priority given to investment both in public spending and in the allocation of credit.

Full employment was maintained in most countries throughout these years. That was certainly the case in Britain, France and Japan. West

Germany began with a rate of unemployment as high as 10 per cent, thanks to migration from the East, but nearly all of the labour force was absorbed into employment by the end of the 1950s. In the United States, the rate was typically around 5 per cent, with some variation over the cycle. This was significantly higher than it had been at the end of the war, although much lower than it had been in the 1930s. It was said that much of the difference between levels of unemployment in Europe and America was due to different rates of turnover in the labour markets. Certainly it is problematic to compare rates of unemployment across countries, whether one is concerned with measuring the pressure of demand, or with assessing social conditions.

The low levels of unemployment in Europe may, nevertheless, be regarded as amongst the most 'golden' aspects of the age. Poverty was reduced, and so was social exclusion. In that respect Beveridge was proved right. It should not be forgotten, however, that societies remained stratified, so that social inclusion might mean membership of a community which was itself excluded from access to many economic opportunities.

The cost of full employment was persistent inflation – or so it was thought at the time. At the start of the 1950s inflation was generally brisk, thanks to the sharp increases in commodity prices at the time of the Korean War. (In 1951, inflation was 7.6 per cent in the USA, 8.7 per cent in West Germany, 9.9 per cent in Britain, 16.5 per cent in Japan and 16.7 per cent in France.) These were quite alarming figures. But, almost immediately after that, commodity prices fell back, and inflation rates in the advanced countries were low or even negative. The system survived a serious inflationary shock with remarkably little trouble. In America the price level was almost stationary for several years in the mid-1950s.

Taking the fifteen years as a whole, the average rates of inflation in the five major countries were as follows: West Germany 2.3 per cent; the USA 1.8 per cent; the UK 3.7 per cent; Japan 4.8 per cent and France 5.4 per cent. (In the case of Japan it is worth adding that the rate of increase of wholesale prices was far lower; the cost of services and the retail mark-up increased as living standards rose.) In 1961 the OEEC published a report called *The Problem of Rising Prices*. Looking back one might question whether the rate of inflation in either Germany or America really constituted a problem at all.

At the time the received opinion was that inflation, even at very moderate rates, was seriously inequitable and also potentially explosive. The OEEC experts put it like this:

It was very sobering that the general level of prices failed to decline in 1958, even though there was a substantial fall in the prices of internationally traded raw materials. This indeed pointed to a future in which average prices would move only one way – given the intention of governments to prevent depression and stagnation – so that after a period of years it would be certain that the price level would be higher and the value of money lower ... Experience has shown the inequities that are caused by inflation and the false incentives it gives for making gains from speculation on rising prices rather than by constructive contributions to national production and higher living standards. (OEEC, 1961, p. 10)

Before dismissing such concerns as exaggerated, it is right to remember that the monetary regime of the time was still linked, if rather tenuously, to gold. This was supposed to mean that the price level could not just drift upwards indefinitely, either in America while the gold price of the dollar was fixed or elsewhere in the absence of exchange rate devaluations. In the long run, under such a regime, inflation even as low as 2 per cent a year must present a problem. The OEEC report also worried that inflation was coming to be anticipated. They thought that this made it more damaging rather than less, although one can argue in theory that inflation causes less misallocation of resources if it is foreseen.

To the extent that the markets expected inflation, interest rates would have to increase in compensation. In this way the borrowers would be prevented from gaining at the expense of the lenders. We can see this happening progressively during this period. In America, for example, the yield on long-term government securities began the 1950s at just 2.3 per cent, far below the current rate of inflation: ten years later the rate was about 4.0 per cent, which implied a modest real return if the going rate of inflation was expected to continue. In Britain the yield on consols was rather higher than that, reaching about 6 per cent in the early 1960s, enough to compensate for a higher expected rate of inflation. Markets were becoming more aware of the problem of rising prices, although of course they failed to anticipate in full what was actually to happen to inflation within the life of a medium- or long-term instrument issued at this time.

It may well be that the tolerance of 'creeping' inflation prepared the way for the much more serious problems of the 1970s. Looking only at the short term, however, it is hard to believe that economic efficiency was seriously damaged by the 'speculation' which the experts deplored. The waste of resources from economising on the holding of cash balances was surely trivial at this time. The main problems were with very long-term contracts specified in nominal terms. Once the stability of the price level is abandoned it becomes very difficult to foresee the value in say twenty years of a mortgage or a pension or a life insurance policy. But against this one must set the argument that adjustment of relative prices is actually made easier by a little inflation, because it spares those responsible for setting wages and prices from the embarrassment of ever having to announce a reduction.

The OEEC report also blamed persistent inflation for the uneven pace of growth in most countries. Under a fixed exchange rate system countries in which inflation was relatively fast were obliged to rein back demand repeatedly because overheating or a loss of competitiveness was causing a deterioration in their balance of payments. Even if the pressure was relieved from time to time by devaluation – as the Bretton Woods rules allowed – the path of output and employment would not be smooth.

In fact the amplitude of fluctuations in output and employment was much less at this time than either before or since. They were ripples, compared either with the waves of the classical cycles in the nineteenth century or with the big recessions of the late twentieth century. So quiet had the scene become by the late 1960s that a conference met to decide whether the business cycle had been abolished (see Bronfenbrenner, 1969). It was observed that the fluctuations in the USA in the 1950s had been relatively tame, and that since the end of that decade it had enjoyed one long period of boom. The mood was optimistic, reflecting the golden age, which was in fact just then coming to an end.

In the USA there were small falls in output in 1954 and 1958; in the UK the same was true of 1952 and 1958. In France and in Japan the stronger upward trend of output meant that no actual annual reductions appear in the data for this period, although the rate of increase was considerably slower in some years than in others, and sometimes unemployment rose. In West Germany the rate of increase was smooth as well as strong, and in every year unemployment fell or stayed at much the same level.

The character, as well as the intensity, of cycles seemed to be different from that of earlier days. Government spending now accounted for a larger share of total spending; it followed its own pattern, different from that of the private sector, sometimes counter-cyclical. The service sector was becoming more important, and manufacturing less so. Prices now lagged so far behind the cycle in activity that they actually appeared to vary inversely with it. Interest rates still went up and down with the cycle, but they were now interpreted as indices of government policy, rather than market confidence.

Robin Matthews suggested that the postwar cycle in Britain might actually be the result of demand management:

> The prominent part played by government has led many, if not most, observers to believe that what has been witnessed is not the old-style business cycle but a new kind of phenomenon known as 'stop-go'. (Matthews, 1969, p. 99)

He likened the behaviour of governments with inadequate reserves of foreign currency to that of the banks in the classical business cycle. They both had to cut short the boom phase of the cycle when their liquidity was threatened. He also suggested that the authorities now went through alternating cycles of optimism and pessimism about the potential growth rate of the economy, similar to those which affected the investment plans of private business. In order to understand the contemporary cycles it was necessary to study the 'reaction function' of the government or the central bank. In some countries their contribution would be to stabilise activity and damp down the fluctuations; in others, especially those with balance of payments problems, the behaviour of the authorities might be itself destabilising.

The experience of Japan could be interpreted in much the same way (Shinohara, 1969). There was, in effect, a ceiling on output; this was not a limit to productive capacity, but a limit to the level of imports which could be afforded. That constraint was put in place by government action, not by market forces as it would have been in the standard theoretical model. In Japan, however, the government did not have to set a floor to the level of output. As in the classical model, the depletion of inventories was enough to initiate recovery spontaneously at the trough of the cycle.

In reading contemporary accounts of economic behaviour during the golden age one is struck by how much of that behaviour is attributed to policymakers, either for good or for ill. It has since become more evident how little is understood, how wrong forecasts can be, and how powerless governments can appear. Perhaps they were not really in charge of events in the 1950s and 1960s, any more than they were later on. The question we might now want to put is about the value of the regime that was then in place, rather than about the merits of particular policy moves. Was the golden age the result of a uniquely well-designed system?

In reviewing the Bretton Woods era, the study by Michael Bordo referred to above asks whether the observed stability of the world economy was a reflection of the Bretton Woods system, or simply the consequence of a period with no major shocks impinging on it. No doubt he had in mind the oil price shocks of the 1970s and the international rivalry and conflicts of earlier decades. Perhaps the golden age was prosperous just because it was uneventful.

It is not easy to quantify the relative scale of different shocks without begging the question of their effects on the world economy. How does one rank the Korean War against that in Vietnam? Were the Arab–Israeli wars of 1967 and 1973 inherently more disruptive than the fighting in Algeria or the British intervention in Suez? Perhaps the moment when the peace of the world was at greatest risk was during the Cuba missiles crisis in 1962. The inflationary threat from commodity prices was perhaps as great in 1951 as in 1972, and yet the former episode was successfully contained whilst the latter proved disastrous.

One striking feature of the golden age is the almost complete absence of major financial panics of any kind. There were no spectacular bank failures, stock market crashes or market manias. This must be due in part to the rather comprehensive regulation present in many countries for most of the time. This did not altogether prevent destabilising speculation, in the foreign exchange markets at least, but it must have limited its scale. More fundamentally, there was confidence that governments would step in to prevent financial chaos, however it arose. Their resolve and their ability to do so were not really tested, but they may have been credible all the same.

It must also be relevant that these were, in the main, years of political consensus and social solidarity in most of the major industrial nations – France being the obvious exception. One can point to the experience of wartime, and to the external threat from the USSR; these have already been identified as important elements in the postwar period. But there was also broad agreement about the scope and character of domestic policy, across political parties and across many interest groups. Virtually everyone was in favour of economic growth, and looked to governments to produce it. If that growth could be maintained then there was benefit for all. It was good for profits, good for wages, good for tax revenue and government spending as well. It was the best possible way of resolving tensions and reinforcing cooperative behaviour.

There is a puzzle here about the direction of causation. Did the economies of the West grow rapidly because of the successful establishment of a new policy regime? Or was the policy regime a success only because the world economy happened to be expanding so fast at the time? Was there a virtuous circle? To begin to answer such questions one has to have some external point of reference, an economy cut off from the influence of America and the new European models, in which a quite different regime was in place. The obvious place to look is the USSR.

It is not easy to find reliable statistics for the growth of the Soviet Union. A recent survey offers a choice of sources (see Kemp, 1995). One gives an annual growth rate of 7.2 per cent in the 1950s, slowing down to just

4.4 per cent in the early 1960s. Another suggests 5.2 per cent, followed by 4.8 per cent for the same years. Overall these figures compare favourably with Britain and the USA, although they do not match those of West Germany or Japan. This comparison cannot do much to resolve the issue, but it does suggest that some of the factors which affected both East and West may help to account for the rapid increase in output in both.

It is beyond the scope of this study to explain the role of all the factors that contributed to the success story of the golden age. Our main concern is with the monetary regimes, both national and international. But they must be seen in their economic and political context. Strong growth worldwide is one very important part of their economic context; support for government intervention was a very important part of their political context; governments were given credit for the growth. The monetary regimes with which we are concerned were part of a new economic strategy and a new philosophy of government. It was the search for the new Utopia.

The visible hand

The popular metaphors for economic policy in the 1950s and 1960s were derived from motoring – car ownership was increasing rapidly at the time. The government was in the driving seat. Sometimes the economy needed a touch on the accelerator, sometimes it was necessary to slam on the brakes. More fundamentally the economy might require a larger engine; and it was the responsibility of government to supply that as well.

But, at the same time, regulations left over from the war were being eased or abolished, so that more reliance was being placed on market forces. The limits of government control and responsibility were often imprecise. Sometimes it was hard to say whether the economy was being guided by the invisible hand of the market or by the more visible hand of the state; the two seemed to work rather well together. All the major countries of the West had what might be called mixed economies, but the proportions were not the same.

Hermann van der Wee (1987) distinguishes three types of mixed economy. The first, which he calls the 'neo-collectivist variant', involved elements of public ownership and indicative planning as well as the management of demand. As examples, he gives France, Britain, Italy and Japan, each of them showing some distinctive features of its own. By the end of the 1950s, in both France and Japan, planning was seen as outstandingly successful; this was a model that other countries wanted to copy. Priority

was given to key sectors where there might be bottlenecks holding up the progress of the economy as a whole. These were chiefly in manufacturing, either capital goods or production for export. Such industries had to be made competitive at home and abroad. Planning was motivated by national rivalries. Countries which were losing their share of world markets, Britain for example, attributed their poor national performance to a lack of central direction.

In the early 1960s, Britain sought to correct this, first by setting up a National Economic Development Council, when the Conservatives were in power, and then by adopting a National Plan under Labour. Both proved largely futile, perhaps because they came too late to prevent the loss of competitiveness, perhaps because they lacked any real authority to allocate resources. In Britain the golden age was also an age of frustration: the performance of the economy, excellent though it was by past standards, never quite matched up to expectations, or to the achievements of other similar economies at the same time.

Two examples of the 'neo-free-market variant' of the mixed economy are the United States and West Germany. After the war the philosophy of government in America reverted to earlier traditions, but the actual size and influence of the public sector was still much greater than before. It did not go unnoticed that the growth rate in America was well below those of most other countries; by the early 1960s the balance of payments was also becoming a cause of concern. There was a perception that prosperity was failing to reach the poorest social groups. In 1961 the Kennedy administration promised a 'new frontier' and also a 'new economics'.

According to van der Wee (1987, p. 305):

> ... it can be contended that during the 1960s in the United States a clear shift from the neo-free-market to the planned variant of the mixed economy took place. So there was increasing convergence with the development in Western Europe.

Certainly a more purposeful management of demand was attempted, using fiscal policy more actively than before, with the intention of stimulating faster growth. In practice, it was easier to win congressional support for tax cuts than for a programme of extra government spending.

But the 'new economics' was not all derived from Keynes. Indicative planning and industrial policies were proposed by influential advisers like J.K. Galbraith. The federal government was given an enhanced role in relation to manpower, the regions and transportation. More significantly, the space

programme and defence spending gave the administration an opportunity to lead developments in many of the highest technology sectors.

In West Germany economic planning was discredited by its past associations. The new regime in Bonn was liberal in its philosophy and its economic policies were intended to encourage competition in the private sector. It remained true, however, that a significant proportion of German industry was publicly owned, that the trades unions were very influential and that big business often chose to cooperate with them. Opinion in Germany, as elsewhere, was impressed by the potential of demand management, preferably by means under the control of government, rather than the central bank. In 1961 the government was given some power to vary its budget for this purpose without first obtaining the approval of the Bundestag.

The third and last type of mixed economy is called the 'central consultation variant', typified by Sweden, the Netherlands, Austria and Belgium. These are all small countries, in which an explicit bargain could be struck between representatives of government, business and the trades unions. The sense of national identity was strong. Many of the individuals involved would know each other personally and were used to working closely together. The difference between this variant and the one called 'neo-collectivist' was a matter of degree. Less formal methods of resolving disputes were possible in smaller states. But the role of the market remained important, perhaps more so in the small states who saw themselves as powerless to resist external pressures from the markets of the world.

In all the variants of the mixed economy of this period the trades unions had economic power and political influence. In the public sector, where the state was the employer, the two were hard to distinguish from one another. Unions were also strong in some of the manufacturing industries which were thought to be most important for growth and national competitiveness. Parties of the left were dependent on trades union support to win elections, so union views on economic policy could not be ignored. In a few cases, France and Italy in particular, the movement was divided, with a large sector supporting the Communist Party; this reduced their power considerably. But in most countries the unions decided that they could serve the interests of their members best by cooperating with governments to maintain full employment and to keep inflation in check.

The OEEC report on rising prices addressed the issue of trades union power. It concluded that, at least in the United States and in Britain, wage increases were a factor independent of the pressure of demand adding to the rate of inflation. The experts wrote:

> Any study of how the labour market has operated leaves no reason-
> able doubt that something besides market forces was at work.
> (OEEC, 1961, p. 48)

They went on to consider whether this meant that they should recommend
an explicit government policy towards wages. On this matter they were
unable to reach agreement.

The majority said that governments should set a norm as a guide to wage
negotiations, indicating what rate of increase would be consistent with
national objectives for employment and prices. They referred to the failure to reach agreement on wages policy in Britain in 1956. But they also
described the success of the French government in setting a figure for wage
rises in 1958, as part of a wider stabilisation plan. It made use of its ability
to set wages in the public sector as well as the national minimum wage.
They also referred favourably to the independent enquiry into sustainable
wage increases set up by the German government in 1959.

The minority (Fellner from America and Lutz from Switzerland) thought
that such intervention was probably unnecessary. The labour market would
work even if there were important elements of collective bargaining. They
said, in any case, that they would not support a wages policy, even if it could
be shown to improve the immediate prospects for reconciling the aims of
full employment and price stability. They wrote:

> Even then, we would not favour moving towards government-regu-
> lated wage and price structures, but in this event we would urge
> making it clear to the public that wage bargaining between power-
> ful groups has become incompatible with a reasonable employment
> policy . . . Whenever the bargaining attitudes should create a last-
> ing conflict between significant policy objectives, the desirable
> solution requires sufficiently modifying the size and the functions of
> the organisational units on both sides of the bargaining table.
> (OEEC, 1961, p. 64)

In other words, the power of trades unions and employers' organisations
may have to be opposed, and not appeased, by government. But these, in
1959, were only the views of a minority.

Whilst most politicians may have thought of economic policy in terms
of negotiations with interest groups, most economists saw it as more like
engineering. More and more professional economists were being employed
in government departments. They offered expertise, insight and specialist
knowledge which the lay public did not possess. Lionel Robbins, of the

London School of Economics, compared the danger of relying on the untutored prejudices of public opinion with the substantial advances which he believed to have been made in applied macroeconomics:

> What does the instinct of the race or the good sense of the common people know of the terms of trade, of over-valued exchanges, of the inflationary gap and similar matters? Yet it is upon knowledge of just such matters as these that economic survival or disaster may depend. It is a big responsibility for professional economists. (Robbins, 1954, p. 11)

Expertise was being applied especially to the mechanics of demand management, and especially in Britain, America and the Netherlands. Economic forecasting was established as a regular routine, using a mixture of formal and informal methods. Econometric models were being developed, as the run of postwar observations increased in length. Surveys of business and consumer confidence were conducted. Forecasters from various countries met to compare their projections and to ensure that a consistent view emerged on the outlook for total world trade and prices. As experience accumulated it was possible to assess the accuracy of forecasts. The results were not very encouraging, and forecasters had to disarm their critics by moderating their own claims. The forecasting exercise was worth doing, because the results were generally more reliable than pure guesswork, but the error margins remained very large. In practice demand management consisted more of reacting to events than of anticipating them.

The question had to be faced, moreover, whether the attempt to stabilise the economy by active management might not have a perverse effect. Control engineers were very familiar with this possibility. A thermostat, for example, which responds to the temperature with a lag, can produce fluctuations of ever-increasing amplitude. In an attempt to 'fine tune' the economy the same result could occur: the control variable, interest rates or taxation, might begin to oscillate violently. It was necessary to design an appropriate control rule, or reaction function, defining how the instrument settings would respond to observed deviations of the target variables from their optimum trajectories (see, for example, Phillips, 1957). The terminology and the mathematics assumed that the economy was a mechanical system governed by unchanging laws of motion, which were invariant to the policy regime. Once those laws had been estimated, using appropriate statistical methods, all that remained to be done was to calculate the best feedback loop. Stabilisation policy was not in fact conducted like that, but there were many economists at the time who wished that it could be.

In the United States there was a school of thought, not very influential as yet, which believed that all such efforts at stabilisation were fundamentally misguided. They advocated policy rules of a different kind, fixed rules which did not respond to events at all. The rules should be simple and inflexible so that the public would come to understand them. For Milton Friedman the main point was that the Federal Reserve System could, and should, keep the money supply growing at a steady rate, just a few per cent a year, come what may. An active policy might well increase the instability that it was supposed to offset. At the time such views were often dismissed as outdated. Most economists, even in America, believed in active intervention, and emphasised fiscal rather than monetary policy as the appropriate instrument to use.

The common view was that changes in tax rates or public expenditure programmes were more potent than changes in interest rates. We find this view expressed in a popular graduate textbook written by Gardner Ackley, chairman of the Council of Economic Advisers under Kennedy:

> One of the most striking changes made by modern macroeconomic thought is that it largely reverses the previously conceived roles of monetary and fiscal policy. Today, monetary effects are recognised, and monetary policy is still seen as important, but the emphasis is on fiscal measures in securing stabilization (or, if badly used, in creating instability). This is the case even where fiscal measures are used in a way which has no effect, direct or indirect, on the quantity of money. (Ackley, 1961, p. 167)

By monetary policy in this passage the author clearly meant the control of interest rates and the money supply. That was commonly regarded as having a very uncertain, possibly very delayed, effect on demand. There was also, however, the possibility of controlling credit much more directly – operating on the assets side of the banks' balance sheets, rather than their liabilities. This was thought to be more powerful and predictable, but also more disruptive. It was appropriate in an emergency rather than in normal times. In several countries the authorities changed quite frequently the terms on which instalment credit and mortgages could be offered.

The principles underlying monetary policy in Britain at the end of the 1950s are exceptionally well documented in the report of the Radcliffe Committee (1959). The Bank of England was seen simply as an agent of the Treasury. Indeed, the committee wanted to do away with any vestige of Bank independence in the implementation of government policy. They thought that interest rates should be set by a standing committee under Treasury chairmanship, and that bank rate changes should be announced by the government. Independent central banks, they thought, were just advocates for the financial institutions that they were supposed to control.

Monetary policy should be an integral part of government strategy, not, as in Germany, a separate activity with its own objectives and responsibilities:

> It is ... no longer appropriate to charge the monetary authorities with unambiguous tasks that can be sharply differentiated from other governmental actions.

They recognised that 'reasonable stability in the value of money' was still a government aim, but they did not think that monetary policy would always be the right method of achieving it.

Any suggestion that the quantity theory of money could be a guide to monetary policy was unambiguously dismissed:

> ... some experts consider that the central task of the monetary authorities is to keep a tight control on the quantity of money. If, it is argued, the central bank has both the will and the means to control the supply of money, and either keeps it fixed or allows it to increase only in step with the growing needs of a growing economy, all will be well. In its extreme form, this doctrine is perhaps not widely held in this country, but its more moderate versions, according to all of which the concept of the supply of money holds the key position, are commonly heard, and were put in evidence to us.
>
> Our view is different. Though we do not regard the supply of money as an unimportant quantity, we view it as only part of the wider structure of liquidity in the economy ...
>
> It is possible, for example, to demonstrate statistically that during the last few years the volume of spending has greatly increased while the supply of money has hardly changed: the velocity of circulation of money has increased. We have not made more use of this concept because we cannot find any reason for supposing, or any experience in monetary history indicating, that there is any limit to the velocity of circulation; it is a statistical concept that tells us nothing directly of the motivation that influences the level of total demand. (Radcliffe Committee, 1959, paras 388, 389 and 391)

The Radcliffean view of monetary policy was that the authorities could influence the liquidity of the economy by acting on the level and structure of interest rates. Liquidity was not directly measurable, although it had a pervasive effect on spending decisions. It would be a mistake to vary interest rates too actively, as this would damage the market for government debt. This did not actually leave much for monetary policy to do.

The role of monetary policy was very different in West Germany, where the Bundesbank took over from the Bank Deutscher Länder in 1957 (see, for example, Marsh, 1992) and succeeded in preserving its independence from the federal government in Bonn. Interest rate decisions were often taken against the wishes of the government, and the Chancellor would on occasion express his displeasure in public. The central bank felt equally free to criticise the government for the laxity of its budgetary position. The president of the Bundesbank was appointed by the government; but even the friends and allies of chancellors became obstinately independent once they were in post. The record was one of disharmony, which some might now call constructive, although it did not seem so at the time.

The Bundesbank set interest rates, but the government was responsible for the exchange rate. That of itself tended to create discord, since the two were intimately related. Moreover, the Bundesbank, at this time, was strongly attached to the principle of exchange rate fixity. It took the view that changing the parity, even to raise it, destroyed the credibility of the counter-inflationary stance. If the exchange rate could go up, it could also go down. If the government could interfere with the external value of the Deutschmark, its internal value was not safe either.

In France, the crisis of 1958, which brought the Fourth Republic to an early end, was accompanied by a move to much stricter financial discipline. Jacques Rueff declared that the very existence of France was threatened; de Gaulle was convinced that French political influence could only be restored once the currency was strong again. A necessary devaluation of the franc was accompanied by greater liberalisation of payments and a more active use of interest rates to control the domestic economy. It would be wrong to describe French policy in this period as Keynesian; it was more like prewar financial orthodoxy, accompanied by intervention on the supply side of the economy.

The political context of monetary policy varied considerably from one country to another in the golden age. It is right to point to some convergence of ideas between America and Europe, as does van der Wee; but there was divergence also, as in the case of France. Yet some propositions which would have been highly debatable a generation before had become almost axiomatic everywhere. Governments had now to accept ultimate responsibility for the performance of national economies. They might discharge

that responsibility by freeing markets rather than by restricting them, but that was for them to decide. If then the markets did not deliver the stability and the prosperity that people wanted, the governments would be to blame.

Fixed, but adjustable

The international monetary regime of the 1950s and 1960s was a compromise between those who wanted the external discipline of fixed exchange rates and those who wanted the national autonomy of floating freely. As time went by it became clear that the system would have to evolve towards one extreme or the other. The choice could be delayed for many years, but only because of the continuation of exchange controls on both current and capital transactions.

The main problem initially was described as a shortage of dollars. It seemed that the American economy was far more productive and efficient than its trading partners, providing goods which all countries wanted to buy, but scarcely needing to import anything in return. It was feared that this was not just a passing phase, but a deeply ingrained structural problem (see MacDougall, 1957). It was by no means certain that exchange rate changes could be the answer. There were plenty of 'elasticity pessimists' who thought that the only significant effect of a devaluation was to add to the import bill. It was also thought politically impossible for the US to abolish its protective duties. Hence the governments of all countries had to be cautious about moving to full convertibility of their currencies. The experience of the British in 1947 was not forgotten. There might be a continuing need to discriminate against American exports, whatever damage that might do to diplomatic relationships.

That was how it appeared in the mid-1950s. Then, gradually and against expectations, the dollar problem solved itself. US military and aid expenditure increased. There was an outflow of private long-term capital as American corporations sought to establish production in lower-cost countries, closer to the fast growing markets. The countries of continental Europe moved to external balance as their export industries thrived. By the beginning of the 1960s, the problem was one of dollar glut.

The movement to current account convertibility, made possible by this turnaround, gathered pace in the late 1950s. The European Payments Union was set up as a first step towards multilateral clearing; it proved a great success and by 1955 payments could be made without much problem between countries in continental Europe. Progress might have been even faster but for the special problems of the pound sterling. The situation in France was also fragile until after the devaluation and reforms of 1958. Thereafter convertibility of European currencies with the dollar was made official. It took rather longer to reach that point in Japan, as the demand for imports was almost insatiable in such a fast growing economy. But exports grew even faster, and the yen was made officially convertible in 1964.

As currencies became convertible they became more exposed to speculative attack. Governments were increasingly required to deny in public that there was any possibility of a parity change. Their prestige came to be associated with the strength of their currency. In private British officials, for example, as early as 1952, debated the case for floating the pound; but nothing of the kind could be said in public. The public commitment to fixity became firmer, going well beyond what was actually required by the Bretton Woods agreement.

There was no real symmetry in the system, despite the intentions of its originators. A country faced with capital inflows did not feel that its national honour was at stake in resisting them. The Germans debated whether a revaluation of the Deutschmark would be a sign of strength or of weakness, and experimented for a time with restrictions on inward transfers. The Canadians took a quite different line: they stopped intervening in the markets and let their dollar float up. That strategy worked to their satisfaction for a number of years, but for the present no other major country followed their example.

An intellectual case for floating rates was being argued vigorously in America, most notably by Milton Friedman. He went so far as to say that floating rates were 'absolutely essential for the fulfilment of our basic economic objective in the achievement and maintenance of a free and prosperous world community enjoying unrestricted multilateral trade' (Friedman, 1953, p. 157). His case rested on the view that the observed instability of flexible exchange rates in the past had been the result of unstable domestic policies, or of an unstable environment. It was better for any turbulence that was unavoidable to show up in the relative prices of currencies and not the level of economic activity. It was deeply damaging to attempt to suppress volatility by regulating currency transactions or trade.

Friedman demonstrated how a fixed but adjustable regime could be the worst of both worlds. Speculators were being offered a one-way bet. It was often obvious in which direction any parity changes would be. Those who anticipated such changes correctly could make vast profits; if the rates stayed the same the speculators would lose almost nothing. Such a system did not do away with uncertainty or offer a stable environment for trade. The real choice was between free floating and something like the classical gold standard. Intermediate positions were not tenable. The virtues of the nineteenth century system were recognised but they were not thought sustainable in the modern world. They required a flexibility of domestic prices and interest rates which would not now be acceptable.

Friedman thought that most speculation under a floating-rate regime would be stabilising. It was in the interest of currency traders to locate the equilibrium in the market, based on the 'fundamentals'. They would buy when a currency was cheap, and sell when it was dear; in that way their behaviour would be both stabilising and profitable. Operators who were not profitable would soon be extinct (for some exceptions to this proposition, see Kemp, 1964, chapter 18).

The economists who supported fixed exchange rates were a mixed group. On the one hand there were those who regarded any market system with suspicion, financial markets most of all. They believed in exchange rates as instruments of policy to be fixed by governments and changed occasionally as part of a plan for economic development. On the other hand there were those who believed that the market system flourished when exchange rates were known with certainty. They did not think of exchange rates as prices allocating real resources, but as dimensions of national monetary policies, and hence as the responsibility of the monetary authorities concerned (see, for example, Robbins, 1954).

In a 'fixed but adjustable' system countries cannot avoid mutual dependence. It has to be managed by agreement amongst them. Those who enjoy surpluses have to lend to those in deficit, and such lending is never devoid of conditionality. The Bretton Woods system was designed to require interdependence and, at least initially, such cooperation was not lacking. There was a general wish to make the new institutions work. Without any surrender of sovereignty, countries agreed to a programme of consultation and surveillance which could in practice limit their freedom of action. The first stand-by agreements were negotiated with the IMF in the early 1950s, with tighter conditions attached to each tranche of the capital that was drawn. As the exchange markets became more active there was all the more need for the monetary authorities to support one another, but such support often had its price. Independence was limited by 'peer pressure, public exhortation and dependence on the possibility of borrowing from an outside institution' (James, 1996, p. 175).

The main institutions for international cooperation were already in existence: The IMF, the OECD, and the BIS. But these were all rather large organisations in which the smaller nations had a disproportionate voice.

If the big countries were to bargain effectively amongst themselves they wanted to do so at gatherings which were more exclusive. To meet this need, the OECD set up a body called Working Party Three, whilst the Group of Ten Deputies had a similar function in relation to the IMF. These rather secretive meetings could be the occasion for real negotiations amongst officials, as well as for the exchange of rhetoric. It could be quite uncomfortable to be isolated at a meeting of this kind.

By the early 1960s a division was emerging between the Anglo-Saxon reserve currency countries and the continental Europeans. Following the Treaty of Rome, signed in 1957, there was a European Economic Community with six member states working more closely together. It did not at this stage have any competence in monetary matters, but it was a sign of the times, pointing towards closer integration. It was not anti-American or anti-British, but it did mean a slight distancing from both. In 1963 de Gaulle vetoed a British application to join.

The Bretton Woods system could, in theory, be understood as a coalition of equals, in which each country set the value of its own currency in relation to gold. In practice, it was not like that: it was a dollar-based system, in which the Americans set the price of gold in relation to the dollar, and many of the other countries set their exchange rates in dollar terms. Reserves were held mainly in dollars, and this was the currency in which central banks intervened. Sterling was a like a planet with a few satellites of its own, but revolving round the dollar. This was the consequence of the circumstances in which the system was set up in the 1940s. It looked less appropriate a decade or so later.

The position of sterling was particularly precarious. It had been chosen as a reserve currency in the past, but now seemed less reliable. The sterling balances, held by countries with which Britain had close historical connections, were becoming a burden rather than a source of strength. They were much too large relative to the British economy and to the reserves in the Bank of England. They could not be converted into dollars or gold without producing a collapse of sterling. They made the British authorities reluctant to introduce convertibility. They made Britain particularly dependent on international support, but reluctant to accept the conditions on which it was available. It did not help that British policymakers of the Radcliffean school had very different views on monetary economics from those being developed by the IMF staff (James, 1996, p. 177).

The sterling balances were not seen as sacrosanct by everyone in Britain itself. Many expected, and hoped, that the incoming Labour government would devalue the pound in 1964. Once that option had been rejected, it became rather unpatriotic to mention it. But that did not stop Fred Hirsch:

A silent censorship on discussion of the exchange rate by those who
understand its economic implications has been accompanied by its
elevation into part of the national heritage by those who do not".
(Hirsch, 1965)

He was particularly bitter about the 'moralistic' attitudes of those who
thought that Britain had a duty to protect the holders of the sterling balances against any loss.

Mixing up morals with money is always dangerous, and often hides
a pretty thick layer of confusion and cant.

He had nothing to say about the issues of commitment and credibility which
were to become so important to the analysis of similar policy dilemmas by
economists a generation later.

It was evident from the early 1960s that the weakness of one reserve
currency could affect the other. At the same time as the British government
was pledging itself to defend the pound, the American government was
looking for ways of safeguarding the dollar. Persistent inflation and the
rapid growth of world trade since the 1940s had left central banks short
of reserves. There was a limit to the amount of gold available, so most of
the additions to reserves took the form of dollar deposits. As the proportion of dollar deposits to gold increased, confidence in the gold value of
the dollar was weakened. It was the US balance of payments deficit which
provided the rest of the world with dollars to hold, but ironically the
very fact of that deficit made the additional dollars less acceptable.
Not only did the situation appear unsustainable, it also seemed unfair.
Why should the Americans be able to pay for their imports, and their
purchase of foreign companies, simply by printing more of their own
currency?

There were rumours that the Kennedy administration would devalue the
dollar, or at least raise the dollar price of gold. On the open market there
was a 'gold rush' in 1960 pushing the price up from $35 per ounce to about
$40. To prevent a recurrence the Americans organised a gold pool in which
the Federal Reserve System and seven other central banks worked together
to stabilise the market price. (It was part of the agreement that the central
banks could buy back any gold they had sold to the United States.) The
French authorities were not helping matters by hoarding any gold they
could get hold of, whilst also campaigning for an increase in its price.

A network of 'swaps' was arranged to enable central banks to intervene
more energetically in the exchange markets, both spot and forward. The

advantage of forward intervention was that one could affect the spot price without actually having to report a loss of scarce reserves. These arrangements were backed up by the General Agreement to Borrow, amongst ten of the major central banks, to cope with short-run problems. For the longer term the Americans were increasingly obliged to denominate their borrowings in foreign currency. Interest rates in the USA were kept at a high level to attract funds, whilst an expansionary fiscal policy kept domestic demand buoyant. This was not a combination that could be sustained for very long.

It was widely recognised, not least in America, that the system was in need of more fundamental reform. There were various attempts to initiate negotiations about the direction of change, but what they revealed was deep-seated disagreement. It was very different from the situation in the 1940s, when only the views of the Americans and the British counted for much. Now a genuinely multilateral constitution was needed: the Americans and the British would have to give up their special privileges and responsibilities. The continental Europeans wanted to see price stability given a higher priority, supported by sound budgetary finance. The Anglo-Saxons at that time were pressing for faster growth in their domestic economies, their governments trying to satisfy the expectations they had aroused when campaigning. American and British leaders both spoke in favour of fixed exchange rates, but were not prepared to act as such a commitment would imply. Neither country was in any mood for austerity. The golden age was drawing to a close.

Economics and politics in the golden age

By the 1960s the teachings of Keynes had been absorbed into the body of economic theory. Academic courses no longer dismissed classical macroeconomics as uninteresting or benighted, but they still regarded the new economics as a great advance on the old. Gardner Ackley, in the textbook already quoted above, put it like this:

> With all its acknowledged deficiencies, the Keynesian analysis still stands as the most useful point of departure in macroeconomic theory. Itself incomplete and imperfect, it remains the foundation of the great majority of the theoretical works in macroeconomics of the past two decades. (Ackley, 1961, p. 418)

That was certainly true of much innovative writing about consumption, investment and the business cycle, but it was not so true of the new departures in monetary theory pioneered at the University of Chicago.

It might have been more appropriate to say that Keynesian and classical economics were now developing in parallel, with various attempts at reconciliation and synthesis. Although Keynesian ideas dominated the policy debate, at the level of high theory the classical school was already making a comeback. Mark Blaug (1962) concluded his history of economic thought with these words:

> Now that the Keynesian revolution has been assimilated, the contrast between the *nouveau* and the *ancien régime* seems much smaller than Keynes himself could ever have anticipated. But this is the fate that time visits on all theoretical innovations. It is doubtful whether Keynes would have made as much of an impression if he had not over-sold his wares. The process of discovering where the older writers really went wrong inevitably leads to a deflation of the innovator's claims. Nevertheless, very little work in economics since 1936 has not reflected, in one way or another, the unmistakable stamp of Keynes' contribution.

In fact, the essentials of classical economics were all being reinstated into the consensus. They were more carefully expressed, but not much changed from pre-Keynesian days. The separation between real and nominal variables in a general equilibrium system was again seen as crucial to the analysis. Money was again treated as neutral, apart from some distributional effects of second-order importance (see Patinkin, 1956). Inflation was, once again, described as a monetary phenomenon; the monetary theory of the balance of payments, dating back to David Hume, was now popular with the staff of the IMF. The quantity theory of money was restated in terms of the Chicago oral tradition (Friedman, 1956). It was even possible again to endorse some form of Say's law, so vigorously attacked in the *General Theory*.

As an academic discipline, and as a useful profession, economics was flourishing as never before. It aspired to the status of a science. Milton Friedman, for example, thought that the uniformity he had discovered in the relationship between money and prices was 'of the same order as many of the uniformities that form the basis of the physical sciences' (Friedman, 1956). It was expected that the controversies between economists of different schools would soon be settled by closer examination of the empirical data. New observations were being collected and better methods of statistical hypothesis testing were being developed. It seemed at the time undeniable that real progress was being made.

Economists of all schools made a sharp distinction between normative and positive statements, between beliefs about how things are, and value judgements about how they should be. It was for politicians to set the priorities, to define, one might say, the shape of the social welfare function. The task of the economist was to explain the constraints on policy choice, to sketch out the set of opportunities. Economics as such was to be free of values, so as not to prejudge what the objectives of policy should be. For example, in macroeconomics there was said to be a trade-off between unemployment and inflation – the less you had of the one, the more you had to accept of the other. It was for economists to say what combinations were possible; then politicians could decide which they preferred. Even in a golden age, there were such choices to be made.

The trade-off between unemployment and inflation was in practice difficult to quantify. The theoretical models then in use made a sharp distinction between full employment and anything that fell short of it. Below full employment there was no inflation; above it inflation might explode. Postwar experience suggested that the fullness of employment might be a matter of degree: the stronger the pressure of demand for labour, the faster wages and prices would rise. Within a certain range it appeared that a choice could be made: one could have relatively low unemployment and relatively high inflation, or vice versa. One country might opt for the first and another for the second. It was a matter of social preference, but also of 'relative prices', the price of one policy objective in terms of the other.

It cannot be said that there was any secure basis in theory for belief in the stability of this trade-off. At this time, it was still intellectually respectable to put forward a macroeconomic hypothesis without providing any microeconomic foundations for it. There was just a general perception that workers were in a stronger bargaining position when unemployment was low. It was, of course, basic to any notion of market clearing that the price of a commodity would rise or fall as demand was greater or less than supply. It was assumed that one could generalise from that, and so infer the behaviour of the general level of wages and prices.

The empirical relationship between unemployment and the increase in money wages became known as the Phillips curve. It was estimated by the same Phillips as had applied the principles of control engineering to the design of stabilisation policy. He plotted annual observations on a graph, tracing out a non-linear relationship which seemed to be much the same in Britain for almost a hundred years (Phillips, 1958). It came to be regarded almost like a physical law of nature. The metaphor of the pressure of demand was taken almost literally. The key parameters of the economy were being identified and measured.

Phillips himself recognised that the behaviour of wages was a little more complicated than that: it depended also on the expected rate of price inflation. He did not think, however, that this made any essential difference to the kind of relationship he was estimating. Expected inflation depends on last period's wage increase, because firms set their prices as a mark-up on costs. All this means is that the effect of demand on wages is greater in the long run than in the short, as the result of an inflationary spiral. He thought that he could take full account of this by allowing for a lag of a few years in the relationship that he was estimating. He does not seem to have recognised the possibility that the spiral would produce ever accelerating inflation even when the pressure of demand was constant. Yet that was precisely what classical theory would imply. A closer examination of the underlying theoretical model would have suggested alternative ways of specifying the hypothesis to be tested.

What most impressed contemporaries was how well the Phillips curve seemed to fit the data, in Britain at least. It was even possible to pick out the rate of unemployment at which inflation would be eliminated altogether. Phillips said that 2.5 per cent unemployment would produce stable prices and 5.5 per cent would produce stable wages. The curve flattened off so that very high rates of unemployment were needed to get wages to fall. At the other extreme, the curvature of the line implied that inflation would become much higher as unemployment fell below about 2 per cent. A reasonable social welfare function would presumably identify an optimum somewhere close to the postwar average.

The statistical methods used in the original paper were not very sophisticated and others tried to improve on them. There were models in which wages and prices were jointly determined and their separate behaviour identified. There were models in which the rate of change of unemployment was important as well as its level, in which special account was taken of import prices and indirect taxes. But the basic hypothesis remained the same: the pressure of demand had a predictable effect on the rate of inflation. Different studies produced different estimates. The results did not appear robust, or consistent across countries. Overall the empirical support for the Phillips curve was always weak – but that did not destroy belief in its existence.

The degree of wage and price 'stickiness' is crucial to the behaviour of the economy. Yet there has never been a good theory to predict or explain it. What one can say, with some confidence, is that experience of inflation is likely to change the degree of 'friction', that is the readiness to make adjustments to nominal variables like prices and wages. It was wrong to expect the same speed of adjustment irrespective of the context and the policy regime. If inflation was persistently high, then the relationships were very likely to shift.

A similar point could be made about the implications of persistently high unemployment. It may well be true that in the 1950s and 1960s there was a reasonably well defined relationship between unemployment and inflation in those countries where both were low. In most countries, inflation tended to speed up towards the peak of the cycle, and to slow down towards the trough, tracing out a sort of Phillips curve. But the behaviour being described must surely have reflected expectations about the range of variation in output and the commitment of governments to economic stability. A trade union will not ask as much in a boom, and an employer will not concede as much, if both expect it to be short-lived, and the converse will be true in a recession. It would be a mistake to conclude from these observations of a regular relationship over the cycle that a lasting shift in the level of unemployment would have a predictable effect on inflation. Yet this was the implication of any discussion of a long-run trade-off between the two variables.

We can now see that the position of the Phillips curve was exceptionally favourable in the 1950s and 1960s. What would now appear to be very low levels of both unemployment and inflation were possible at the same time. We may look for an explanation either in economic or in political theory. Economic theory, as usually understood, attributes prosperity and efficiency to competition and flexibility. So far as macroeconomic performance is concerned, this must mean principally the flexibility of the price level and of market interest rates. Yet one would certainly not naturally characterise behaviour in this period as flexible in this sense. The rise in prices did not eliminate excess demand, neither it seems did interest rates adjust to the going rates of inflation. Too much of the wartime apparatus of controls was retained for the market system to operate effectively. Should one, therefore, conclude that economic theory is mistaken about market flexibility? Does regulation in fact deliver better results?

From a free-market perspective the best response might be that this was not a golden age at all! The preferences of individuals were not allowed to determine the outcome. It was an age, perhaps, of over-full employment: if there had been less demand for labour then workers would have enjoyed more leisure, with shorter working hours and earlier retirement. If more workers had experienced longer periods out of work then there might have been a better matching of people to jobs. Perhaps unemployment was held below the level at which resources are used with greatest efficiency. If one believes that the market always knows best, then one might well take that view.

Similarly, one might suggest that there was too much investment in fixed capital at this time, especially in fast-growing economies like that of Japan. Interest rates ought to have risen in response to inflation; instead they were held artificially low by the monetary authorities. Perhaps the optimum rate of growth was not so fast. If investment had not been so high there could have been more consumption and a higher standard of living for that generation – many people in the so-called advanced economies were still living in absolute poverty. The Russians are often blamed for pressing ahead with investment too fast; perhaps the same criticism could be applied in some measure to the West. In a really free and competitive market the growth rate would perhaps have been lower – but that would have been all to the good.

Such reasoning would have seemed very strange at the time. The market was not revered in that way. Instead it was seen as serving the purposes of the community as a whole, purposes which found their expression in the political arena. Since people voted for parties that promised them full employment and rapid growth, that must have been what they wanted, and what was good for them. It was a golden age because the declared objectives of policy were, to an unusual extent, achieved.

One might go further and say that the behaviour of firms and trades unions was also governed as much by a kind of politics as by economic motives. The system was not fully competitive, as an efficient market should be, but relied instead on a sort of social solidarity. We have already suggested that solidarity was relatively easy to maintain when technical progress was delivering such abundance. Firms might, for example, keep on more workers than they really needed because they were earning good profits and could afford to be generous. They might take pride in the size of their business and the number of jobs they could provide. It is difficult to rationalise such behaviour in terms of the standard economic theory – but it may have existed all the same.

Let us suppose, then, that the golden age was a political rather than an economic success story. Does this mean that the monetary regime was irrelevant? It need not be so. It was recognised from the beginning of the period that a government commitment to full employment risked causing explosive inflation. The goodwill of union leaders might prevent such a disaster, but it would be helpful to have some other safeguard in place as well. A fixed exchange rate would provide an added incentive for wage moderation and would also require governments to keep demand under control. In that respect its inflexibility was a virtue; had it been totally inflexible it might have worked even better. But, of course, a system which cannot bend is more likely to break.

The behaviour one observes under a successful fixed-rate system appears conducive to price stability. Governments do not borrow excessively for fear of destroying international confidence in their currency. Central banks are obliged to keep monetary growth under control. Firms worry about price competitiveness, and hesitate to raise their prices; workers worry about the security of their jobs. Both have an interest in low inflation. The strength and stability of the national currency becomes a matter of national pride – an absurd feeling, perhaps, but one which may reinforce stability. All these considerations were of some importance under the Bretton Woods system. Observing such stable behaviour one might be tempted to say that the constraint of a fixed exchange rate was not really needed. Such reasonable people did not need an external discipline. It was only after that external discipline was removed that it became evident just how necessary it had been.

6   Policy failure (1965–1980)

Neither full employment nor price stability

The golden age did not have an abrupt end. One cannot point to one particular event which destroyed it, or to a particular year in which it became clear that the combination of high employment and low inflation was no longer achievable. In the late 1960s and early 1970s, a succession of adverse shocks and policy failures indicated that underlying conditions were changing – and changing for the worse. The policy regime which had worked so well in the 1950s and early 1960s was now breaking down.

The Vietnam War demonstrated the limits of American power, both military and economic. The devaluation of sterling in 1967 showed the fragility of the international monetary system. Student revolt, especially the 'events' of 1968 in Paris, suggested that social consensus might be an illusion. Already, before the end of the 1960s, the foundations of the postwar mixed economy were becoming insecure. The growth rate of output was still rapid, and unemployment was still very low in many countries, but the accompanying rate of inflation was accelerating, and faster than previous experience would lead one to predict.

Then, in the 1970s, the performance of the world economy deteriorated sharply. Between 1971 and 1973, the system of fixed-but-adjustable exchange rates fell apart, being replaced by floating rates with official intervention. At the same time, partly as a consequence, output surged ahead in many countries simultaneously. The result was a commodity price boom which pushed inflation higher still. Then came the first oil price shock, which raised world prices and reduced world output, creating a condition popularly called 'stagflation'.

For the remainder of the decade and beyond, the aims of economic policy

Table 6.1 *Consumer price inflation, 1965–1980, per cent*

	USA	UK	France	Germany	Japan
1965	1.8	4.4	4.3	3.2	7.7
1966	2.9	3.9	2.7	3.5	5.2
1967	2.8	2.5	2.7	1.4	3.0
1968	4.2	4.7	4.5	2.9	5.1
1969	5.4	5.4	6.4	1.9	4.6
1970	5.9	6.4	5.2	3.4	6.5
1971	4.3	9.4	5.5	5.3	6.5
1972	3.3	7.1	6.2	5.5	4.8
1973	6.2	9.2	7.3	6.9	11.7
1974	11.0	16.0	13.7	7.0	23.0
1975	9.1	24.2	11.8	6.0	11.8
1976	5.8	16.5	9.6	4.5	9.5
1977	6.5	15.8	9.4	3.7	8.1
1978	7.7	8.3	9.1	2.7	4.1
1979	11.3	13.4	10.8	4.1	3.9
1980	13.5	18.0	13.6	5.5	7.8

Source: OECD.

proved impossible to achieve. The recovery of output in the late 1970s was generally weak, and unemployment stayed high almost everywhere; inflation abated somewhat, but then rose to a second peak around the end of the decade, when there was a second oil price shock. By that time, confidence in the ability of governments to manage the economy had been largely destroyed. Keynesian theories had lost their credibility. The attempt to preserve the postwar regime was finally abandoned and a new regime was being designed to take its place.

Changing perceptions of the severity of the situation can be documented in contemporary reports. A useful starting point is the report entitled *Inflation – The Present Problem* (OECD, 1970a). In 1970 inflation in the OECD area as a whole had reached about 5 per cent, more than twice the rate in the early 1960s. The increase was especially marked in America and in France – less so in Germany. It came as a disappointment after the successes of policy just a few years before. The report identified some disquieting new developments.

There was a greater public awareness of inflation than before. In collective bargaining the unions were seeking to safeguard against it by means of indexation clauses. This was perhaps the phenomenon which was later called a 'change of gear' (Flemming, 1976). The recent rate of inflation, or even perhaps its acceleration, was projected into the future. Certainly work-

Table 6.2 *Growth rates of GDP, 1965–1980, per cent*

	USA	UK	France	Germany	Japan
1965	6.3	2.6	4.7	5.4	5.8
1966	6.0	2.0	5.2	2.8	10.6
1967	2.6	2.6	4.7	–0.3	11.1
1968	4.7	4.1	4.3	5.5	12.9
1969	2.8	1.5	7.0	7.5	12.5
1970	–0.2	2.2	5.7	5.1	10.7
1971	3.4	2.7	5.4	2.9	4.3
1972	5.5	2.2	5.9	4.2	8.2
1973	5.4	7.5	5.4	4.7	7.6
1974	–0.6	–1.0	3.2	0.3	–0.6
1975	–0.9	–0.6	0.2	–1.6	2.8
1976	5.4	3.6	5.2	5.4	4.2
1977	5.4	1.3	3.1	3.0	4.7
1978	4.4	3.3	3.8	2.9	4.9
1979	2.5	2.8	3.2	4.2	5.5
1980	–0.5	–2.2	1.6	1.0	3.6

Source: OECD.

ers were becoming more militant, very successfully so in France. There was a new generation in the labour force with no recollection of high unemployment. As the report put it, 'fears of recession have receded'. The very success of demand management could be the cause of inflation persistence (see also Cagan, 1979).

Despite this interpretation of events, the report does not recommend that the commitment to full employment should be abandoned, or even qualified. It refers to certain 'hardliners' who suggest that governments should 'lock the levers of monetary and fiscal policy in a non-inflationary position', but it concludes that this would be to 'turn back the clock' too far. It questions whether the social and political fabric would be strong enough to sustain such policies.

The following passage was written when the unrest of 1968 was still a recent memory:

> Today, a serious recession would be clearly recognised to be the result of a deliberate policy being followed by the government. The experience of those few countries which, at one time or another in the 1960s, fell short of their potential growth rates for some period of time, suggests that the under-currents of social and political discontent thus generated may eventually have rather violent economic

Table 6.3 *Short-term interest rates, 1965–1980, per cent*

	US, Treasury bill rate	UK, Treasury bill rate	Germany, call money rate	Japan, call money rate
1965	3.95	5.91	4.1	6.97
1966	4.88	6.10	5.3	5.84
1967	4.33	5.82	3.4	6.39
1968	5.35	7.09	2.6	7.88
1969	6.69	7.64	4.8	7.70
1970	6.44	7.02	8.7	8.28
1971	4.34	5.58	6.1	6.41
1972	4.07	5.52	4.3	4.72
1973	7.03	9.34	10.5	7.16
1974	7.87	11.37	8.9	12.54
1975	5.82	10.17	4.4	10.67
1976	4.99	11.12	3.9	6.98
1977	5.27	7.68	4.1	5.68
1978	7.22	7.84	3.4	4.38
1979	10.04	12.97	5.9	5.86
1980	11.62	15.16	9.1	10.93

Source: IMF *International Financial Statistics Yearbook*, 1985.

repercussions in the form of wage explosions which are difficult to foresee or control. (OECD, 1970a, p. 35)

With these dangers in mind the report falls back on the familiar plea for a combination of demand management with a policy for incomes. The targets for inflation should be realistic, and appropriate to the conditions in each country. Little is said about monetary policy or the consequences of exchange rate changes. It is assumed that the commitment to rapid growth and full employment remains securely in place.

1970 was in fact a recession year in the USA, although rapid growth continued elsewhere. Then in the next upswing the problem of inflation changed in character, becoming a great deal more serious. There was in effect a last 'dash for growth' and other objectives were forgotten in the process. The freeing of exchange rates was seen as a green light. In Britain the view was popular that fast growth was good for inflation because it reduced unit costs (Dow, 1964, p. 402). In Japan it was argued that inflation would help to hold the exchange rate down (Cargill *et al.*, 1997, p. 35). The result was the first commodity price boom for more than twenty years.

Table 6.4 *Unemployment, 1965–1980, per cent*

	USA	UK[a]	Germany
1965	4.5	1.5	0.6
1966	3.8	1.5	0.7
1967	3.8	2.4	2.1
1968	3.6	2.4	1.5
1969	3.5	2.3	0.9
1970	4.9	2.5	0.7
1971	5.9	3.4	0.8
1972	5.6	3.7	1.1
1973	4.9	2.6	1.2
1974	5.6	2.5	2.6
1975	8.3	3.9	4.7
1976	7.6	5.4	4.6
1977	6.9	5.7	4.5
1978	6.0	5.6	4.3
1979	5.8	3.9	3.8
1980	7.0	5.0	3.8

Source: Mitchell (1998).
Note: (a) Great Britain only.

The index of all commodity prices compiled by the IMF rose by 13 per cent in 1972, 53 per cent in 1973 and a further 28 per cent in 1974. The *Economist* sterling-based index, which excludes oil, rose by 24 per cent, 68 per cent and 25 per cent in those same years. This is the largest increase on record (the previous peak year, 1950, showed a rise of 48 per cent). The surge in food prices owed something to special factors, for example the running down of American grain stocks to feed the Russians, but it was essentially a speculative boom of the classical kind, with antecedents back to the nineteenth century and before. As ever, it reflected buoyant world markets and political tensions; as ever it was fuelled by an excess of world liquidity. Fear of inflation played a part, helping to make those fears come true.

The oil price increase was, of course, a rather different kind of event from the more general increase in commodity prices. It was imposed by the OPEC cartel, and it was originally presented as motivated by political, rather than economic, considerations. It was the Arabs' way of hitting back at the industrial countries that supported Israel in the Middle East War. As such it could become an excuse for the subsequent failures of economic policy worldwide. It was an exogenous shock, an event which could not be

Table 6.5 *World money and prices, 1965–1980*

	Growth of 'world[a] money' %	'World[a] price inflation' %	Commodity prices[b] 1999=100	Oil price, $ per barrel	Gold price, $ per ounce
1965	6.8	3.0			
1966	6.4	3.5			
1967	5.9	2.8	36.0	9.2	35.2
1968	8.0	3.9	35.5	9.2	41.9
1969	8.0	4.7	37.3	9.2	35.2
1970	6.2	5.6	38.8	9.2	37.4
1971	11.1	5.2	38.1	11.2	43.6
1972	11.6	4.7	41.0	12.2	64.9
1973	11.0	7.7	66.4	13.7	112.3
1974	8.2	13.3	80.5	48.9	186.5
1975	8.7	11.2	67.3	16.1	140.3
1976	10.2	8.4	74.2	51.5	134.8
1977	8.8	8.6	82.1	55.9	165.0
1978	10.9	7.3	83.4	56.4	226.0
1979	9.9	9.3	101.0	127.2	512.0
1980	5.9	12.0	107.1	159.7	589.5

Source: IMF, *IFS Yearbooks*.
Notes: (a) Industrialised countries; (b) non-fuel index, in $.

foreseen or prevented. Governments could not be blamed if their policies were seriously damaged by this unexpected blow.

A different interpretation is possible. In the inflationary environment of the early 1970s some increase in the price of oil was inevitable. The dollar was no longer seen as a reliable measure of value. Other commodities had increased in value dramatically. If the growth of the world economy continued at its current rate, fuel would become increasingly scarce (see, for example, Meadows *et al.*, 1972). Looked at this way, the oil price rise was the consequence of the economic policies of the industrial countries. The date and the extent of the increase cannot be explained along these lines, but the policies made a very large increase around this time quite probable.

The industrial economies were particularly vulnerable to an external shock of this kind. Indexation may seem a fairly harmless convention when all prices are relatively inflexible upwards as well as down. The same is not true when important elements in the cost of living can suddenly jump up. Then the attempt to preserve living standards and profit margins can be a recipe for runaway inflation. This danger was particularly well illustrated in Britain, where inflation reached 24 per cent in 1975 (Britton, 1991, chapter 3).

Once exchange rates were free to vary, rates of inflation could be very different from one country to another. All countries allowed inflation to rise in the 1970s, but some tolerated far more than others. For the OECD area as a whole the average rate of inflation over the decade was 8.4 per cent, the annual rate peaking at 13.4 in 1974 (arithmetic average of annual rates, 1970–9). In the United States the average was a little lower than that, but it tended to increase rather than decrease through the decade. In Japan, by contrast, the rate in 1974 was as high as 24.5 per cent, but after a sharp tightening of policy it was actually lower in 1979 than it had been in the 1960s. In Germany the average rate was just under 5 per cent, contrasting with France where it was nearly 9 per cent. Britain was even less successful in curbing inflation, which remained in double figures for most of the decade, with an average of 12.6 per cent.

In none of the large industrial countries did inflation get completely out of control, although it clearly threatened to do so both in Britain and in Japan. There was sufficient public concern, and sufficient political stability, to maintain some form of economic management, even if the results were far from satisfactory. Everywhere policy decisions were taken, however reluctantly, to restrict demand by one means or another. The consequence was recession almost everywhere, either in 1974 or in 1975; in both of those years total OECD output was virtually static. One could attribute this to the effects of oil prices on real incomes and hence on demand. But equally one could say that governments were introducing severely contractionary policies even before the OPEC shock.

The tightness of monetary policy is difficult to assess by reference to interest rates, since the real cost of borrowing must depend also on the expected rate of inflation. In purely nominal terms rates were certainly higher in the 1970s than they had been in the 1960s. In the United States, for example, the Treasury bill rate averaged about 6 per cent , as against about 4 per cent. In the United Kingdom the increase was rather greater, from about 5½ per cent to nearly 9 per cent. It might seem that *real* interest rates had actually fallen, but this would be misleading as an index of the policy stance. With imperfect access to capital markets, high nominal rates can inhibit spending even when real rates are low or negative. Moreover, quantitative controls on the availability of credit were tightened, and this may have been at least as effective in dampening down demand as an increase in its cost (OECD, 1975).

The OECD report of 1970 said that a recession would no longer be seen as a natural disaster but rather as a deliberate act of government policy. That may have been true of the recessions in the mid-1970s, despite the excuse provided by OPEC. Even so they did not result in the kind of political backlash which the report anticipated. They did, however, result in levels of unemployment which seemed very high at the time. The average rate for all OECD countries was just 2.6 per cent in 1965; by 1972 it was 3.7 per cent and after the recession it reached 5.2 per cent in 1975. Very little of this increase could be explained by identifiable structural factors. In the main it was seen at the time as Keynesian unemployment, caused by a deficiency of aggregate demand. Many governments wanted to eliminate it by expansionary measures, and were only prevented from doing so by the fear of inflation.

Even decades after the event, it is not easy to draw a clear distinction between unemployment which is cyclical and unemployment which is structural. If inflation is accelerating, as it was in most countries towards the end of the 1970s, that might be taken to mean that unemployment is below the sustainable, or 'natural' level. If so, the increase in that 'natural' rate was quite substantial, reaching perhaps 7 per cent in America, perhaps 6 per cent in Britain and France. But this increase had occurred in the aftermath of recession. It is natural therefore to speculate that the experience of recession had changed the behaviour of employers and of workers, with lasting consequences for the level of unemployment which was sustainable without adding to inflation. Cyclical unemployment, if it is allowed to persist, can become structural and that process may be very difficult to reverse. Thus contractionary policies could do permanent damage to the real economy.

A similar question can be asked about the growth rate of output after the recessions of the mid-1970s. At the beginning of the decade there was no sign of a general slowing down. A long-range forecast prepared in 1970 projected an average growth rate of 5.3 per cent for the OECD countries over the next ten years (OECD, 1970b, p. 80). The actual was only 3.1 per cent, with two years of virtual standstill in 1974–5. The impression is that the ground lost in the recession was never regained; when output began to grow again in 1976 it scarcely grew at the previous average rate, when one might have hoped for a spurt to get back onto the previous trend path. It is as if the supply potential of the world economy had marked time for two years (see Dow, 1998).

There are, however, plenty of alternative explanations for the deceleration of output growth in this period (see, for example, Matthews, 1982). Inflation itself may have reduced economic efficiency; the oil price increase may have had damaging effects on supply as well as on demand; government social programmes may have reduced the incentive to work; the potential for other countries to catch up with the technological leaders may have been exhausted – and so on.

It is particularly interesting to look at the case of Japan. In that country the growth rate had been consistently above 10 per cent a year in the 1960s; this continued almost uninterrupted until the sharp slowdown and recession in 1974. Thereafter the growth rate was steady at a mere 5 per cent a year. In this case at least it seems clear enough that the set-back of the recession and the tightening of policy does not offer a full explanation of the change in trend. A rather similar pattern is found in Britain and in France. It was not just a matter of failing to make up for the loss of momentum in the recession: the growth rates were actually *lower* after the recession than before.

In an earlier part of this study the temptation has been resisted to attribute fast growth in the golden age to the conduct of monetary policy or to the nature of the regime. It also seems wrong to put all the blame for slow growth in later periods on the failures of policy or the inadequacies of the regime. It is more plausible that causation runs mainly in the other direction. Rapid growth helped to sustain postwar social harmony and discipline; less rapid growth in subsequent decades necessitated a change of regime.

Contemporary economists and policymakers were aware of the complexity of the problems facing the world economy in the late 1970s. As ever, the OECD provided some of the best commentary and analysis. A major enquiry into the causes of inflation and unemployment was undertaken, chaired by Paul McCraken, the former chairman of the United States Council of Economic Advisors (OECD, 1977). Their report concluded in relatively optimistic terms. Nothing had changed so fundamentally that the objectives of price stability and full employment could no longer be pursued. The world economy had been through a very difficult few years, but policymakers should be able to put that experience behind them, and try to do better in the future. The report said:

> Our reading of recent history is that the most important feature was an unusual bunching of unfortunate disturbances unlikely to be repeated on the same scale, the impact of which was compounded by some avoidable errors in economic policy.

They continued to favour discretionary demand management as against inflexible monetary rules. The task is to 'steer demand along the relatively narrow path consistent with achieving a sustained recovery'. They recognise that this will not be easy, but they imply that it will not be impossible:

> It will be difficult to combine rising employment and capacity utilisation with a further reduction in the rate of inflation. . . To bring

inflation progressively down to an acceptably low level will therefore require skilful and determined use of monetary and fiscal policy,
and, where appropriate, prices and incomes policy.

In retrospect it must seem that the report fails to discern the severity of
the policy dilemma. More was required than skill and determination. The
path back to full employment and price stability, using conventional means
of demand management, was not just narrow: it was non-existent. Even if
full employment was approached slowly and cautiously, it would still be
incompatible with the objective of price stability. And the record of prices
and incomes policies, as the experts themselves acknowledged, was not at
all encouraging.

Elsewhere the report makes a much more radical suggestion. Perhaps the
commitment to full employment was itself the cause of inflation. This was
not a new idea, but it was certainly gaining support at the time:

> The route to full employment lies in recognising that governments
> cannot guarantee full employment regardless of developments in
> prices and wages.

This paradox points towards a very different policy regime from that still
being pursued by many governments at the time. In the 1970 report quoted
above (pp. 151–2) it is maintained that governments have to give such a
guarantee in order to preserve social peace and harmony. Seven years later,
attitudes were hardening. Sometimes, there was no alternative to policies
which were 'strongly restrictive'.

The McCracken report also recognised that attitudes to governments had
changed. They were no longer seen to be effectively in charge of events:

> Public confidence in the ability of governments to manage demand
> has waned.

Considering the disarray of policy in many countries at the time, this is
hardly surprising. But the problem went deeper than that. The task faced
by those who sought to manage demand had become much more difficult,
probably impossible. The report went on to say:

> To restore confidence is, perhaps, the most important though the
> least tangible facet of the task facing governments.

What the report did not say was that confidence could only be restored when governments set themselves targets which they could actually achieve.

Disillusion with government

The regime of the golden age was built on trust in government – confidence that 'the authorities' in finance ministries and central banks knew how to manage the economy and had the necessary political support to do so. That confidence was lost in the 1970s, mainly because governments failed in the task. But this should also be seen as part of a wider disillusion with government, not confined to its economic role.

With reference to the United States in particular, Ben Friedman, writing at the end of the decade, summed up the situation like this:

> Economic events have probably not been the sole cause of the decline in confidence in America's economic prospects that set in during the 1970s. Loss of the Vietnam war, apparent erosion of American influence in world affairs, failure to meet domestic social objectives set in the 1960s, increased emphasis on pollution and other intangible costs typically associated with the economic process, and the political trauma of Watergate all contributed to the feeling, widely reported in surveys of business and consumer opinion, that the future looked less bright than the postwar past. (Friedman, 1980, p. 15)

Arguably what happened was that governments attempted too much, over-estimating the capability of the political systems on which they were dependent. At the end of the 1960s, the Americans were overstretched by military commitments, whilst at the same time they were seeking to build a more equal and open society at home. This was not only too expensive in simple financial terms, it was also too costly in terms of the strains that it put on political consensus and social harmony. At the beginning of the 1970s the view was already gaining ground that governments should not try to do too much. But the need to win and to keep the support of voters tempted politicians to promise more than they could deliver.

The scandals of the Nixon administration obviously damaged the prestige of government, confirming the cynics. Similarly the Lockheed affair in Japan hurt the reputation of the ruling LDP Party. Perhaps in a different context these episodes would have damaged only the individuals directly involved; as it was, in an atmosphere of disenchantment, they confirmed the impression of weakness and incompetence amongst politicians, and the feeling that they could not be relied on to ensure economic prosperity.

Disillusion did not result in a simple movement to the left or the right along the political spectrum. Typically what happened was that any party which was in power around the middle of the 1970s lost popular support. Thus it was, in the first instance, the Republicans in America and the Conservatives in Britain who took the blame; but their successors from the Democrat or the Labour camp did no better in the next few years. In France the Gaullists were replaced by a succession of governments, each pursuing different and short-lived strategies. In Germany the SPD needed the support of coalition partners to retain power, and had difficulty in implementing any consistent set of policies.

In the late 1960s, Germany made a late conversion to Keynesian principles under the guidance of Karl Schiller. A law of 1967 on the promotion of stability and growth enlarged the powers and responsibilities of government accordingly. Much hope was placed in 'concerted action', that is cooperation between government, employers and trades unions. The election of Willy Brandt as Chancellor in 1969 has been described as 'the great watershed in German politics' (Kettenacker, 1997, p. 141) and it was greeted with euphoria. Yet by the mid-1970s, the SPD was barely able to cling to power, and its approach to economic management had been largely discredited.

The rhetoric of policy still assumed that governments were in control of the economy, pursuing much the same objectives as hitherto. Perhaps the best example of this is to be found towards the end of the decade in the United States with the passing of the Humphrey–Hawkins Bill requiring the administration to maintain unemployment at no more than 4 per cent. The later comment on this piece of legislation by Herbert Stein, although not unbiased, is not unjustified:

> Every informed person knew that the whole idea – including 4 per cent unemployment – was nonsense and that the bill could only be stomached on the assumption, which proved to be correct, that it would be forgotten as soon as it was enacted. (Stein, 1984, p. 218)

Academic economics reflected the changing mood. For most of the postwar period economists addressed questions about how governments ought to discharge their responsibilities in controlling the economy. The economist was the expert, and the government was the client. From the 1960s onwards however some of the attention shifted to the quite different question of how governments do in fact behave. Whose interests do they serve? How do they reach decisions? The theory of public choice developed, based on the same axioms of rational self-interest as economic theory applies to market behaviour. The appeal of this new sub-discipline may be explained by a certain distancing of intellectual debate from the actual process of policy formation. The social theorist now stood back, seeking to understand political choice, rather than to influence it. The conclusion was that, even in a democracy, the influence of government need not be benign.

Disillusion with government in the West did not imply admiration for the Communist rulers of the East. The new radical movements on the left were hostile to any form of bureaucracy or coercion. They believed in the rights of minorities, in decision-making at a local level, the ability of every person to control her or his own life. This was a different kind of idealism, a different vision of Utopia, from that which had inspired the welfare state and created the mixed economy. That vision was now decried as paternalistic. The demand now was for something more genuinely democratic and inclusive (see, for example, van der Wee, 1987).

The political consensus until the 1960s was built around the objective of economic growth. This satisfied the aspirations of many conflicting interest groups, workers and management, rich and poor alike. In the 1970s this aim was increasingly questioned. If poverty was a relative concept then no amount of growth would abolish it. The distribution of income was again becoming the main political issue, and greater equality was seen to be inconsistent with maximising the size of the average share. It was also being asked, more insistently, whether an increase in the measured standard of living meant that people were actually getting to be any happier.

The harmful by-products of growth were more noticeable. Pollution was becoming, for the first time, a political issue. In 1967 the popular slogans in Japan were 'Blue Skies over Tokyo' and 'To Hell with GNP' (Takafusa, 1994). The quality of the environment was now, for some people, more important than the quantity of goods and services being produced. There were fears for the exhaustion of natural resources, summarised (and exaggerated) in a famous report of the Club of Rome (Meadows *et al.*, 1972). There was also at least a suggestion that people were working too hard, allowing themselves too little time to enjoy life to the full.

The case against growth was ably summed up in a book by Ed Mishan (1969), all the more effective for the orthodoxy of its economic theory. He wrote:

> ... so entrenched are the interests involved, commercial, institutional and scientific, and so pervasive the influence of modern communications, that economic growth has embedded itself in the ethos of our civilisation. Despite the manifold disamenities caused by the

postwar economic expansion, no one seeking to advance his position in the hierarchy of government or business fails to pay homage to this sovereign concept. The general conclusion of this volume is that the continued pursuit of economic growth by Western societies is more likely on balance to reduce rather than to increase social welfare.

These were the views of a dissenting minority. The political parties of the left which actually gained, or shared, power in the 1970s were not much affected by the new radicalism. They still believed in growth, in economic planning and in the management of demand. They were still trying to govern according to the maxims of the golden age. The problem was that they could no longer rely on the broad consensus which had made that regime so successful in the past. Economics was becoming an even more contentious and disputatious subject than before. The divisions over economic theory and policy were hardening along party political lines.

In Britain, for example, the Conservative government was brought down in 1974 in large part by the industrial action of militant trades unions. The Labour government which succeeded it was obliged to work very closely with the Trades Union Congress. This determined the character of its incomes policies, its industrial policies and even at times its fiscal and monetary policies. It sought to establish a 'social contract' in which the government delivered full employment in exchange for wage moderation and industrial peace. It was a development of postwar 'Keynesianism', but it rested on an alliance with just one of the 'social partners'. It was not a strategy which could enjoy much cross-party support. In opposition the Conservatives regrouped around a new philosophy, which disowned the past. It disowned the recent attempts to placate the unions; more significantly it also disowned most of the postwar Conservative record, its support for demand management and the mixed economy. A new radicalism of the right was gaining ground.

Whilst economists and politicians argued about the aims and methods of economic policy, the fact was that almost all economic policies were becoming less effective. The market system was taking over from the state, whether governments surrendered influence voluntarily or not. One historian has expressed it like this:

Nobody knew what to do about the vagaries of the world economy or possessed instruments to manage them. The major instruments for doing so in the Golden Age, government policy, national or internationally coordinated, no longer worked. The crisis decades were the era when the national state lost its economic powers.

> . . . the model was . . . undermined by the globalisation of the economy after 1970, which put governments of all states – except perhaps the USA, with its enormous economy – at the mercy of an uncontrollable 'world market'. (Hobsbawm, 1995, pp. 408 and 411)

These rather sweeping generalisations are more appropriate to some areas of policy than others. In the 1970s governments could still set their own objectives for social policy and employment regulation. Different structures of taxation still coexisted, even in neighbouring states. There was actually an intensification of trade restrictions, usually in the form of quotas rather than tariffs. In Europe the scope of Community legislation was certainly expanding, but it was not always very rigorously enforced.

In industrial policy and economic planning, the state was indeed losing the initiative. Many large firms were adopting strategies directed to the world market, rather than concentrating on their customers 'at home'. It was sometimes difficult to say where their 'home' market was. They did not identify their own success or failure with that of the country in which they originated, even if they still had their world headquarters in a small Swiss town, or even if they flew the Japanese flag over their production lines throughout the world. The policies of a company located in one country might well be settled by its parent located elsewhere. This did not mean that industrial policy was becoming less important. In fact the competition to attract multinationals was becoming more fierce than ever. But there was not the same possibility of formulating a plan on the basis of national advantage, of doing deals, open or tacit, which favoured national champions at the expense of foreign rivals. It was more often the case that governments came under pressure to fit in with the plans of big companies who could create or destroy jobs.

The most striking changes were in relation to macroeconomic policy. Governments became far more dependent on market confidence, that is on the expectations and beliefs of individuals and financial institutions throughout the world. Thanks to the recessions and to the oil price increases, most governments found themselves obliged to borrow far more than they would have wished. This put their credit ratings at risk, forcing interest rates up and currencies down. The British government was viewed with more suspicion than most; in the mid-1970s it faced what was called a 'strike' in the gilts market – long-term debt could not be marketed at an acceptable price until the government announced changes in its fiscal plans. The price of independence was financial austerity.

In the 1970s the actual conduct of monetary policy also changed, giving much greater influence to market forces. Some of the changes were deliberate, motivated by the wish to stimulate competition and efficiency; others were the unintended side-effects of national regulations. If one set of institutions was kept under official control, then often another set of institutions would spring up to take business from it.

In America, Regulation Q limited the rates of interest that could be charged on bank loans. The result was to encourage the growth of non-bank lending, as well as off-balance-sheet transactions in which banks acted as intermediaries. It also encouraged the growth of the vast eurodollar market in which the overseas subsidiaries of US banks played a large part. World liquidity expanded rapidly, outside the control of any central bank.

For several years in the early 1970s it is questionable whether central banks were even in control of their domestic liquidity. In Japan, for example, the central bank had been able to limit credit by issuing instructions to the commercial banks (Argy and Stein, 1997). The inflow of funds, speculating on the appreciation of the yen, made such control methods inadequate. The authorities may have been happy to see a rapid growth of liquidity and prices, but it is doubtful whether they could have stopped it if they had tried. Eventually the Finance Minister had to bring about a 'credit crunch' more severe than any contraction since the Dodge reform postwar. Thereafter the Bank of Japan became more independent in practice than it was in theory and began to focus attention on the growth of monetary aggregates. The liberalisation of financial markets went ahead very slowly, with regulated and unregulated markets existing side by side.

The French also relied on quantitative controls to limit and to direct credit through the banking system until the late 1960s. They too found it difficult, perhaps impossible, to restrain the growth of bank lending by these means when money came pouring in from abroad. In 1970–73 there was, in the words of one national source, 'an extraordinary development of credit and liquidity that monetary policy could control only with difficulty' (Patat and Lutfalla, 1990). The Banque de France had to introduce a system of 'supplementary reserves' to enforce the norm it had set for credit expansion.

The Bundesbank faced an even more serious problem in coping with inflows of foreign capital in the early 1970s. It could not reconcile its aims of exchange rate and price stability. It could not rely on its established methods of controlling bank liquidity. In 1973 it considered copying the French system of credit control, but decided against it, because it was too 'dirigiste', and also because it would compromise the independence of monetary policy by requiring cooperation with the Ministry of Finance (von Hagen, 1998). An experiment with refusing to meet the banks' demand for reserves was abandoned on the grounds that it made market interest rates too volatile.

Instead, the Bundesbank announced that it would set its interest rates with the intention of meeting medium-term targets for the growth of 'central bank money'. This was, in effect, a weighted average of currency and bank deposits. Typically the targets were not met, but the reputation of the Bundesbank was such that this did not seem to damage confidence in monetary control.

In Britain, the Bank of England did not enjoy the same independence or public confidence. In 1971 a new method of operation was introduced, called 'Competition and Credit Control'. The aim was to allow more freedom to the banks and other financial institutions, but the effect was to allow runaway growth in liquidity. It was necessary to reintroduce quantitative controls, now called 'supplementary special deposits', or 'the corset'. The British authorities were reluctant converts to the discipline of published monetary targets, introduced under pressure from financial markets and the IMF. The Fund prescribed limits on domestic credit expansion, to prevent domestic demand growing at the expense of the balance of payments, a natural preoccupation for international lenders; the UK authorities preferred to focus on a broad definition of the money supply, which they thought was amenable to influence by fiscal as well as by monetary policy.

As confidence in governments waned, the responsibility of central banks for the design and implementation of monetary policy became clearer. Theory suggested that elected politicians would always be tempted by the short-term benefits of monetary expansion, but central bankers would be more tough-minded, provided that they were given job security. Opinion shifted a long way on this issue in the course of the 1970s. In the mid-1960s, Harry Johnson, a sympathetic expositor of monetarist theory, had seen no merit at all in central bank independence. He put it like this, writing in the *US Federal Reserve Bulletin*:

> I would judge that few economists now would be prepared to advocate an 'independent' central bank, as proposed in the literature published between the World Wars; that is a bank whose first duty is to protect the value of money against the inflationary propensities of the elected politicians. Such a function is consistent with neither democracy nor modern concepts of the economic responsibilities of government. And, even if it was, the historical record provides little evidence of the capacity of central banks to perform it wisely. (Johnson, 1964)

Fifteen years later many central banks had quietly asserted their independence by imposing greater monetary control when democratically elected governments seemed to be reluctant or unable to do so. The most admired economic institution in the world was the Bundesbank. It was admired both for its tactical skill and for its firm commitment to price stability in the medium term. It was seen as the guardian of a sound currency; control of the money supply was itself a powerful symbol of reliability and rectitude.

The political philosophy behind the monetarist counter-revolution had its roots in the nineteenth century, and before. A good ruler would always provide sound money, and would not exploit the rights of coinage for private gain. This precept went with a very limited view of the role of government in the economy – enforcing contracts and keeping the peace, but not much beyond that. Money which carried the 'image and superscription' of the ruler had some of his majesty attached to it. It was potent, whether for good or for evil. There is a certain mystery about money, even in modern times. (For a very readable history of money as a symbol and an obsession, see Buchan, 1997.)

This all seemed seriously anachronistic when it was revived as a political philosophy towards the end of the twentieth century. No financial transactions, beyond the most trivial, were conducted in coin of the realm. There was no clear way of distinguishing those assets which could function as a means of payment. In any case, governments had no direct means of controlling the supply of liquid assets, nothing comparable to the control of the mint in ancient times, or to the control of the printing press in more recent centuries. At best, governments and central banks could use their influence, and in the last resort their authority, to prevent excessive expansions or contractions of short-term instruments. The political philosophy of one era was being lifted into another, where it did not so naturally belong.

Yet the symbolic appeal of 'money' was needed to support the change of policy regime being forced on governments at this time. The fact that 'money' was an anachronistic concept was actually part of that appeal. People were disillusioned with 'modern concepts of the responsibilities of government' and they needed something else to trust instead. The new regime made use of the rhetoric of the nineteenth century and before, although it did not actually try to reverse a hundred years of institutional and political change.

Floating exchange rates

The transition from fixed to floating exchange rates has to be counted as a policy failure because most governments resisted it at the time. They did so with considerable tenacity and at great cost, in terms of their other policy objectives and also in terms of their reputations. After the event, as is usually the case when policy fails, governments and their advisers have found plenty of reasons why the new regime is better than the old. By the mid-1970s they knew that they could not go back to fixed rates, and in most cases they no longer wished that they could.

The break-up of the Bretton Woods system provides some close parallels with the break-up of the gold exchange standard in the 1930s. The drama was re-enacted, with several members of the cast playing the same roles as before. Again sterling was in the front line, and again its fall exposed the weakness of the dollar. Again the French helped to destabilise the system, which again they would have preferred to reform rather than destroy. Again many economists favoured flexibility; again most bankers wanted to preserve discipline and respect pre-commitments. Again there were politicians of the left who wanted to demonstrate their financial rectitude, and again they were accused of doing so at the expense of their supporters. It is strange how little had changed in thirty-five years.

Sterling was devalued in 1967, after a succession of crises and of measures to correct the chronic British payments deficit. It was intended as a parity change within the rules of the Bretton Woods system, not as a move to initiate a change of regime. It would allow an export-led recovery and bring a traumatic period of deflation to an end. Alternatively it was a once-for-all adjustment needed to meet the foreign exchange costs of prospective membership of the European Community (Brittan, 1971).

Yet sterling remained weak even after the devaluation. Meanwhile a wider crisis of confidence was developing. The Americans had opposed the devaluation because they believed, rightly, that it damaged the credibility of the system as a whole. In 1968, the gold pool was abandoned. As the free market price of gold was pushed up by speculation, the Americans were being asked to provide gold to other central banks at $35 an ounce, which they could then resell for over $40 an ounce. To prevent this happening, the dollar was made inconvertible. This made the system even more objectionable to the governments of some countries.

It was clear by the end of the 1960s that the international monetary system would have to be reformed. On the one hand the surplus countries of Europe and Japan were unwilling to accept a regime which allowed the Americans to print money which the whole world had to use. On the other hand the Americans, trying to pay for both the Vietnam War and the Great Society programmes, were unwilling to rein back their spending. Negotiations and international conferences did little to reconcile these positions.

In 1969, the French devalued, having conceded increases in minimum wages which were bound to be inflationary. The Germans, with more reluctance, allowed the Deutschmark to float upwards. The Japanese refused to revalue the yen, which was described abroad as 'super-competitive', because they wanted to protect their export industries. Indeed the Bank of Japan insisted on tightening credit so as to moderate domestic inflation. The balance of payments moved even further into surplus.

In 1971, the Nixon administration abruptly reversed its economic policies and forced a dollar devaluation on the rest of the world. Orthodox policies did not seem to be working in America: they were adding to unemployment, but they were not reducing inflation. So Nixon declared himself a Keynesian, announcing a wage freeze and a surcharge on imports. After a period of disarray, a new set of parities was negotiated at the Smithsonian, to be surrounded by wider bands. The Germans and even the Japanese were obliged to revalue in order to get the surcharge removed.

By this stage it was clear that governments collectively did not have the will to preserve the Bretton Woods system. When any serious conflict arose between domestic priorities and international commitments, it was the commitments that had to give way. The British Chancellor of the Exchequer said so, quite explicitly, in his Budget Statement of 1972. The American attitude to the dollar was now one of 'benign neglect'. Policy statements did less and less to discourage currency speculation. It is unlikely that any set of parities would have been defensible for long after 1971, however determined that defence might be; in fact most countries by then were not trying very hard to defend their exchange rates at all.

Multilateral floating was formally accepted as the new regime in 1973. Most countries continued to intervene heavily in the exchange markets, but generally they did so to preserve what they regarded as orderly conditions. When they set themselves targets for their exchange rates they often kept them very secret, in the hope of outwitting the market. Few countries were really indifferent to their exchange rates or willing to trust the markets to set them on their own.

The advantage of floating exchange rates was popularly supposed to be that governments were set free from an external constraint. They could choose how tight they wanted their policies to be, worrying only about the domestic situation. Experience during the 1970s showed that this was just wishful thinking. A collapse of the exchange rate was as much a crisis as a haemorrhage of reserves; both required an immediate response. It was as important as ever to keep the confidence of the market, and the actions which that required remained the same. One could compare the sterling crises of 1967 under Bretton Woods and of 1976 under the new regime. In both cases Britain had to do what was needed to satisfy the 'gnomes of Zurich', as the exchange market was popularly described. The constraint was still there. Even in America floating did not spell freedom, according to the chairman of the Federal Reserve Board, Arthur Burns. 'Under the present regime of floating rates', he said in 1975, 'it is more necessary than ever to proceed cautiously in executing an expansionary policy'.

This quotation comes from a contemporary study by Stanley Black (1977) of the effects of floating on five major countries in the 1970s. He concluded that the new system allowed exchange rates to compensate for different inflationary trends, although it did not neutralise short-term disturbances. Different countries responded to the inflationary shocks of the decade with differing degrees of accommodation. This would not have been possible before. Some countries adapted better to the new conditions than others.

In Black's view the transition to floating was good for America. The Federal Reserve System had sufficient autonomy to set credible domestic monetary targets. The same was true of Germany, despite the confusion over exchange rate policies in Europe. Britain was a more problematic case: he thought that the UK authorities had misunderstood the implications of the new order and had allowed it to reinforce the inflationary tendencies of their economy. The French also got things wrong: they tried to rely on an external discipline that was no longer enforceable.

One could also ask a more difficult, and more fundamental, question: would the world economy as a whole have performed better if the Bretton Woods system had been strengthened and preserved? One can conduct a kind of thought experiment. Clearly the rate of inflation in the 1970s would have had to be roughly the same in all, or most, countries. There might have been a round of realignments after the oil price shock, since it had different effects on the trade balances of different countries. The price level would have been increased everywhere by the direct effect of the OPEC action; perhaps the appropriate response under the Bretton Woods system would have been to issue more reserve assets, or raise the price of gold. But would the effects on wage levels and the consequent inflationary spirals have been anything like as big? It is hard to believe that the sequel would have been world inflation averaging 10 per cent over the next seven years. The natural comparison is with the commodity price boom of the Korean War. That also produced a burst of inflation and a permanently higher world price level; but it was followed by several years when inflation was close to zero. The history of the 1970s could have been very different if there had been a credible international monetary regime in place.

The member states of the European Community tried to preserve a regime of fixed exchange rates amongst themselves long after the world system had changed. They were almost completely unsuccessful throughout the 1970s, but the attempt was never abandoned. It was part of a search for ever closer union, political as well as economic. More immediately the member states more prone to inflation wanted to use an exchange rate regime as a discipline for their domestic economies.

The Treaty of Rome had almost nothing to say about monetary policy, except that member states should consult one another. In 1964 a committee of central bank governors was set up. But, so long as de Gaulle was in power, no further progress could be made. Then the exchange crises of 1969 brought the issue to the fore. The Common Agricultural Policy had been designed on the assumption that rates were fixed. When the franc was devalued and the mark floated up, it was thought necessary to introduce border taxes and subsidies to compensate. The Community was convinced that the aim must ultimately be a monetary union. The Werner Committee was set up, and it reported in 1970.

The target date for monetary union was 1980. Two different routes were considered, one favoured by the 'economists', the other by the 'monetarists'. (Neither of these terms kept their common meanings in this context.) The 'economists', supported by the Germans, required convergence of economic behaviour before a common monetary policy was in place. The 'monetarist' plan, supported by France, would put the common monetary policy first, and assume that convergence would then follow. It is a perennial debate in monetary economics: does the regime determine behaviour, or should behaviour determine the design of the regime? On this occasion, a compromise was reached, but much was left undecided.

Negotiations concentrated on the first stage of the programme, which was to be implemented straight away. Parities were to be fixed, and intervention margins narrowed. The French urgently needed German support to prevent another devaluation of the franc. For the Germans, on the other hand, it was the ultimate goal of union that mattered most. They insisted that the first stage would lapse unless agreement could be reached on the programme as a whole.

These plans all came to nothing in the turbulence of the next few years. European countries found their currencies floating independently of each other. They were supposed to stay within a narrow band, inside the broader range of variation against the dollar – 'the snake in the tunnel'. In practice they were often obliged to shift their relative positions, or to take 'leave of absence' from the band altogether. The British, who were at last admitted to membership of the Community, only lasted a few weeks in the 'snake'. By 1974 it was clear that the first stage of the Werner programme was not effective. In the same year member states failed to reach agreement on the later stages and the whole project was at an end.

This was not, however, the end of the quest for monetary union in Europe. Roy Jenkins, as President of the Commission, revived the idea in 1977, and agreement was reached between the French and the Germans at the Copenhagen summit meeting in the following year. The new Exchange Rate Mechanism came into effect in 1979. Technically it was an advance on previous designs, involving calculations of divergence in each currency from the average, as well as limiting the extent of any cross rate. But at the time it did not look very different from the old 'snake'. The British decided to stay out. The provision for changing parities still seemed to invite destabilising speculation. It was still a very long way indeed from monetary union. There was really no reason why it should succeed, except for the obstinate determination of some politicians that it should (Krause and Salant, 1973; Magnifico, 1973; Kruse, 1980).

Meanwhile, in the latter half of the 1970s, the Americans were preoccupied with a rather different agenda. World monetary relations had to be recast now that exchange rates were floating, and capital controls were becoming less effective. The vast surpluses earned by the OPEC countries had to be recycled through the world financial markets so as to finance the deficits of the oil importers. The IMF had to establish itself in a new role appropriate to a very different environment from that in which it was born.

The dollar retained its supreme position as the currency for international transactions. Most central bank intervention in the markets was conducted in dollars. The OPEC countries accumulated most of their financial assets in dollars – although not usually in America. Gold was officially demonetised in 1976, despite the protests of the French. The use of 'Special Drawing Rights' as a substitute for dollars was curtailed. American dominance in the IMF was consolidated, giving the US administration influence over the domestic policies of many countries. The concept of a multipolar system was not realised. The end of the Bretton Woods system did not spell the end of American hegemony.

Under the Carter administration the United States looked abroad for help in addressing its continuing problems of inflation and unemployment. It sought cooperation in propping up the dollar against the mark and the yen. It also sought agreement for a coordinated expansion of demand across all major industrial countries. The scheme naturally appealed to the frustrated Keynesians who still saw an external constraint as the main inhibition on demand reflation. The plan was for the surplus countries to lead the way, allowing others to follow. Popularly known as the 'locomotive' theory, the idea was warmly supported by the British government, who also wanted to find an engine that would pull their economy up the hill.

At the Bonn summit meeting of world leaders a coordinated approach was agreed. Helmut Schmidt, as host, felt pressed into offering some relaxation of the German fiscal stance, and the Japanese Prime Minister was persuaded to make a similar concession, though neither felt able to relax monetary policy. It was greeted as a triumph of diplomacy, but, as with most agreements of this kind, the measures announced were, in the main, steps which the governments concerned had been planning to take well before the meeting took place.

Unfortunately, the next year saw a revival of inflation. This was to be followed by another oil price shock and another world recession. Most of the world leaders who met at Bonn were soon to be replaced. New ideas also replaced the consensus reached on that occasion. The cause of policy coordination was itself set back. It became all too easy to blame the failures of domestic policy on the pressures exerted by governments abroad.

The monetarist counter-revolution

In 1972, Michael Stewart published a book in Britain about Keynesian economics. It began like this:

> John Maynard Keynes is generally described as an economist of genius, ranking with such giants of the past as Adam Smith and Karl Marx. No doubt this is true, but it is not the whole truth. He certainly possessed superlative intellectual power: more than one good judge said that he was the cleverest man that they had ever met. But he was not simply a very high-powered academic: he had a practical grasp of the economic and political problems of the real world. (Stewart, 1972)

The book concludes on a similar note of uncritical adulation:

> Keynes' great contribution to economics was to show that the modern economy did not work in the way everyone had supposed, and to provide a new and completely convincing explanation of how it did work. This new explanation has become the foundation of modern economics.

And, finally:

Whatever the qualifications, the basic fact is that with the acceptance of the *General Theory*, the days of uncontrollable mass
unemployment are over. Other economic problems may threaten;
this one, at least, has passed into history.

Such intellectual hubris tempts fate. Even as these confident words were
being written, academic opinion in America was questioning the validity
of Keynes' theoretical reasoning and the merits of his policy prescriptions.
Even in Britain, by the end of the 1960s students were expected to assess
both the strengths and the weaknesses of the Keynesian and the classical
schools. (The author of this book was a student of Harry Johnson at the
London School of Economics.) By the mid-1970s it was all too evident that
the days of 'uncontrollable mass unemployment' had returned, and that
Keynesian economics could not provide a cure.

Nevertheless, macroeconomics of the Keynesian school continued to
flourish in the 1970s, and beyond. One response to the failure of simple
models to predict or explain the simultaneous rise of inflation and unemployment was to construct larger, more complex, models. It was thus
possible to incorporate, for example, the effects of oil prices on demand,
or the effects of exchange rates on domestic prices. In 1978 one of the big
American macroeconomic models was used retrospectively to explain what
had caused the recession a few years before (Eckstein, 1978). It could identify separately the effects of fiscal and monetary tightening, of world food
prices and of the OPEC shock. Significantly, however, it left some of the
downturn unexplained; it was the result of a collapse in confidence, an 'old-
fashioned' panic, the 'worst financial crisis since the Great Depression'.

Typically, the big models were rather good at explaining the relationships
between quantities, between personal incomes and consumer spending, for
example, or output and trade; they were less good at explaining how output affected inflation. The Phillips curve had at one time appeared to show
a stable relationship between unemployment and the increase in wages.
Now it seemed to shift around unpredictably. Even if the relationship was
re-specified to include the expected rise in consumer prices, it did not prove
reliable. An even more serious problem was caused by the behaviour of
exchange rates after 1973. Attempts to explain them, using relative interest rates, or relative prices, or the balance of payments, were all in vain. If
exchange rates could not be explained, then the models could not give a
good account of how monetary policy affected inflation.

With the passage of time it became possible to assess how much of the
variation from year to year in output and prices was predictable, using
models of this kind. The record of actual published forecasts for a decade

or so could be compared with the subsequent outturn data. The forecasters themselves knew that the error margins were large, and they did not claim to predict as much as half of the variation in output growth a year ahead (for example, Savage, 1983). All that could really be claimed was that the forecasts, and hence the models used and the theories underlying them, contained some useful knowledge, however incomplete, about the true behaviour of the economy.

Meanwhile a different kind of applied economics was being developed as a rival to the mainstream Keynesian models. Milton Friedman and his followers had long claimed that the growth of the money supply caused inflation. The relationship had been traced and documented in America year by year. The response was not immediate, neither was the timing always the same, but each percentage point added to the growth of money was an extra percentage point, sooner or later, on inflation. It was necessary to scrutinise the data closely, and with the right presuppositions, in order to be convinced. Moreover, the same account could not so easily be given of money and inflation in countries other than the USA. But now, in the 1970s, this all changed. For the first time it could be claimed that one could see a relationship between money and prices in the aggregate world data. And it was so good a fit that it needed no elaborate econometrics to demonstrate it. It was clearly visible to the naked eye.

The IMF series for total monetary growth in all the industrial countries shows a marked acceleration in the early 1970s; this is followed about two years later by a similar increase in the average rate of inflation. A single observation of this kind may not be very impressive. But, towards the end of the decade the same pattern appeared again. Monetary growth re-accelerated to a peak in 1978, and inflation duly reached its peak in 1980. (See Table 6.5 on p. 154 above.) This is just what the monetarists had predicted before the event. Could it be a mere coincidence?

The monetarist case did not rest solely on crude observation like this. There were more systematic attempts to estimate the impact of money on prices, and to test the stability of the key behavioural relationships involved. The most important issue was the stability of the demand for money. If the quantity of money held by the public was predictably linked to output and prices, then the equation could be inverted and used for control. By limiting the amount of money available to the public, the authorities could determine the growth of output and prices, affecting output in the short term and in the long term controlling inflation. The results of estimation varied from country to country, and also from time to time. They were better for the narrower monetary aggregates than for the broader ones. But, by the usual criteria of econometrics, they were as respectable as most of the key equations in the big macroeconomic models of the time (Broughton, 1979).

It would be wrong, however, to suggest that the monetarist counter-revolution was based mainly on econometric evidence. Something much more fundamental was changing in the way that economists went about their work. The events of the 1970s vindicated theory against observation. The classical economists reasoned from first principles, whilst the Keynesians had reacted to what they saw happening all around them. It had always been a simple deduction from the axioms of rational choice that the price level as such had no lasting significance for the condition of the real economy. In the long run, therefore, inflation was a separate phenomenon from such things as growth or unemployment. Keynes and his followers had seen that this dichotomy did not hold in practice, so they relegated the classical theory to an irrelevant long run. In the 1970s that long run finally caught up with them, and proved them wrong.

The counter-revolution was not just about the importance of money: it was a revival of classical and neoclassical views about rational behaviour and market clearing. It meant, for example, reinterpreting the phenomenon of persistent unemployment. This was not, as Keynes had taught, the result of disequilibrium and demand deficiency. It was now to be understood as the result of rational choices by workers and employers, or of the organisations to which they belonged. Workers had chosen to search longer for a better job, or to put off working until real wages rose. Employers had decided to keep on the workforce they knew, rather than sack them and hire others who would accept a lower wage. According to the classical theory, unemployment was not a macroeconomic problem at all. If governments wanted to reduce it – and it was not entirely clear why they should – they would have to cut social security payments, or reduce the powers of trades unions.

This was not just a return to classical economics as it was in the nineteenth century. The 'new classical' school broke new ground as well. It applied the methods of classical economics more consistently than ever before. In particular it invented a new approach to the theory of monetary economics and of the business cycle. It was now assumed that the economy was in a continuous state of equilibrium. Markets never failed to clear. Certainly outputs could not adjust instantaneously to changes in prices, but the speed of adjustment was itself the result of a calculation by producers of the most efficient response to make. Both producers and consumers knew what they were doing; they understood the economy at least as well as any government official or economist.

The new classical school put forward the hypothesis of rational expectations. Market participants should be assumed to know as much as could be known about the markets in which they traded. This was especially important in financial markets. Expectations were not always correct, but they were not systematically wrong. Thus exchange rates, bond prices, even the value of real estate, took full account of all relevant information as soon as it became available. News caused prices to jump straight away to their new equilibrium. There were no profit opportunities to be exploited by studying the past behaviour of prices. Any information which was public knowledge would already be 'in the market'.

It is no accident that the hypothesis of rational expectations became the standard model under a regime of floating exchange rates. Clearly economists could not ignore expectations or treat them as purely random and arbitrary. That would be to abandon the attempt to understand and explain behaviour. They could not assume that expectations were based on misunderstandings or on wrong information, because that would be to deny the rationality of agents. They did not want to assert that foresight was perfect, which would also be implausible, but any model which involved agents learning gradually by trial and error was likely to be complex and unfruitful. There was no very promising rival to the rational expectations hypothesis, and usually it won by default. Moreover, the attempts to refute the hypothesis using data from financial markets were generally unsuccessful.

Rationality became the foundation of macroeconomics, as it had always been the foundation of microeconomics. It became necessary for any macroeconomic theory to have 'micro-foundations'. It was no longer good enough to assert, as Keynes had done in the *General Theory*, that there was a 'fundamental psychological law' determining consumer behaviour; the law had to be deduced from the rational choices of a representative household. Thus mainstream macroeconomics from the 1970s, even if it retained some Keynesian features, accepted the same methodological principles as those which governed other branches of economic theory. Anything else was likely to be dismissed as essentially *ad hoc*.

These were years of transition in economics, as well as in the economy. The counter-revolution spread gradually, and it was never complete. Controversy continued, and on most fronts no conclusions were ever reached. One compromise was to apply Keynesian economics to the short term – that is behaviour from one year to the next – and classical economics to the long run – say five years or more. One could readily construct a mathematical model which had those properties. Yet this would not satisfy all the protagonists: the behaviour of markets with rational expectations could make the propositions of classical economics hold instantaneously; conversely the legacy of a Keynesian recession might change the structure of the economy and hence persist for ever.

Who was right, then, and who was wrong? That is not as straightforward a question as it may seem. Beliefs and expectations can themselves affect behaviour. If people think that the money supply determines the price level, it will certainly affect the exchange rate, and hence have a powerful influence on the price level as well. If firms think that unemployment is structural rather than cyclical they may be less inclined to increase production. So much, in macroeconomics, depends on what people think, that it is hard to distinguish perception from the reality underneath.

Behaviour will, in any case, reflect the character of the monetary regime. The change from fixed to floating exchange rates made much of previous experience obsolete. Expectations of inflation would be formed in a different way, changing the conventions of wage and price setting. The response of international trade flows to relative cost advantage would be different when changes in competitiveness could be reversed overnight. During the 1970s the ideas governing both fiscal and monetary policy evolved. To the extent that the ideas behind the counter-revolution in economics came to influence policy, they were also changing the behaviour that policy was designed to control.

Robert Lucas (1976), in a famous article, insisted that one could not evaluate the effects of a change in policy regime, using a model estimated on old data. This point is not applicable only to formally estimated models and their use in policy simulation. A much more general conclusion can be drawn: the observation of behaviour under one regime is of limited value in predicting behaviour under any other. Even if the underlying preferences of consumers and the technology of production stay the same, almost everything else can change: the institutions of bargaining, the 'stickiness' of prices, attitudes to risk and the investment plans of firms. All these are factors which might distinguish a Keynesian economy from a classical one.

As we have seen, the 1970s were a transitional period in which governments were progressively giving up the tasks they had taken on in the postwar period. It was a period rather like the 1930s, only in reverse. In the Great Depression, confidence in the market system was destroyed, and reliance on the state began to take its place. In the years of 'stagflation', it was the other way round: confidence in the state was severely damaged, and there was more inclination to think that the market might be right. But, for some years during both transitions, there was little confidence in anything at all.

There are some similarities between the 1930s and the 1970s, but important differences as well. Both were periods of slow growth and of unemployment. Both experienced financial disorder and unexpected changes in prices. In both there was turbulence in the international monetary system. Yet international relations remained reasonably cordial in the 1970s. Most financial institutions and markets weathered the storms reasonably well. There were bank failures, in America and in Germany, but nothing like the collapse seen in the interwar period. Governments did become unpopular, but democracy survived.

At the end of the 1970s there was a widespread perception that a new design of policy was required. It could no longer be a matter of patching up the old regime, as governments had been attempting for more than ten years. There was no way back to Utopia and the golden age. There was growing support for a very different approach to economic policy. The age of Reagan and Thatcher was about to begin.

7   Liberalisation (1980–1990)

Disinflation

The 1980s began with a sharp re-acceleration in the rate of inflation. There was a second OPEC oil price shock, administered in the context of the war between Iran and Iraq. There was also another surge in the prices of non-oil commodities: the IMF dollar price index rose by nearly 30 per cent in two years at the end of the 1970s. In the United States the annual increase in consumer prices was 13.5 per cent in 1980, well above the figure recorded in 1974. In the other major industrial countries this second peak in inflation, following the second oil price shock, was rather lower than the peak which had followed the first. This was most strikingly true of Japan, where the rate of inflation this second time round reached only 8 per cent. It was a nice question therefore whether the trend of world inflation was rising or falling. On one interpretation the situation was serious but under control; on the other the drift towards hyperinflation was continuing, and a change of regime was essential.

One could argue about the precise nature and timing of the policy changes which took place at the end of the 1970s and the start of the 1980s. Some took place quietly; others, no more significant, were announced as revolutionary. There were elements of continuity, despite the political slogans. What undoubtedly did happen was a sharp rise in interest rates in America, to a level far higher than they had been in the 1970s. At about the same time there were steep rises elsewhere, most notably in the United Kingdom. Monetary growth in the industrial countries as a whole slowed down abruptly, from 11 per cent in 1978 to 6 per cent in 1980: in real terms the reduction was from plus 3.6 per cent to minus 6.1 per cent.

What followed was a very rapid reduction in inflation, not just

Table 7.1 *Consumer price inflation, 1980–1990, per cent*

	USA	UK	France	Germany	Japan
1980	13.5	18.0	13.6	5.5	8.0
1981	10.4	12.0	13.4	6.3	4.9
1982	6.1	8.6	11.8	5.3	2.7
1983	3.2	4.5	9.6	3.3	1.9
1984	4.3	5.0	7.4	2.4	2.2
1985	3.5	6.1	5.8	2.2	2.0
1986	2.2	3.4	2.7	−0.1	0.6
1987	4.3	4.1	3.1	0.2	0.1
1988	4.2	4.9	2.7	1.3	0.7
1989	4.9	7.8	3.6	2.8	2.3
1990	5.2	9.5	3.4	2.7	3.1

Source: OECD.

reversing the acceleration of the late 1970s, but actually getting back to rates not recorded since the 1960s. In America the rate fell from 13.5 per cent in 1980 to just 3.2 per cent in 1983, a reduction of 10 percentage points in just three years. Similarly the rate fell from 18.0 per cent to just 4.5 per cent in the same period in Britain. By one means or another, the medicine worked.

It is possible to argue that all of the slowdown in inflation between 1980 and 1982 is attributable to the behaviour of commodity prices (Beckerman and Jenkinson, 1986). The fall in the IMF (non-fuel) index in the two years following 1980 reversed the rise in the two years before. That could account for the whole of the deceleration in the average rate of inflation worldwide, assuming that wages were in effect indexed to prices. The more spectacular reductions in the USA and the UK can be explained by the appreciation of the dollar and the pound.

This would accord well with the theory of financial markets. The announcement of a policy change, and the signal of a sharp rise in interest rates to lend it credibility, should have a much quicker effect on commodities and currencies than on anything else. Wages and the prices of finished goods would respond much more slowly to the pressure of demand. Later analysis showed that labour market pressure did eventually make itself felt, contributing to the further reductions in inflation later in the decade (Brown, 1988; Coe *et al.*, 1988).

Exchange rate appreciation can be seen as exporting inflation from one country to others. Yet, on this occasion, inflation was also reduced in Germany and France, even though their currencies were depreciating in the first

Table 7.2 *Growth rate of GDP, 1980–1990, per cent*

	USA	UK	France	Germany	Japan
1980	−0.5	−2.2	1.6	1.0	3.6
1981	1.8	−1.3	1.2	0.1	3.6
1982	−2.2	1.7	2.5	−0.9	3.2
1983	3.9	3.7	0.7	1.8	2.7
1984	6.2	2.3	1.3	2.8	4.3
1985	3.2	3.7	1.9	2.0	5.0
1986	2.9	4.4	2.5	2.3	2.6
1987	3.1	4.8	2.3	1.5	4.1
1988	3.9	5.0	4.5	3.7	6.2
1989	2.5	2.2	4.3	3.6	4.7
1990	1.2	0.4	2.5	5.7	4.8

Source: OECD.

half of the 1980s. The same was true of Japan, if one measures the change in the effective exchange rate index from 1978. The shift to a stricter monetary discipline was virtually universal at this time, although not generally as dramatic elsewhere as it was in America and Great Britain. The timing, and the rhetoric, varied from one country to another, but the results were similar in character.

The reductions in the rates of inflation left real interest rates unusually high. If one subtracts the contemporaneous rise in the consumer price index from the short-term interest rate, then the figures for the average of real interest rates from 1981 to 1985 are as follows: America, 4.6 per cent; Britain, 3.8 per cent; Germany, 3.3 per cent. This was a sharp contrast with the 1970s when real rates calculated in this way were typically negative. When nominal rates were raised so as to combat inflation, the expectation was that ultimately they would end up lower than they had been at the start of the operation. In fact they remained high despite the fall in inflation, because the monetary authorities thought that it was too risky to reduce them any further. Why did they have to remain so high for so long?

The popular explanation among economists, especially in Europe, was that the fiscal deficit in the United States was much too large (Atkinson and Chouraqui, 1985). The Reagan administration had pressed ahead with tax cuts although Congress would not agree to cuts in government spending. As a result the financial balance of the government sector in the USA moved from a surplus of 0.6 per cent of GNP in 1979 to a deficit of 3.8 per cent in 1982, with little change for the next three years. The counterpart to the fiscal deficit was a deficit on the current account of the balance of payments.

Table 7.3 *Short-term interest rates, 1980–1990, per cent*

	US, Treasury bill rate	UK, Treasury bill rate	Germany, call money rate	Japan, call money rate
1980	11.62	15.16	9.1	10.93
1981	14.08	13.03	11.3	7.43
1982	10.78	11.47	8.7	6.94
1983	8.62	9.59	5.4	6.39
1984	9.57	9.30	5.5	6.10
1985	7.49	11.56	5.2	6.46
1986	5.97	10.37	4.6	4.79
1987	5.83	9.25	3.7	3.51
1988	6.67	9.78	4.0	3.62
1989	8.11	13.05	6.6	4.87
1990	7.51	14.08	7.9	7.24

Source: IMF, *IFS Yearbook*, 1993.

As the US government borrowed more it raised the cost of capital to other borrowers all over the world. Another way of describing the situation was to say that the tax cuts had stimulated private sector demand, requiring the Federal Reserve to raise real interest rates to offset that effect.

Some alternative explanations were also possible. The liberalisation of financial markets must have reduced, even eliminated, many forms of non-price rationing. A higher cost of borrowing had to substitute for quantitative controls. This story fits the British case, since the Thatcher government matched fiscal with monetary restraint, whilst at the same time abolishing controls on personal borrowing and instalment credit. This may explain how demand was able to recover so well in the late 1980s.

Before that, higher real interest rates, and the expectation of a tough policy stance for the foreseeable future, had an immediate effect in depressing demand and output levels. Early in the 1980s there were two years of falling output in America, and an even deeper recession in Britain: Germany followed suit in 1982. France experienced stagnation, whilst in Japan output continued to grow at a much reduced rate. Unemployment generally rose sharply, lagging a short distance behind the output cycle. The only exception was in Japan, where the effect on labour demand was cushioned by security of tenure and variation in hours of work.

In America, unemployment reached 9.5 per cent in the early 1980s, the highest level since before the war. Looking back over the preceding decades at the time it appeared that the trend was gently upwards, although the level was still far below that of the 1930s. In Britain, unemployment

Table 7.4 *Unemployment, 1980–1990, per cent*

	USA	UK[a]	France	Germany
1980	7.0	5.0	6.3	3.8
1981	7.3	8.0	7.4	5.5
1982	9.5	9.4	8.1	7.5
1983	9.5	10.4	8.3	9.1
1984	7.5	10.6	9.7	9.1
1985	7.2	10.8	10.2	9.3
1986	7.0	10.9	10.4	9.0
1987	6.2	9.8	10.6	8.9
1988	5.5	7.8	10.1	8.7
1989	5.3	6.3	9.4	8.0
1990	5.5	5.9	8.9	7.0

Source: Mitchell (1998).
Note: (a) Great Britain only.

(as then recorded) reached 12.4 per cent in 1983, and it was still rising – although suhbsequently the definition was revised. This was far higher than any earlier postwar peak and contrasted painfully with recent memories of full employment, and with the expectations created by the Conservative government when they won the 1979 election with the slogan, 'Labour isn't Working'. It was not far below the rates recorded in Britain in the 1930s. It appeared that firms were shedding labour faster than the fall in output could explain. A structural change was going on in the economy, with government support and encouragement, at the same time as the counter-inflation strategy was producing a deep recession.

In France, the rise in unemployment was steady but unrelenting, reaching 10 per cent in 1985. It was very difficult to judge how far this was due to the slow growth of output, how far to problems of structural adjustment. The situation seemed better in Germany, where unemployment peaked in 1985, and then began to fall a little. In the early 1980s, unemployment rates in Germany were similar to those in America. There was little to suggest that the German social model was obsolete, or in need of fundamental reform.

The downward pressure on inflation continued in the mid-1980s, despite a general recovery in output. Then in 1986 the process was reinforced by a large fall in the price of oil, about enough to reverse the increase at the start of the decade. The power of the OPEC cartel had been broken, not just by the slow growth of the world economy, but by the development of new oil fields and by the introduction of new energy-saving technologies.

The two large oil price increases had raised inflation and reduced output throughout the world. Now a large oil price reduction was to have a similar effect in reverse.

The exchange rate changes of the early 1980s were also being unwound. The dollar and the pound were now falling; the Deutschmark, the franc and the yen were now rising. Hence it was in Germany and Japan that the lowest rates of inflation were recorded in 1986: a negligible price rise in Germany and a small fall in prices in Japan. In America inflation was only 2.2 per cent despite the fall in the dollar; in Britain it was 3.4 per cent, the lowest rate since 1967. At this point it would have been easy to assume that inflation was finished for good. In fact there was to be a mild recurrence of the disease, before the cure was complete.

In the latter half of the decade it became increasingly clear that the relationship between the growth of the money supply – however defined – and the rate of inflation had changed. Through the 1970s the increase in the world money supply had been a good indicator of world inflation two years on. In the 1980s the growth of the world money supply was not much slower than in the 1970s – yet inflation almost stopped. The irony was that the 'monetarist' policies had achieved their ultimate goal, whilst completely failing to hit the intermediate target which was supposed to be an essential step on the way.

The explanation can be found in the process of liberalisation which was going on in parallel with the contraction of demand. Banks were making their services more attractive and competing for deposits. The size of their balance sheets was no longer constrained by regulations or even by moral suasion. The definition of a bank was becoming hazy, and hence the definition of money more problematical than ever. It is doubtful whether the monetary statistics since the 1980s are really measuring the same things as those from earlier decades.

The late 1980s were years of prosperity, even of euphoria. It seemed that at last the austerity of the new monetary policies had paid off. It had taken longer than expected but it had not been in vain. It was possible now to bring interest rates down a little since the outlook for inflation was so much more favourable. Moreover the structural reforms which had been introduced were now themselves helping to increase demand. The long-standing restrictions on the banks had been eased, or indeed abolished, in most countries. Financial services generally were booming; despite productivity gains from the introduction of information technology, they were at this stage taking on more staff. Tax rates were being cut, stimulating both supply and demand. The prospect of an end to the Cold War encouraged the expectation of more tax cuts to come – the so-called 'peace dividend'. There was every reason to expect growth to continue at a rapid pace for many years to come. Those who were most hardworking, and most ambitious, would profit most – these were the characteristics that were most admired, and most rewarded, at the time.

The revival of confidence was evident in asset prices. Stock market prices rose strongly and fortunes were made with comparative ease. Employees sometimes attached more importance to their share options than to their salaries. Property prices also increased rapidly and homeowners found themselves far richer than they had ever dreamed possible. It was difficult to judge what levels of asset prices were sustainable, since so many changes of institutions, regulations and behaviour had taken place since previous peaks more than a decade earlier. Then in 1987 there was a spectacular one-day fall in share prices. The press was full of comparisons with 1929, but events did not follow the same pattern at all. Monetary policy was eased to compensate, perhaps eased too much. Growth continued at a rather more modest pace, but fast enough to encounter capacity shortages in some industries in some countries. The dangers of inflation were becoming evident once more.

Commodity prices (non-fuel, in dollars) rose by 30 per cent between 1986 and 1988, returning close to the levels of 1980. As at the end of the 1970s, this contributed to a recurrence of inflation in most industrial countries, although not to the same degree as ten years earlier. In America the rate was close to 5 per cent in 1989. In Britain it went much higher: 7.8 per cent in 1989 and actually 9.5 per cent in 1990. The figures for Germany, France and Japan were all much lower. The continental countries did not share the Anglo-Saxon exuberance, even though they recorded quite satisfactory rates of growth.

The increase in inflation in America owed something to the fall of the dollar, which was initially encouraged by the authorities after 1985. By 1989 the US real exchange rate (weighted by trade shares) was down by about a quarter, and back to where it had been ten years previously. Even a country as large and self-sufficient as the United States must feel the effects of exchange rate swings of this magnitude.

The fall in the dollar helped to stimulate demand. By the end of the decade unemployment in America was not much over 5 per cent, actually lower than it had been in the late 1970s. The impression of an upward trend in the sustainable rate of unemployment had disappeared. The productivity trend in America continued to disappoint, but this meant that the growth of output was accompanied by growth in employment, mainly in the service sector, and often low skilled. Real wages on average failed to increase, and for the low skilled they were falling significantly. There was much talk of the need to cut costs so as to meet the challenge from the developing countries, and of the bias of new technology towards higher levels of skill and education. Jobs could be created by the market system, but they would not always be attractive or well paid.

In Europe, similar circumstances produced a different response. In France, for example, unemployment remained on a high plateau, close to 10 per cent. In Europe generally, real wages continued to rise, and even the low-paid shared in the increase. Very few new jobs were created, except in the public sector. The UK, as so often, was to be found about halfway between the Continent and America: there was some increase in real wages, except for the poor; unemployment did fall a little, but that was thanks largely to a number of 'schemes' and 'special measures'.

The measures to liberalise the labour market, especially in Britain, were intended to increase efficiency and reduce unemployment. Trades union power was challenged, employment protection was qualified, social security benefits were not increased in line with wages and some minimum wage regulations were abolished. The intention was to make the market clear, as it could be seen to do in America. The European model was regarded, even by many in Europe, as too rigid and rule-bound. No wonder then that unemployment was lowest in countries where the labour market was most flexible. On closer inspection, however, the relationship between flexibility and efficiency was not so simple. There were some countries, in Scandinavia for example, where the labour market was highly regulated but where unemployment was exceptionally low. There seemed to be a 'humped' relationship, with the most successful economies at either extreme and the least successful ones in the middle (Calmfors, 1993).

At the end of the 1980s it was becoming clear that many economies were in danger of overheating. Short-term interest rates were being raised again: to 8 per cent in America, 6–7 per cent in Germany and as high as 13 per cent in Britain. Real interest rates, which had eased back a little, were again exceptionally high. In retrospect we may be able to detect the signs of an approaching recession. Few contemporary observers saw it coming. There was no clear signal, like the oil price increases of 1974 and 1979. A liberalised world economy was capable of generating its own downturns, as it had done under earlier regimes. But in the late 1980s the transition to a more liberal system created some unique problems and there was no recent experience to indicate how a liberalised regime could behave. The economic system could still surprise.

Neo-liberals in power

The term 'neo-liberal' is used by Skidelsky to describe the ideas which guided the politicians of the right who gained power in the 1980s.

> The widespread perception that misguided government policies were responsible for both the inflationary explosion and the growth slowdown of the early 1970s led to the revival of neo-liberal economics, proclaimed by Milton Friedman, and pursued by Ronald Reagan in the USA and Margaret Thatcher in Britain. (Skidelsky, 1998)

The slogan was that government is the problem, not the solution. Governments should do less, and do it better.

The change in macroeconomic policy should be seen as part of a much wider programme. There was certainly a popular reaction against the economic failures of the 1970s, but it did not stop there. The inheritance of the 1960s was repudiated as well. In America, there was a return to confrontation with the Soviet Union, both military and ideological. In Britain there was a reassertion of nationalism, manifested in the Falklands War. Reagan had the support of the religious right, who sought to restore traditional moral codes. Perhaps all of this was a nostalgia for the 1950s, but in other respects the appeal was to an even more remote past.

The neo-liberals were set on reversing historical trends going right back to the beginning of the century. It was not just postwar Utopianism which they thought mistaken – Keynes was wrong, and the New Deal of the 1930s was misguided. The rise of trades unionism and the expansion of the welfare state were at the root of the problem as they saw it. Government spending (except on defence and the police) was much too high; taxes should be reduced quite drastically. The philosophy was not so much conservative or reactionary as revivalist, although it was not always clear what period of history it sought to recapture.

For most of the world it was enough to imitate contemporary America. That meant deregulating industry, privatising public corporations, freeing financial markets, reducing tax rates, restraining welfare payments and curtailing the influence of trades unions. In Britain, the Conservative Party became staunch in support of the Atlantic Alliance, and deeply divided over anything European. But on the Continent too there were those who saw America as a model to copy, more efficient than the European versions of the market economy.

Within this political philosophy, monetary policy had a limited but essential role to play. Its task was to restore and maintain price stability. Any additional aim would be a distraction and a temptation to compromise. If price stability was achieved, then the free market system would take care of the rest – full employment, growth and the distribution of income. The key to price stability was control of the money supply, which it was perfectly possible to maintain. Monetary growth should be constant, predictable and slow.

On these issues neo-liberals everywhere were in agreement. The main issue that divided them was the role of fiscal policy. In America, the orthodox view was that the control of the money supply was both necessary and sufficient to ensure price stability. If the fiscal deficit increased then it would be necessary to sell more bonds to finance it. Provided that the government did not borrow more from the central bank, it would not undermine monetary control.

The Reagan administration went ahead and borrowed more. Apparently they believed at the start that cutting tax rates would stimulate supply very quickly, and hence would increase government revenue almost at once (Krugman, 1994). Failing that, it was hoped that Congress would agree to cut social spending once the size of the deficit became clear. In practice, the deficit remained very large. There were moves to amend the constitution so as to require Congress or the administration to balance the budget. An Act was passed in 1985 mandating proportional cuts in expenditure across the board, but it was subsequently thrown out by the Supreme Court. In the end it was mainly the robust growth of the tax base, helped by deregulation and the easing of monetary policy, which brought the federal budget back to balance.

In the rest of the world fiscal discipline was regarded as essential to monetary control. That would certainly be the advice offered to any country by the IMF. Most governments did not have access to large domestic markets for long-term debt. If they borrowed on a large scale it was from the banks. Moreover, if they did succeed in financing a large deficit by non-inflationary means, it would have the effect of 'crowding out' borrowers in the private sector. Thus they would reduce fixed investment by industry and jeopardise the growth rate of the economy.

The neo-liberals did not trust government. As they understood the political process, politicians were always making promises and then breaking them. There was a problem of 'time inconsistency'. That is to say, the policy which was optimal *ex ante* (when the announcement could affect expectations and hence the behaviour of the economy) was not optimal *ex post*. Governments would promise, for example, to reduce inflation, but when the time came for action they preferred to keep unemployment low instead.

They were like soldiers who were prepared to threaten war, but not to wage it. Neo-liberals, when they gained power, did not expect their own promises to be believed, so they adopted precommitment strategies. They undertook to bind their own hands, so that their statements of intent would carry conviction.

For those with long historical memories the obvious commitment strategy was to revive the gold standard. There were influential voices in America at the end of the 1970s calling for just such a regime. In 1980, when Carter was still President, Congress set up the Gold Commission, with Anna Schwartz as its staff director. It reported in 1982 under the Reagan administration (Cagan, 1986). Some members believed in discretionary management of the economy and thought that the whole idea of going back to the start of the century was absurd. Others, including Anna Schwartz, were less dismissive of the suggestion. They wanted a firm commitment to price stability and they recognised that the gold standard did provide one. The suspension of convertibility, although not impossible, was 'a dramatic act hard to initiate'. Nevertheless, they argued that a similar commitment could be made to monetary stability without reference to gold or any other commodity. By the time they reported they had allies in power.

The nearest the monetarists came to advocating a gold standard was to insist that the central bank should control the monetary base. This consists of currency and the reserves of the commercial banks, and at one time it would have been gold. The argument was that banks need reserves in proportion to their deposits, and only the central bank can provide them. By controlling the base, the growth of total bank deposits, and hence the money supply, was ensured. The proposal was widely supported in America and Britain, by right-wing politicians and economists. The notion of a firm commitment to a rule required some measurable quantity which the authorities could control directly. The money supply itself was too remote from the levers of policy. The monetary base was closer to hand. With some changes in operating procedures, it was believed, it could be controlled with certainty and precision.

Central bankers were less enthusiastic. The system was untried, except perhaps in Switzerland, which was far from being a typical economy. In 1979 the Federal Reserve System had adopted a new method of operation which focused on 'unborrowed reserves', a concept not unrelated to the monetary base. The result was much greater volatility in short-term interest rates, which the money markets and the Fed itself found quite alarming (Bryant, 1983). Moreover it was argued that, under a strict monetary base regime, the banks would feel obliged to hold far more excess reserves, so that the ratio of reserves to bank deposits would become even less predictable. There would be institutional changes, which would make the monetary statistics impossible to interpret for many years. The politicians and economists were advised not to meddle with a delicate system which they did not fully understand.

If monetary base control was impractical, the precommitment would have to be to the money supply itself, even if it could not be controlled directly. The difficulty was to find words which made that commitment sufficiently precise to be credible, but not too precise to keep. The British government, in its Medium Term Financial Strategy, drew a distinction between the rule for the money supply and discretion in the means of achieving it:

> To maintain a progressive reduction in monetary growth in these circumstances it may be necessary to change policy in ways not reflected in the above projections. The Government would face a number of options for policy changes to achieve this aim, including changes in interest rates, taxes and public expenditure. But there would be no question of departing from the money supply policy, which is essential to the success of any anti-inflationary strategy.

Yet, within a few months, the government had to accept that it did not have any means of keeping the chosen monetary aggregate close to the path it had indicated for it (Britton, 1991).

By the early 1980s, most major countries had adopted some form of monetary targets. This did not necessarily mean that their monetary authorities had been converted to monetarism. A paper by a Bank of England economist distinguished three reasons for setting monetary targets (Foot, 1981). The first was to monitor the economy as part of a traditional policy of demand management. It was very difficult to judge the stringency of financial conditions from the level of nominal interest rates when one could not say what rate of inflation was anticipated by the markets. The second reason was to provide an anchor for the price level in an era of floating exchange rates. The third reason was rather more subtle.

It was necessary to have a monetary target in order to reassure the markets, because most market participants believed that the money supply was important. This was the rationale for what came to be called 'unbelieving' monetarism. Even if the money supply figures contained no useful information about 'fundamentals' at all, they were important for their effect on market confidence. The authorities had to behave as if they believed in monetarist doctrine, even if they were in fact complete sceptics. Foot's paper concludes that, having set targets it is necessary to hit them:

> Economists may differ over the value of monetary targets but most
> would agree that to set them as a key policy aim and then persist-
> ently to overshoot them may, in a sense, afford the worst of both
> worlds.

That may have seemed obviously true, but experience in Britain over the
next few years was to prove it false. The money supply targets were missed
by a large margin, but that did not matter, because inflation itself did come
down. Thus the whole apparatus of 'technical monetarism' was called into
question. What really impressed the markets was the willingness of the
British government to allow unemployment to rise so high, and the fact that
it had raised tax rates even in the depths of a recession.

Germany had learned its lessons about the value of monetary targets in
the 1970s. The Bundesbank had already established its credibility as the
guardian of the currency, regularly announcing monetary targets, although
not always hitting them. What changed in the 1980s was not the conduct
of monetary policy but the economic philosophy of the federal government.
In 1982 Kohl replaced Schmidt as Chancellor and introduced an explicit
austerity programme to reduce the budget deficit. After a year of recession,
a slow but steady recovery got under way. Fiscal policy was not to be used
for demand management any more. A deaf ear was turned to those abroad
who still wanted Germany to lead a coordinated fiscal expansion. As one
senior German economist put it:

> With cyclical recovery gaining ground, this position lost much of its
> intellectual appeal and gradually degenerated into a relic for a he-
> retical group of economists with strong ties to unions or the more
> extreme political left. (Giersch, 1992)

From 1982 to 1987, Japan had a strong and popular leader in Nakasone
Yasuhiro. He too was determined to enforce fiscal prudence after a period
of excessive government borrowing. He was strongly nationalist in style,
like many neo-liberals. He was a friend and ally of Reagan. He introduced
a programme of privatisation, in imitation of Thatcherism. The continuing strength of the Japanese economy, now classed as an 'economic
super-power', earned him much personal support (Smith, 1995).

The one major country which seemed out of step in the early 1980s was
France. Mitterrand was elected President in 1981 with a socialist programme of nationalisation, economic planning, redistribution and the

expansion of aggregate demand. In contrast to the neo-liberals, the philosophy was in part Keynesian and in part Marxian. The first priority was to raise the incomes of the poor: social security benefits were raised by 20 or 25 per cent and the SMIC (the national minimum wage) by 10 per cent. The working week was to be cut and more jobs created in the public sector. Considered as a reflationary package, the measures announced were not on a grand scale. But they came at a time when any reflation at all was bound to be risky (Baker *et al.*, 1984; Machin and Wright, 1985).

It might have been anticipated that the franc would collapse as soon as the result of the election became predictable. In fact it did not come under pressure until 1982 as the balance of payments deteriorated. The French economy was not growing fast, but it had escaped the sharp recession experienced elsewhere; hence its imports increased whilst the market for its exports declined. After a severe loss of reserves, the French were obliged to devalue twice. To reassure the markets, and to win the support of their partners in the European Monetary System, it was necessary to change course.

This attempt at a socialist programme did not only come to grief in the foreign exchange markets; it failed also at home. The attempt to breathe new life into the planning system served only to demonstrate how dependent the French economy now was on foreign capital and technology. Membership of the European Community limited the scope for industrial as well as commercial policy. Even nationalisation, or the threat of it, did not really enable government to dictate to industry. The traditions of dirigisme had weakened, even in France. The unions were divided, and generally unhelpful. Mitterrand remained as President, but he had to 'cohabit' with governments of a quite different persuasion. In the tactful words of an OECD report, France was obliged to adopt 'a medium term approach which was rather similar to that of many other OECD countries' (OECD, 1988).

The failure of socialism in France, together with the marginalisation of dissent in Germany and even in Britain, confirmed the view that there was 'no alternative' to the new neo-liberal consensus. The programme of reforms went ahead, through the rest of the 1980s and beyond. Following Christopher Hood (1994) we can distinguish six policy reversals: deregulation of the private sector, privatisation, reduced public spending, reform of taxation, new methods of management in the public sector and the new macroeconomic regime. He emphasises that none of these policy reversals was widely foreseen by political scientists before the event. In a search for explanations, he identifies in each case new intellectual ideas, new interest groupings, new social and technological contexts and the potential for the old policies to destroy themselves. He likens the abandonment of the old policies to the extinction of the dinosaurs, asking for example whether it was a monetarist 'meteor' that killed off Keynesianism, or whether it perished as a result of a post-Fordian 'climate change' in employment practices.

Such a piecemeal analysis of the New Right agenda is useful, but it should not allow the big picture to be lost in a mass of detail. The policy reversals of the 1980s clearly all belong together, and derive from a common vision. They involve the rejection of the vision of the preceding generation, but also the enthusiastic acceptance of a different ideal. It is also important to recognise that the ideals of the New Right were not themselves new. They were derived from history. The neo-liberal ideas were once thought themselves to be extinct. The surprise was that the 'dinosaurs' of the nineteenth century had come back to life.

Policy coordination

If macroeconomic policymaking is viewed as a problem in control engineering, then there is clear advantage in coordinating the actions of governments and central banks in all countries. The decisions of the Federal Reserve Board, for example, do not just affect output and prices in America; neither is the American economy unaffected by the decisions of the Bundesbank. If each central bank has one instrument and one target, so that there are as many instruments and targets as there are countries, then the optimum assignment must be calculated for all of them simultaneously. This was one line of argument used in the 1980s to justify the renewed attempt to persuade all countries to work together for the common good within the framework of OECD, the IMF or the economic summit meetings.

Not everyone accepted this conclusion. To some it sounded like a defence of central economic planning (Vaubel, 1983). True democrats would not support international coordination. Just as each consumer knows best what will satisfy his or her needs, so each government knows best what policies will please its own electorate. Moreover, there could be merit in a variety of policy approaches, all competing to demonstrate their advantages. Many of the neo-liberals were also nationalistic, and they did not take easily to coordination.

When the predominantly right-wing governments took office at the start of the decade, there was initially very little interest in international cooperation. They put their faith in domestic monetary control: the implications for exchange rates were for the market to decide. The same was true of interest rates, the other channel through which the most visible spillovers flowed from one country to another. If it was suggested that the rise in American interest rates, or the appreciation of the dollar, was creating problems for the rest of the world, the response might be that these were the inevitable side effects of reimposing proper monetary discipline, and it was up to each country to keep its own house in order. It would also have been said that these problems would soon sort themselves out, as the economy completed its adjustment to the new policy framework.

Around the middle years of the decade, attitudes changed (James, 1996). The persistently high value of the dollar was becoming an embarrassment for the American government itself. Exports were suffering from the effects of relative costs, and protectionist measures were being introduced into Congress. The US administration decided that coordination might be a good thing after all. In 1985, a basis for joint action was agreed at a meeting of the Group of Five at the Plaza Hotel in New York.

One view of policy coordination was that it should focus on exchange markets themselves. The central banks should present a common front to the markets and impress them with a show of strength. The authorities in America let it be known that they thought that the dollar had gone too high. They supported market intervention by central banks in Germany and Japan to drive the dollar down. Another view was that exchange rates were better influenced indirectly, by coordinating the settings of domestic policy instruments in such a way as to bring about the exchange rates which the authorities thought appropriate. About the time of the Plaza agreement there was progress towards policy agreement on a wide front.

Most European countries wanted to see a reduction in the US fiscal deficit, in the expectation that this would reduce interest rates worldwide. As the US government pointed out, this was not in its gift; however an Act of Congress seemed to promise an end to fiscal extravagance by one route or another within a few years. The next stage was a concerted reduction in interest rates by central banks in many countries at once, proving to the markets that the easing of policy did not favour any one currency at the expense of another.

The Plaza agreement was successful in one respect: the dollar began to fall. As sentiment changed, it fell of its own accord, and no further intervention was required. It cannot be said, however, that the authorities of the Group of Five really had the situation under control. They were able to agree only on broad objectives, not on a specific set of rates. There were plans for 'target zones', but no great readiness to expend reserves, or to sacrifice domestic objectives, to achieve them. There was no enthusiasm for a return to Bretton Woods. At most what was wanted was some compromise between domestic and international stability, but the weight attached to each was not made explicit – perhaps it never could be.

By 1987, the Americans were convinced that the depreciation of the dollar had gone far enough. They wanted to avoid any further boost to US inflation. On the other hand they were not keen to bring this about by raising interest rates and bringing the boom in output to an end. The meeting at the Louvre in Paris was intended to remove their difficulties. The French, as hosts, had a rather different agenda, seeking to promote exchange rate stability as an end in itself, and to stop the buoyancy of the Deutschmark disrupting cross rates in Europe. Although the meeting itself was regarded as a success, it proved difficult to implement the exchange rate tactics as agreed.

Later that year it became clear that the whole project of international policy coordination was under threat. The Germans were reluctant to reduce their interest rates simply to help the Americans – or even the French. The position of the Bundesbank was, as ever, that its duty was to maintain price stability at home. If the federal government wanted to cooperate with other countries then it could use instruments of its own. This meant in practice that the Federal Reserve would have to raise its interest rates, as the only effective means of supporting the dollar. The fear of such a move was one factor contributing to a dramatic stock market collapse.

The world economy survived that 'electronic panic' reasonably well – for the present at least. The episode did help, however, to discredit the idea of policy coordination. High profile meetings involving heads of state could easily do more harm than good. They would damage confidence if they failed to deliver impressively phrased promises of mutual support. To hold regular quiet meetings between like-minded officials from different countries was one thing; to parade a group of temperamental politicians in front of the cameras, pronouncing on issues that they did not fully understand, was another. By the end of the decade much less was expected from policy coordination. The authorities in each country were much more concerned to please the markets than they were to please one another.

It is difficult, even now, to find a satisfactory explanation of exchange rate behaviour in the 1980s (de Grauwe, 1996). The current theory, based on 'rational expectations', would suggest that there would be short-term volatility and 'overshooting', but not the long swings and persistent departures from Purchasing Power Parity which were typical of this decade. One interpretation is that this kind of market behaviour reflects a state of radical uncertainty. 'Rational' expectations cannot be formed in a totally strange environment, such as might well face traders in the years immediately after the removal of long-standing controls and regulations. How were traders to judge where the long-term equilibrium of the market might be? Nothing quite like Reaganomics or Thatcherism had been experienced before. They might tend to assume, for want of any other model, that rates would continue to drift in the directions that they had taken in the recent past. In such a market the levels of rates could be 'chaotic', within certain bounds. Beyond those bounds, some kind of logic would reassert itself, helped perhaps by policy action or official statements. A trend which lacked any economic justification would eventually be reversed, but only after it had gone far enough to cause serious disruption to international commerce and investment.

The removal of controls on banks, and the abolition of exchange restrictions, produced a rapid expansion of international lending and the development of new market instruments. Here too there was great uncertainty as to how markets would behave, what kind of borrower was a good risk and how the financial system as a whole would be supported if confidence began to crack. The need for some kind of international cooperation was made very evident by a succession of debt crises resulting from imprudent commercial lending to developing countries.

In the 1970s, when real interest rates were actually negative, it became very attractive for governments to borrow abroad. It allowed countries, especially in Latin America, to put off the evil day when they would have to get their international trade into balance. It was seen as a good way of 'recycling' the surpluses of the oil producing countries. The banks in America and Europe seem to have been under the impression that such lending was relatively safe. They did not monitor conditions in the borrowing countries very closely, or share with one another what information they had. All this changed rather abruptly in 1979 when the Federal Reserve tightened monetary policy and allowed interest rates to escalate. The chairman of Citibank said that Volker should be held personally responsible for what happened next.

In 1982 Mexico suspended debt service payments. It suddenly became clear that both borrowers and lenders had seriously miscalculated. The solvency of some of the largest international financial institutions was called into question (Davis, 1992). There was a rush of capital fleeing from other indebted countries in Latin America, East Asia and eastern Europe. There was an urgent need for some institution to step in and stop the panic from growing. No single national central bank could achieve much on its own, since the crisis was global in scale.

The Federal Reserve concluded that policy in America could now be eased a little – indeed they had no wish to see their own commercial banks destroyed by a collapse of confidence in developing-country debt. But America could not act alone. The outcome showed that international co-operation was both possible and very necessary. A procedure was established on this occasion which set a precedent for the response to similar crises in later years. The IMF had a crucial part to play. As an intergovernmental agency, it could negotiate with the Mexican authorities and require them to put policy measures in place which would improve the outlook for resuming debt service. This was a role that the IMF had often played before, essentially to protect its own assets; now it was acting to protect the assets of commercial banks as well.

The commercial banks were also required to play their part. More money had to be lent to Mexico so as to protect the value of the money which had been lent already. All the creditors had to act together. The situation was not unlike that which could arise in any country during a financial crisis. Banks generally do have an incentive to act together and support one another – up to a point. Experience in the interwar years had shown that such spontaneous cooperation was not always enough. There was a need for an element of coercion by the central bank as well. Now, in a world financial crisis, all the major central banks had to act together. It is arguable that cooperation of this kind in the 1980s saved the world from a financial disaster on the scale of the 1930s.

Cooperation was needed to cope with the problem borrowers. The US Treasury played a key part in arranging the resumption of official lending from the mid-1980s, so as to allow the more creditworthy of the less developed countries to resume investment. By the end of the decade the rich countries were even prepared to write off some official debts to ease the situation of the most deserving, or poorest, nations. But cooperation was also needed to cope with the problem lenders. Banking supervision had to follow a common pattern in all the major countries if all were to be asked to help one another in an emergency. The Basle Accord in 1988 set common standards of prudence, so as to prevent an international competition in cheap and risky lending.

The liberalisation of world capital markets in the 1980s was not a return to the conditions of 1900, or even of the 1920s. Governments and central banks did not abdicate responsibility for the stability of the system as a whole. The intention was to replace one kind of supervision with another. The authorities would not give directives to individual institutions, or stop them competing on equal terms with one another. Instead there would be a clear code of practice applied to all. Finance would not be rationed, and governments would not tell private institutions how they should lend and to whom. The implication was that institutions should not expect the authorities to bail them out if they were unwise in their lending, or even if they were just unlucky. In practice, the authorities seemed to err on the side of caution, to be overgenerous in using taxpayers' money to keep institutions afloat and shelter depositors from the consequences of their ignorance. Certainly the American authorities were prepared to spend a vast sum to rescue the so-called 'thrifts', which helped to finance home ownership, from the difficulties, largely of their own making, which they got into in the late 1980s.

International finance in the 1980s was, of course, very different from international finance at the start of the century, because it had to face exchange rate risk as well as the risk of default. Some would say that this must prevent the creation of a single world market, however liberal the regulations might be. That was the view taken by the architects of the European Monetary System. This was international policy coordination taken a step further, pointing towards the limiting case of economic and monetary union.

Initially the exchange rate mechanism in place from 1979 did not seem to be much of an advance on previous attempts to build a zone of stability in a turbulent world. By 1982 there had already been six realignments, as inflation rates in member states failed to converge. But the system was not operated so as to accommodate different price trends in full. Each time that the franc and the lira were devalued, only about half of their real appreciation against the Deutschmark was reversed. Thus the countries whose currencies were relatively weak were kept under constant pressure to restrict domestic demand, so as to offset their loss of international competitiveness. Gradually, in the latter half of the decade, with unemployment remaining high in many countries, European rates of inflation came closer together, and closer to the ultimate goal of price stability.

Initially, when the Exchange Rate Mechanism was set up, capital controls were tightened to give it a better chance of success. (They did not prove very effective, however, in stopping capital flight from France during the socialist episode under Mitterrand.) As realignments became smaller and less frequent controls were relaxed, and eventually removed. This was an essential part of the single market programme. The intention was to remove all barriers to trade and investment within the European Community, so as to create an economic unit of a size comparable to the United States. Germany had no exchange controls, and those in Britain were abolished in 1979, so removing barriers to investment meant allowing capital to flow freely, not just within Europe, but anywhere in the world. To help support the weaker currencies in this more open market, the rules for intervention were changed in 1987, increasing the obligations of the countries whose currencies were strong.

The ERM was seen as increasing the credibility of anti-inflation policy in Europe. The reputation of the Bundesbank was being used to underwrite the commitment of other central banks – even though the Bundesbank itself was far from enthusiastic about the whole project. The connection was clear enough: governments generally were committed, for political as much as economic reasons, to the goal of European unity; but this required a common currency, and hence a common rate of inflation; to satisfy the Germans this must mean price stability all over Europe. Hence the French, the Italians and the rest must enforce price stability in their own countries, whether public opinion there supported that objective or not. The commitment in the more inflation-prone countries was all the more credible because it was being imposed on them from outside. The cost of failing to curb inflation would be exclusion from the inner circle of European unity. The hope was that such a firm commitment would impress the foreign exchange markets and also those setting wages and prices at home.

The one large member state of the European Community which did not initially participate in the ERM was Great Britain. The Thatcher government was at least as firmly committed to domestic monetary control as was the Reagan administration in America. As in America, the consequence was a sharp increase in the exchange rate – helped in this case by the perception of sterling as a 'petrocurrency'. At first this was a welcome reinforcement in the fight against inflation. The official position remained that Britain would join the ERM when the time was right, a formula which appeared to allow indefinite procrastination.

From the mid-1980s, the British position began to shift. Industry felt uncomfortable about being left out of the plans for a large and uniform single market; the City wondered whether its dominant position in international finance could be preserved. There were also those who thought that Britain, like France and Italy, could benefit from borrowing some of the credibility of the Bundesbank. This was a time when inflation in Britain was approaching 10 per cent. The government was divided on the issue. The money supply had proved such an unreliable indicator of inflationary pressure that it was no longer regarded as a satisfactory anchor for price stability. The exchange rate was understood to play a very important part in the transmission of any monetary policy, so it was becoming the main focus of attention. Given the existence of the ERM, it was natural to monitor the rate against the Deutschmark, rather than against the dollar.

At the end of the decade interest rates in Britain were several percentage points above those in most other European countries. One reason for supporting ERM membership was to get rates down, and encourage economic growth. On the other hand, sterling was at a high level against other currencies. So another reason for supporting ERM membership was to prevent a depreciation which would add to inflation. These essentially incompatible arguments reinforced the view that the time might at last be right. This was to ignore completely the signals that Europe, and especially Germany, was about to experience a major political disturbance. Britain could hardly have chosen a less appropriate moment to join the ERM.

Market imperfections

In 1984 Robert Barro published a college textbook on macroeconomics. He explained that it was written because existing books at this level did not adopt the 'market clearing' approach to the subject which was now becoming standard in the more advanced literature. His text included only a brief reference to Keynesian economics, towards the end, in the chapter on business fluctuations. One is reminded of the treatment of classical macroeconomics in the early editions of Samuelson's *Economics*. Soon, perhaps, Keynes would rate no more than a scholarly footnote. (It is ironic that Barro himself had made significant contributions to Keynesian economics at an earlier stage in his career.)

It was not even certain that macroeconomics would survive as a separate subject. Only one methodological style was now acceptable to some ultra-orthodox schools of economics. Those who took a more eclectic view of the subject were in danger of marginalisation within the profession. To insist that macroeconomics was different from microeconomics might sound like heresy. Robert Lucas wrote:

> The most recent developments in macreconomic theory seem to me describable as the reincorporation of aggregate problems such as inflation and the business cycle into the framework of 'microeconomic' theory. If these developments succeed the term 'macreconomics' will simply disappear from use and the modifier 'micro' will become superfluous. We will speak simply, as did Smith, Ricardo, Marshall and Walras, of economic theory. (Lucas, 1987)

Clearly what he had in mind was not a synthesis of 'macro' and 'micro', but a takeover of the former by the latter.

This does not mean that economists now believed that all markets were efficient and perfectly competitive. On the contrary, some of the most innovative ideas of the 1980s concerned the causes and consequences of market imperfections. They took the classical assumption of individual rationality, and worked out its implications in situations where the market mechanism could not work very well, for example because of exceptionally high transactions costs. Some practitioners called this 'New Keynesianism', although its method was not that of Keynes and his original followers. Moreover, the rigorous analysis of imperfect markets did not in general lend support to traditional Keynesian policies. Barro made this point with a fine flourish:

> When we allow for incomplete information and various adjustment costs, we find that the coordination of economic activity is a hard problem for the private sector to solve. Thus, there are often mistakes, which sometimes show up as unemployment and underproduction. But the key challenge to the Keynesian analysis is to explain why these problems are eased if the government occasionally throws in a lot of money or steps up its purchases of goods. (Barro, 1984)

The range of market imperfections which were being studied is indicated in another, rather more advanced, textbook of the 1980s written by Blanchard and Fischer (1989). They say in the preface that macroeconomists do not really disagree amongst themselves nearly as much as outsiders suppose:

> Behind the public relations gimmicks and the strong incentives that exist in academia to differentiate products, macroeconomics shares many basic models and views. We believe that macroeconomics exists as a science, an admittedly young, hesitant, and difficult one. Its inherent difficulties stem from the need to draw from all branches of microeconomics, deal with aggregation, make contact with data, and eventually make policy recommendations.

Such was the new image of the subject. The origins of macroeconomics actually went back half a century. From the 1930s to the 1960s macroeconomists would hardly have been described as 'hesitant', and many of them did not study much microeconomics at all.

Six whole chapters of Blanchard and Fischer are devoted to the exposition of an essentially classical model, in which markets all clear and even speculative bubbles are explained as the consequence of rational individual behaviour. It is then pointed out that some of the implications of this model are incompatible with observed patterns in output and prices, for example the effects of aggregate demand changes on output and employment. Any departure from the equilibrium approach requires a lengthy justification, but provided that it is based on individual rationality it is permitted to proceed.

There follows a chapter on the implications of stickiness in the adjustment of wages and prices. This shows how some kinds of nominal rigidity can cause changes in the money supply to have effects on output as well as on prices – a small step in the direction of the real world perhaps. But no theory can claim to be complete if it begins by merely *assuming* price rigidity. It has to be shown that such rigidity is inevitable, or that it is optimal from the point of view of those who set prices. The next chapter therefore delves deeper into the nature of markets, for goods, for labour and for credit, explaining in turn why each may rely on the adjustment of quantities rather than prices to reach an equilibrium.

The conclusions from this research agenda are admitted to be incomplete. There is no single insight which might set off another counter-revolution. The authors do not identify any particular imperfection as a reason for losing all faith in the market mechanism. On the contrary, they actually support the neoclassical consensus, subject only to some important qualifications. They plead for more time to establish just how important those qualifications really should be:

> At this stage we cannot discern which model or combination of models will 20 years hence be regarded as absolutely essential to serious macroeconomic theory . . . However, we can give educated guesses. In the labor markets, notions of efficiency wages have a definite ring of truth. So does monopolistic competition . . . in the goods market. We believe that the recent work attempting to account for certain features of the financial markets from the viewpoint of asymmetric information is extremely important and that it will be increasingly integrated in complete macroeconomic models. Finally we are quite sure that nominal rigidities are an important part of any account of macroeconomic fluctuations and that staggering of price and wage decisions is an important element in any complete story.

This presentation of the state of macroeconomic theory is clearly at home in the 1980s. The dominant theme of the time is the working of the market system, in which society has come to place its trust. Under normal conditions it works well enough, but it is not perfect. One thinks of the deep recessions at the beginning of the decade which were needed before the change of monetary policy worked through to prices. One also thinks of the persistence of high unemployment in Europe. One thinks of the debt crisis, a clear case of imperfection in the world market for credit. All these suggest that there is still a task for government to do. That task, of course, is to preserve and encourage the market system, not to replace it.

The agnostic conclusions of Blanchard and Fischer are also typical of the period. The contending certainties of the monetarists and the Keynesians were giving way to more balanced and more tentative judgements. One could admit to a great deal of ignorance. Nevertheless, as the authors admit in their final chapter, policymaking must go on, even in a state of ignorance.

Those who were actually responsible for giving economic advice to governments and central banks had to make use of much more concrete and specific economic models. There was a strange contrast between the generality of the theoretical debate in the 1980s and the estimated models which claimed to show exactly how hundreds of economic magnitudes would be affected by a change in a policy instrument. This was a period of scepticism amongst many academic economists, but it was also the period in which the use of large models became well established within finance ministries and central banks.

Modelbuilders do not deny the existence of uncertainty; on the contrary they try to address it logically. There are two kinds of uncertainty: the economy is, like politics and the weather, subject to unpredictable shocks caused by events which economists would not claim to understand; but, in addition, our knowledge of the way the economy works is itself fallible and incomplete. In a mathematical model, the first kind of uncertainty is represented by stochastic or random error terms that are added to each behavioural equation; the second kind of uncertainty concerns the parameters in the equations themselves, and the way in which they are specified. It is much easier to cope with the first kind of uncertainty than with the second. One has only to estimate the scale and time structure of the error terms affecting the relationship in the past.

The Brookings Institution organised an international conference of modelbuilders in Washington in 1990 to compare the properties of different models, and to address the implications of stochastic errors. The issue at stake was the choice between alternative monetary regimes (Bryant *et al.*, 1993). By the choice of 'regime', the organisers meant something rather narrower than the sense in which the word is used in this book. A regime was defined by a simple mathematical rule, or 'reaction function', which the authorities might choose to follow – for example to raise interest rates by a half percentage point for each percentage deviation of the money supply above its target path. Rules of this kind can very easily be programmed into a mathematical model, and the effects of alternative rules on the properties of the model can be compared.

The main question addressed on this occasion was how closely the variables that really matter – like the rate of inflation or the level of output – could be controlled under different regimes related to intermediate targets such as the exchange rate or a monetary aggregate. The technique used was called 'stochastic simulation'; it involves repeated solution of the model in response to sequences of shocks produced by a random number generator. The large computers becoming available in the 1980s made this a possible, and a rather appealing, task.

As this was an international conference, the models for the simulations were models of the world economy. Typically each world model comprised a set of small models representing the major economies, all linked together by relationships for trade and capital flows; they also contained equations to represent the determination of commodity prices and of the trade balances of other country groups. Such models were widely available to policymakers at the end of the 1980s. They included MPS and MX3, both developed by the Federal Reserve System, MULTMOD developed by the staff at the IMF, GEM developed by the NIESR in London and widely used by central banks in Europe, and INTERLINK developed at the OECD. Purely domestic models were also used in many finance ministries and central banks, both for forecasting and for policy analysis.

Stochastic simulations, although burdensome in terms of calculations, are relatively straightforward to produce. On this occasion they showed that neither exchange rate targets nor monetary rules were very good at stabilising output and inflation. If one wanted to devise a simple feedback rule, or reaction function, for the authorities to use, then it was more effective to respond to data on output and inflation themselves. In fact, given the complexity of the models, the best feedback rule in every case would be far from simple. These results were certainly of some interest, but they could be no better than the models from which they were derived. The exercise took account only of the shocks to which the world economy might be subjected; it could take no account of uncertainty about the workings of the world economy itself. It was as if the models being used were taken to be accurate representations of the real world. But everyone knew, of course, that this could not be the case.

The equations which describe behaviour in a model may be misspecified. Theory does not tell us for certain what variables should be included in an equation to describe, for example, the demand for employment. No doubt it should include the level of real wages, and probably the cost of capital as well. But should it include the exchange rate or other variables which could influence the output expectations of employers? It is very difficult to know where to draw the line. If all variables are included in all equations, then it will be impossible to distinguish one from another (Sims, 1980).

That is just the beginning of the uncertainty about the models. Even if the specification was known to be correct, there would be severe problems of estimation. Econometricians in the 1980s were particularly worried about the problems of 'bogus regressions'. If two variables have a common trend, as is so often the case in economic data, then it is all too easy to fit an equation suggesting that one is influencing the other. New and more powerful statistical tests were devised to establish which coefficients really were significant. The only difficulty was that they needed large samples of data if they were to be decisive.

Typically models are constructed using about twenty years' quarterly observations – far less information than the methods really require. Because of this limitation, the same set of data would be used over and over again, in the search for plausible coefficient values and satisfactory test statistics. Unfortunately the process of repeated search must itself invalidate the test procedures. In practice, many of the coefficients in some models were not estimated at all, but 'imposed' or 'calibrated' so as to produce answers which the modelbuilders themselves found convincing.

In the 1980s, the estimation period being used for most applied macroeconomics was the 1960s and 1970s. One could not go much further back than that, because the data had never been collected. This was, no doubt, an interesting and varied sample of history, including some quite extreme changes in the rates of inflation and real growth. It was, however, quite different from the circumstances of the late 1980s. Financial variables, in particular, had clearly been affected profoundly by the measures of liberalisation and the consequent institutional change. An equation for the outflow of capital from France, for example, estimated on data for the 1970s, would be of little relevance to the situation ten years later. This type of issue became particularly worrying when the models were used to simulate the implications of different policy regimes. As had already been recognised and accepted in the 1970s, the nature of the policy regime must itself influence the behaviour of the economy that it is designed to control.

The issue which occupied most of the attention of modelbuilders in this decade was the treatment of expectations. An equation for fixed investment must obviously include the real rate of interest, but that depends on the expected rate of inflation. Early models assumed that the expected rate of inflation was equal to the rate of inflation in the recent past – making expectations 'adaptive'. Theory insisted, however, that individual agents are rational and can forecast inflation as intelligently as the model itself. Hence, the convention was established that expectations should be specified so as to be 'model consistent': thus the variable which stands for expectations about inflation should be equal to the actual rate of inflation forecast by the model, using information available up to that date. With large, fast computers, it was possible to use an iterative solution method which ensured that such consistency held.

One implication, however, was not entirely plausible. Suppose that we have two alternative views as to how the real world works, a Keynesian view and a neoclassical one. If expectations are to be 'model consistent', then in the Keynesian model, everyone is assumed to be a Keynesian, whilst in the neoclassical they are all neoclassicals. We know that, in the real uncertain world, some people must hold mistaken views, and that some expectations at least must be systematically wrong.

In such an uncertain world, the search is for policies which are robust. That was one reason for the kind of conference which was organised at the Brookings Institution. The results of many different models could be compared and contrasted. Policy conclusions which were supported by many different models would be preferred to those which depended crucially on one particular view of the world. Unfortunately the sceptic could not dispose of models altogether. If the use of formal mathematical models was abandoned, then policymakers would fall back on naïve rules of thumb, or on models which were neither explicit nor internally consistent. If any purposeful action was to be taken at all, then a view had to be adopted as to how the economy works and how those actions would affect it.

A sceptical view of the results of economic research also has implications for market efficiency. The markets which determine exchange rates, interest rates and asset prices can work well only if the 'fundamentals' which determine equilibrium values are known with some certainty. These 'fundamentals' comprise macroeconomics, both the underlying theory and the empirical facts of particular economies at particular points in time. Such knowledge was especially difficult to establish in the 1980s.

Knowledge of macroeconomics is always uncertain and incomplete. It is especially so in the aftermath of major reforms. Thus, the neo-liberals were caught for some years by a rather paradoxical consequence of implementing their programme. They saw a need to free the market and to rely on its wisdom rather than that of government officials. In the case of 'microeconomic' markets for particular products, the market might have more specialist knowledge than was available to any central planner. But, so far as macroeconomics is concerned, the market does not have access to more or better information than do governments or central banks. Everyone is dependent on the same small and inadequate sets of data. Governments handed over more responsibility to the market for maintaining stability just at the time when the task had been made much more difficult.

8   Back to the beginning? (1990–1999)

Full circle?

Around the start of the 1990s all the major economies experienced years of recession or stagnation, although the timing was not the same in every case. The exuberance of the late 1980s can be seen in retrospect to have been taken too far. It may be true that the programmes of liberalisation had improved growth potential, but not by so much as to make the rapid expansion of that period sustainable. A downturn was an inevitable correction. In the USA output fell by about 1 per cent in 1991; in Britain the recession was both longer and deeper, with a fall of about 2 per cent in 1991 and no recovery in the next year. In Germany and France the recession year was 1993, whilst in Japan there was virtually no growth from 1992 to 1996.

Although the scale and time profiles were different, all these contractions had some common characteristics. Financial deregulation appears to have been an important factor, especially in America and in Britain. It had made possible an excessive increase in the debt owed by both households and firms. Once the associated boom came to an end, both borrowers and lenders took fright. There was a scramble to rebuild balance sheet positions: many banks introduced tighter criteria for lending as bad debts accumulated; firms sought to avoid bankruptcy by shedding labour and running down inventories. Events followed a course which was all too familiar a hundred years before. It was a 'commercial crisis' from the classical mould.

Previous recessions in the postwar era appeared to result from some external shock – the oil price increases for example, or deliberate deflation by the monetary or fiscal authorities. This one, by contrast, appeared out of a blue sky. It was not widely predicted, and it was not well understood

Table 8.1 *Consumer price inflation, 1990–1999, per cent*

	USA	UK	France	Germany	Japan
1990	5.2	9.5	3.4	2.7	3.1
1991	4.3	5.9	3.2	3.6	3.3
1992	3.3	4.7	2.4	4.0	1.7
1993	2.7	3.5	2.1	3.6	1.3
1994	2.0	2.2	1.7	2.6	0.8
1995	2.2	2.9	2.0	1.9	−0.5
1996	2.0	3.1	1.9	1.9	0.1
1997	1.7	2.5	1.4	1.7	1.7
1998	0.9	2.5	0.7	0.9	0.2
1999	1.6	2.5	0.8	0.8	−0.4

Sources: OECD; *National Institute Economic Review*.

at the time. Dow, in his study of recessions treats this one as exceptional:

> My conclusion is that this recession, unlike all the previous four, was
> not due to exogenous shocks, but was entirely due to a reversal of
> the over-confidence that had been built up in the preceding boom
> years. (Dow, 1998, p. 352)

The revival of an endogenous cycle in output seems to have been the consequence of liberalisation. But two rather different interpretations are possible. The first would be that the new regime had much in common with that of the period before the First World War, so it was only to be expected that the path of output would show a similar pattern. The other, perhaps more optimistic, view was that this recession was part of a transition. The process of liberalisation caused the excess of borrowing, and hence the re-action to it. Once that lesson had been learned, it would not have to be repeated.

Experience over the rest of the decade appeared to support the second interpretation. Once the recovery got under way, growth rates in many countries were remarkably steady, although not exceptionally fast. In the USA, output growth varied between about 2.5 and about 4 per cent from 1992 to 1999. This was one of the longest periods of sustained growth on record. It was kept going mainly by the buoyancy of consumer demand, financed by new borrowing or by the realisation of capital gains. This was another period of jubilation in capital markets. Share prices had risen to levels which could only be justified if the growth of corporate earnings could continue well above trend. Perhaps, it was hoped, new information tech-

Table 8.2 *Growth rate of GDP, 1990–1999, per cent*

	USA	UK	France	Germany	Japan
1990	1.2	0.4	2.5	5.7	4.8
1991	−0.6	−2.0	0.8	5.0	4.3
1992	2.7	0.1	1.3	2.2	1.1
1993	2.3	2.3	−1.5	−1.2	−0.2
1994	4.0	4.4	1.8	2.4	0.7
1995	2.7	2.8	1.8	1.8	1.4
1996	3.7	2.6	1.2	0.8	5.2
1997	4.5	3.5	2.0	1.6	1.6
1998	4.3	2.2	3.4	2.0	−2.5
1999	4.1	1.9	2.8	1.4	0.7

Sources: OECD; *National Institute Economic Review.*

nologies really had transformed production possibilities, although to less sanguine commentators these stories of 'new paradigms' sounded all too like the siren songs of the 1980s replayed. Yet, whatever the sequel might be, the 1990s was undoubtedly a decade of success for the American economy. It was, as it had been at the start of the century, the envy of the rest of the world.

The decade was not quite such a good one for the economies of Europe. The unification of Germany prolonged the boom in Europe until 1992, but it was then brought to an abrupt halt. The terms on which the East was united with the West were generous. The federal government was left with a very large bill to pay, to subsidise inefficient producers, to pay Western style benefits and to cope with resulting levels of unemployment. An increase in the fiscal deficit was probably inevitable, and perhaps justified, but taxes were not raised enough to offset the effect of the extra spending on aggregate demand. Inflation threatened; the Bundesbank raised its interest rates; under the terms of the European Monetary System, the other central banks were obliged to follow suit.

From 1994 to the end of the decade, growth in most of Europe was steady but slow. These were years of fiscal consolidation in preparation for monetary union. One could not hope, at the same time, to use fiscal policy to stimulate demand. On the contrary, the first priority was to reduce inflation or to keep it low. Doubts were also expressed about the dynamism and flexibility of the European economies. They did not seem able to respond well to the competition from cheap imports coming from the Far East, or indeed from eastern Europe. They did not seem to be as able as America to benefit from the new technology. Clearly there was a more

Table 8.3 *Inflation in Europe, 1992 and 1999, per cent*

	1992	1999
UK	4.7	1.4
France	2.4	0.6
Germany	4.7	0.7
Italy	5.5	1.6
Spain	6.4	2.2
Netherlands	3.0	2.0
Belgium	2.4	1.1

Sources: *National Institute Economic Review*, 1995 and 2000.

expansionary policy towards demand in America than in Europe at this time, but that may not have been the sole explanation for the differences in performance.

But the really problematic economy in the 1990s was Japan. Between 1992 and 1999, the average growth rate was only 1 per cent a year. This compares with an average of over 4.5 per cent in the preceding eight years, and much higher rates than that in previous periods. There was just one good year, in 1996, but there was then another even more calamitous downturn towards the end of the decade, with a fall of more than 2 per cent in output in 1998. The economy seemed to be unable to pull itself out of the rut.

Japan did not respond at all well to the liberalisation of markets. It had been the star performer under the regime of economic management and control. The confidence which sustained its years of achievement was based on traditions of cooperation and team spirit. There was not much trust in the market mechanism or the merits of competition and individual enterprise. The financial system in particular rested on conventions of mutual obligation between related businesses, rather than accountability or objective measures of credit risk.

The attempt to reform the Japanese economic system following the American design proved much more difficult than expected. The financial institutions clearly did not meet international standards of conduct and disclosure. As this became clear, confidence in the whole economic system was lost; demand then contracted and the financial institutions became weaker still. Even at the end of the decade there was no sign that the transition had been successfully made. Far from it: in the late 1990s similar problems hit other countries in East Asia, compounding the vicious circle of financial and economic instability in the region.

These different experiences of output growth across countries were as-

Table 8.4 *Unemployment in Europe, 1999, per cent*

Austria	4.4
Belgium	9.0
Denmark	4.5
Finland	10.2
France	11.1
Germany	9.1
Greece	9.9
Ireland	6.7
Italy	11.3
Netherlands	3.2
Portugal	4.7
Spain	15.9
Sweden	7.0
UK	6.0
EU	9.2
Euro Area	10.0

sociated with different levels of unemployment. The recessions at the start of the 1990s took unemployment to levels without precedent in the post-war era. It was, for a few years, the main focus of policy debate. In 1994 the OECD published a major report on the subject. It was a response to concern, not only in Europe but also in America, where it had been a campaigning issue for the new Democratic administration. The report began by supporting this political priority:

> Unemployment of 35 million, some 8.5 per cent of the OECD labour force, represents an enormous waste of human resources, reflects an important amount of inefficiency in economic systems, and causes a disturbing degree of social distress. (OECD, 1994)

Unlike previous reports from the same body, however, it did not regard the problem as primarily one of demand management.

There was a need, as everyone recognised, to climb out of the recession, but the main interest of the report was in longer-term trends. It made a distinction between the situation in America and in Europe. In America the trend was flat, or even falling, and the average duration of unemployment was short; in Europe the trend was still rising, and the average duration was long. The main explanation of unemployment in the report was that labour markets were not flexible enough to cope with the changes in employment patterns required by changes in technology and international competition. The remedies proposed consisted largely of Europe becoming more like America – although the writers would not have dreamt of putting it so bluntly. There should be more incentive for the unemployed to seek work and more incentive for firms to employ them.

So far as macroeconomics was concerned, the message was a now familiar one. There should be a framework of stability. Inflation should be kept low; booms should be avoided, because they were followed by busts. Governments should borrow less, so that real interest rates could come down and private investment flourish. This was the conventional wisdom of the 1990s, as it had been of the pre-Keynesian eras.

In the same year, the European Commission (1994) published a White Paper covering much the same ground. It began with a similar expression of concern:

> Why this White Paper? The one and only reason is unemployment.
> We are aware of its scale, and its consequences too. The difficult
> thing, as experience has taught us, is knowing how to tackle it.

It also emphasised the need for flexibility, whilst recognising also the merits of solidarity. It set a target of creating 15 million extra jobs by the end of the century – as if it were a quantified economic plan. But its actual macroeconomic philosophy was not much different from that of the OECD. Where it was rather more concrete was in its recommendations on the structure of taxation. It supported an increase in the tax on energy, partly on environmental grounds, and it suggested that the opportunity could be taken to reduce non-wage labour costs in Europe.

All this analysis and debate did not produce any pronounced shifts in policy. Certainly there were later innovations, like the 1997 New Deal for young people in Britain, but they were essentially adaptations of the existing programmes of 'special measures' aimed at helping various groups of the unemployed back into work. But the main characteristics of the regime remained the same. Neither was there any substantial change in the pattern of unemployment itself.

As the recovery got under way, unemployment figures fell somewhat, and the urgency of the problem seemed to be reduced. Total OECD unemployment eased gradually from 8.3 per cent in 1993 to 6.8 per cent in 1999. The divergence between America and Europe widened. As rates in the USA fell below 5 per cent, without adverse effects on inflation, estimates of the 'natural' or 'structural' rate were revised down. In the UK the rate came down from a typically European level of 10.5 per cent in 1993, to a more 'mid-Atlantic' figure of 6.3 per cent. But the rate in united Germany was about 9 per cent, whilst in France it stayed at around 11 per cent. The objectives of the European Commission White Paper seemed unobtainable. Meanwhile in Japan, where unemployment figures had remained very low even in the early 1990s, the rate was beginning to climb. At the end of the decade it had reached about 5 per cent, similar to that in America.

Whilst progress was uneven towards the goal of full employment, price stability seemed to be secured. The problem of inflation in the major industrial countries was dormant from the mid-1990s, perhaps actually dead. For the OECD area as a whole, the increase in consumer prices averaged below 2 per cent from 1994 to 1999. Given the uncertainty of measurement, this is not far from zero. There was a remarkable convergence of inflation rates in Europe as a preparation for monetary union. In Italy for example the rate was down to just 2 per cent by 1999. Even in Greece, which failed to qualify for membership of the EU by that year, the rate was coming into line. Everywhere the prices of many goods were actually falling. In Japan there were years when the whole price index fell. Monetary policy, almost everywhere, was seen as a great success.

In a period of low and steady inflation, one would expect the rate of interest to settle at a level determined by the long-term demand for savings and for investment, not by short-term considerations of monetary policy. As the fear of inflation receded in the later 1990s, US bond yields eased from around 7 to around 5.5 per cent, implying a real return of perhaps 3 to 4 per cent. Yields in Europe settled rather lower than that, perhaps because the euro was thought to be undervalued relative to the dollar. In crisis-hit Japan short-term rates were under 1 per cent after 1996. Had it been possible to cut rates further, the Bank of Japan might well have wished to do so. Bond yields were driven down to under 2 per cent, about as far as was feasible. As in the American Great Depression, nominal interest rates had reached their floor.

As we have seen, the behaviour of the world economy in the final decade of the century was, in many respects, more like the first than it was like anything that had gone between. Both were periods of price stability without full employment; both were periods of relatively strong growth, interrupted by brief recessions. In both periods, the growth of output was faster in America than in Europe.

Rates of inflation at the start of the century were close to zero, but slightly positive. They were similar in all the major countries, locked together by the gold standard. Rates were also low and similar in those countries at the end of the century, although exchange rates were floating. Commodity prices fell in the recession of 1991, as they had in the recession of 1908.

But price indices generally had become less volatile over the years, as the service components became more important.

The level of real interest rates is difficult to measure, but at the end of the century the real yield on long bonds seems to have been around 2 to 4 per cent. This would be just a little higher than the yield on consols in Britain before the First World War. But a small premium may have been needed in the later period to compensate for greater volatility.

It goes without saying that the world economy changed profoundly in the course of a hundred years: technology advanced, living standards rose, the composition of output changed, and so on. But these are not the factors which determine macroeconomic performance. The rate of inflation, the amplitude of the cycle, and the risk of financial crisis all depend rather on the monetary regime in place, and on public confidence in it. In 1900, people put their trust in the market system, in the rule of law and in the prudent management of the financial institutions. For much of the century they transferred that faith to the wisdom and benevolence of governments – and the behaviour of the macroeconomy changed accordingly. There were periods of turbulence when people did not really trust the system at all. But the closing years were relatively calm ones, in which a basic confidence in the market system, the rule of law and financial prudence seemed to be restored.

The end of history?

At the end of the 1980s the Soviet Union and the communist states of eastern Europe collapsed and fell to pieces. A threat to the liberal democracies, which had been perceived for most of the twentieth century, was lifted. This was, most obviously, the triumph of political freedom over authoritarian rule, but it could also be seen as the triumph of the market economy over state control. Economists who had preached the classical doctrine of laissez faire could, for the first time in three generations, say with confidence that history had proved them right.

A wave of optimism left its mark in the literature of the early 1990s:

> If the early twentieth century's major political innovation was the invention of the strong states of totalitarian Germany or Russia, then the past few decades have revealed a tremendous weakness at their core. And this weakness, so massive and unexpected, suggests that the pessimistic lessons about history that our century supposedly taught us need to be rethought from the beginning. (Fukuyama, 1992)

The grand narrative had reached its triumphant conclusion:

> From the beginning, the most serious and systematic attempts to write Universal Histories saw the central issue in history as the development of Freedom. History was not a blind concatenation of events, but a meaningful whole in which human ideas concerning the nature of a just social and political order developed and played themselves out. And if we are now at a point where we cannot imagine a world substantially different from our own, in which there is no apparent or obvious way in which the future will represent a fundamental improvement over our current order, then we must also take into consideration the possibility that History itself might be at an end.

It was now the destiny of all the diverse peoples and societies to unite within a global market system with one culture based on liberal economic institutions:

> The enormously productive and dynamic economic world created by advancing technology and the rational organization of labor has a tremendous homogenizing power. It is capable of linking different societies around the world to one another physically through the creation of global markets, and of creating parallel economic aspirations and practices in a host of diverse societies. The attractive power of this world creates a very strong *predisposition* for all human societies to participate in it, while success in this participation requires the adoption of the principles of economic liberalism.

It was, no doubt, appropriate that such hymns of victory should be sung at that time. The reality of the world without communism in the closing years of the century was a more sombre affair. The political and economic tribulations in Russia showed just how difficult it could be to make the transition from the old regime to the new. There was very little bloodshed, but there was real and lasting hardship for most of the population.

A radical reform of the Russian economy was begun in 1991, following the failure of an attempted coup by the old guard. The reformers, and their Western advisers, believed that they had to move fast, introducing simultaneously both liberalisation and macroeconomic stabilisation (Åslund, 1995; Flemming and Matthews, 1994). As soon as prices were set free, the latent pressures of inflation were manifest. The central bank was unable or unwilling to impose a consistently tight control on the quantity of money;

the exchange rate of the rouble was extremely volatile. It proved impossible to make adequate cuts in government spending, or to raise an adequate
level of taxation. It could be claimed that Russia escaped outright hyperinflation, unlike some other republics of the former Soviet Union, but it did
not escape prolonged and crippling monetary disorder.

By the middle years of the 1990s the old system had largely been dismantled and a market system of a kind was in place. But the troubles were not
over. The slower pace of inflation in 1997 owed too much to an unsustainable exchange rate and an unsustainable level of real interest rates. A second
crisis hit the country in 1998, with another collapse of the currency, an effective default on rouble debts and a breakdown of the payments system.
The type of monetary regime which was working so well in America and
Western Europe did not seem to be so suitable to a country with such a
different history and culture, and so much social and political instability.

It was always accepted that the transition from communism to the free
market would result in some temporary loss of output. In fact the fall went
on throughout the decade. The scale of the reduction in GDP cannot be
measured accurately, but it seems to have been of the order of 40 per cent
between 1989 and 1999 (OECD, 1997–9). Evidently the living standard
of the vast majority of the population fell very sharply indeed. Unemployment, which was unknown or concealed in the old Soviet Union, was estimated
at 11–12 per cent at the end of the decade. It was not surprising then that popular support for the market system in Russia was weak, and getting weaker.
There might well be plenty more 'History' in that part of the world.

In America and western Europe the collapse of communism confirmed
the ascendancy of the liberal philosophy already established in the 1980s.
It was possible to portray democratic socialism and indicative planning as
just pale imitations of the discredited regime in the East. The political parties of the left had to dissociate themselves, not only from the failed
'socialism' of the Soviet Union, but also from their own past. In order to
regain political support they had to find a 'Third Way', which was neither
the way of the 1970s, nor that of the 1980s. As electoral tactics this proved
extremely successful, especially in America and Britain, but doubts remained about the substance beneath the slogans.

The Third Way recognised the imperfections of the market and the need
for regulation, but it did so from within the mainstream of neoclassical
economics. It believed that there was a role for the public sector, but it introduced there the management practices of the private sector. It believed
in redistributing resources to help the poor, but it insisted that such assistance should be precisely targeted so as to reduce the burden of taxation
on the majority of the population.

In its approach to macroeconomic policy, the Third Way was not fundamentally different from the second. Budgetary policy was dominated by considerations of fiscal prudence. Under the Democrats, the US federal budget was at last brought under control and a surplus was recorded in 1998. In Britain the New Labour government laid down the 'golden rule' that there should be no net borrowing except to finance net public investment. In most of Europe governments of any political party were constrained by the Stability Pact and the convergence criteria for membership of the new monetary union.

The teachings of Keynes, and demand management as a means of securing full employment, were almost forgotten. They did appear from time to time, not in discussions of policy in America or in Europe, but in the advice that Europeans and Americans offered to Japan. Explanations of the prolonged stagnation in that country did refer to demand deficiency, and the suggested remedies did include fiscal and monetary reflation. Ironically the Japanese themselves did not see their problems in the same way, although they were willing enough to undertake public works.

Everywhere, it was regarded as axiomatic that the purpose of monetary policy was to establish and maintain price stability. Finance ministers might still back this up with exhortations to trades unions and employers about the evils of excessive wage increases. But, in the larger economies at least, the idea of an explicit incomes policy or a deal with the 'social partners' seemed rather quaint and anachronistic even to politicians of the centre left.

The assignment of monetary policy to control the price level meant that the monetarists had won their long-running campaign against the Keynesians. But, at the same time, the importance of the money supply itself to the conduct of monetary policy was being downgraded. Experience had shown that the monetary aggregates as actually measured were not reliable guides, month by month, or year by year, to the prospects for inflation. It was an easy and logical step to dismiss them as redundant. The authorities could target inflation itself, making use of such information as the monetary aggregates contained along with every other available indicator. This became the practice in Britain, in Canada, and in half-a-dozen other countries. It was accepted as one of the ways of defining the operations of the new European Central Bank. As long ago as 1911, the neoclassical economist Irving Fisher had advocated replacing the gold standard with a regime in which central banks varied the rate of growth of the money supply so as to keep the price level stable. At the end of the century this proposal was at last being adopted.

The substitution of inflation targets for money supply targets was explained by the practical problems of monetary statistics. Yet it can also be seen as a resolution of the old debate between the advocates of rules and of discretion.

> By imposing a conceptual structure and its inherent discipline on the central bank, but without eliminating all flexibility, inflation targeting combines some of the advantages traditionally ascribed to rules with those ascribed to discretion. (Bernanke *et al.*, 1999)

In effect, the debate was being settled in favour of rules, but with some small concession to the other side. The rules were to be strategic, the discretion only tactical. The requirement that the European Central Bank should aim at price stability was actually written into its constitution, like that of the Bundesbank. There was no suggestion that it had the discretion to adopt priorities like those revealed in the past by the monetary authorities in Britain or in France.

The distinction between strategy and tactics was institutionalised as a separation of responsibility between government and the central bank. The political philosophy of the 1990s drew a clearer line than ever before between the formation of policy and its execution. This distinction was made across the whole range of government – for example between decisions about the public provision of health and education on the one hand, and the delivery of those services on the other; so far as possible the 'purchaser' and the 'provider' should be separated. In much the same spirit government ministers were expected to set the objectives for monetary policy, whilst central banks were expected to achieve them. The key word was 'accountability'.

The intention was to take monetary policy out of the political arena. It was claimed that countries with independent central banks had better records of price stability, and no worse records of unemployment, growth and real interest rates (Alesina and Summers, 1993). Theory suggested that voters might actually prefer to see monetary policy entrusted to central bankers who had a reputation for being tough-minded, rather than to politicians who would be tempted to buy their votes with concessions to pleas for lower interest rates and more economic activity. Although politicians had to retain the ultimate responsibility, the separation of powers would require them to say 'vote for a more relaxed inflation target', and that would sound less appealing than to say 'vote for a lower rate of interest'. Actually setting interest rates would be a purely technical matter, best left to the experts at the central bank.

One cost of this assignment was that fiscal and monetary policy came under separate control. This could lead to an inefficient use of both instruments. Moreover, a finance minister who was reluctant to raise taxes might be able to escape the odium of the consequent increase in interest rates. That, it has been argued above, was what happened in Germany at the time of unification. One can see why there was a move at the time to limit the discretion of finance ministers as well as central bankers, for example by means of the European Stability Pact.

In practice, the conduct of monetary policy in the 1990s took on some of the characteristics of demand management under previous regimes. Its aim was to control inflation, but to do so it needed to influence aggregate demand and output as well. The philosophy behind monetarism had been that the central bank could and should control the money supply directly, by operating on the monetary base or the reserves of the banking system. Inflation targeting abandoned that model and recognised that the central bank had to control the demand for money rather than the supply of it, that is to say control the economy as a whole. It could do so through its control of interest rates and through its ability to change expectations and prices in financial markets of every kind.

The technique for setting interest rates, in Britain at least, was very dependent on short-term forecasting. Each month the members of the Monetary Policy Committee had to take a view of the future course of inflation a year or two ahead, assuming that the rate of interest was unchanged. To do this they used macroeconomic models, just like their predecessors in the Treasury in the 1960s or 1970s. The models also told them how much interest rates would have to be changed now in order to get the inflation forecast into the centre of the target range. The procedure was highly dependent both on econometrics and on less formal judgement. Given the margins of error known to surround inflation forecasts, it was rather surprising that the procedure worked as well as it did.

The insulation of monetary policy from politics recreated a situation which was taken for granted before the First World War. To that extent history had come full circle. Yet the role of the monetary authorities was not the same at the end of the century as it had been at the beginning. The emphasis now was on *price* stability, which had once been ensured, at least for the medium term, by adherence to the gold standard. The need to preserve *financial* stability was as great as ever, but it was not now the sole responsibility of the central bank.

A distinction can be made between the stability of financial *institutions* and the stability of financial *markets*, although the two are obviously connected (Federal Reserve Bank of Kansas City, 1997). Increasingly, the regulation of institutions was seen as an issue of consumer protection. The main requirement was disclosure; and the hope was that the market might then impose its own discipline. It was no longer thought enough for the central bank to exercise an informal oversight of institutions which were 'too big to fail'.

The multiplicity of financial instruments or 'products' made the overseeing of markets increasingly difficult. The danger from speculative 'bubbles' was as acute as ever, but central bankers were reluctant to intervene. Their responsibilities were being defined more precisely, and also more narrowly. They were not so keen to be diverted from their main job, which was to combat inflation.

Where did this leave the traditional function of the central banker as 'lender of last resort'? The question could not be clearly answered at the end of the 1990s, although the potential need for such a function could not be denied. In the nineteenth century this would have been described as the main justification for the existence of central banks. It was inevitable that the stability of the banking system would remain a matter of crucial importance, however monetary policy was defined. As recently as the 1980s, the Federal Reserve Board had relaxed monetary policy so as to avert a banking crisis, even though this delayed the reduction in inflation. Interest rates were reduced on that occasion, and the need for extensive support of the banks was thus avoided. Events around the close of the 1990s, in Russia, in Latin America and in the Far East made clear that a similar situation could easily arise again.

For most of the 1990s America and western Europe enjoyed a period of relative economic tranquillity. It did indeed appear that some of the conflicts and crises which defined economic history for most of the twentieth century were at an end. But this was certainly not true of the world as a whole. It was not true of Japan and the other countries of Pacific Asia; it was not true of Russia and eastern Europe; it was not true of the poorest countries burdened by international debt. And, if it was not true for all these countries and regions, it could not be true for the world as a whole. The integration of the world economy was such that economic history was indivisible. Somewhere there was a new grand narrative waiting to unfold.

One market, one money

Economic and Monetary Union (EMU) became a reality in Europe, after so many set-backs, at the end of the 1990s. The transition was made possible by relatively tranquil conditions in the world economy and by relative harmony in European politics. Even so, the outcome was in serious doubt for much of the decade. It was uncertain whether the project had sufficient popular support and how the scepticism of financial markets could be overcome (Taylor, 1995). When it came, it was not heralded as a triumphant achievement, but it was accepted as an appropriate evolution, perhaps an inevitable one.

The Treaty of Maastricht was negotiated in 1991 but not ratified in all member states until 1993. It defined in detail the constitution of the new European Central Bank (ECB), modelled on that of the Bundesbank. Its independence was safeguarded and its accountability defined. Its task was to maintain price stability. Responsibility for the exchange rate of the new currency was given to a committee of ministers, although they were to consult with the ECB. It was not given all the traditional functions of a central bank. It was not to lend to governments or to mount rescue operations for them if they got into financial difficulties. It was not made responsible for the supervision of commercial banks or for preserving stability in financial markets.

The transition to EMU was to be in three stages, on the lines set out in the Delors Report (European Commission, 1989). The first stage did not differ greatly from the position already reached when the Treaty was negotiated; in the second stage, to begin in 1994, the ECB would come into being as an embryo called the European Monetary Institute. The real change was to be in Stage 3 when the ECB would take control of setting interest rates, and when the exchange rates of the participating countries would be locked together. The Treaty set the date, 1 January 1999, on which this would happen, unless it was decided to bring the date forward. It did not contemplate the possibility that Stage 3 would be cancelled or postponed. All that would remain to be done after that would be to replace the old notes and coins with the new ones, and to change the denominations of financial assets and liabilities.

The Treaty could not define the membership of the monetary union, since that would depend on the countries meeting certain convergence criteria. The requirements for inflation, interest rates, government debt and financial deficits were all quantified precisely – although there was to be some scope for indulgence in the way that one or two of them were to be interpreted. It was not generally expected at the time that all, or even most, member states would be able to meet these conditions. It was also necessary that participant countries had a central bank which was independent of government, so that it could take its instructions from the ECB. Countries were also required to have kept their exchange rates stable for a period within the old Exchange Rate Mechanism prior to joining the new EMU.

One of the chief stumbling blocks in the course of the negotiations was the position adopted by the British. They would have liked to have vetoed the whole programme, but could not do so. They were likely to meet the convergence criteria, but they did not want to join the union. Their problems were political rather than economic. In most of Europe a majority could be mustered to vote in favour of the programme, but in Britain that would clearly be impossible at that time. The solution was to include an 'opt-out' clause in the Treaty which applied specifically to Britain.

Monetary union in Europe satisfied two quite different aspirations, one mainly economic, the other mainly political. The first was the search for exchange rate stability, which had never been altogether abandoned in Europe since the demise of the classical gold standard. Money functions better, both as a unit of account and as a medium of exchange, if the same currency is used in many countries. Moreover the function of money as a store of value will be best served when governments are made subject to an external discipline. These long-familiar arguments were now deployed by the advocates of EMU, and reinforced as being especially relevant to Europe as economic integration increased. As the barriers to trade, and to the movement of people and of capital, came down, it became more and more advantageous to have a single currency to complement the single market (European Commission, 1990).

The other, more political, aspiration was the 'ever closer' union of Europe. Those who favoured a federal European state naturally saw monetary policy as an appropriate function for a federal institution. They might recognise that problems of coordination could arise if monetary policy was centralised whilst other aspects of economic policy were not. From their point of view that might even be welcome, since the resulting tension could be resolved by creating further European institutions with responsibility in such areas as taxation or the supervision of financial markets. This half-hidden agenda of further centralisation won support for EMU in some countries, most importantly in Germany, but it alienated opinion in others, most notably in the UK.

Debate centred on the area of fiscal or budgetary policy. Some argued that individual member states needed more, not less, independence in this respect so as to compensate for the loss of the monetary instrument as a means of managing demand. They were concerned particularly with the possibility of 'asymmetric shocks', that is disturbances to demand which impacted differently on different member states. An increase in world oil prices was an often quoted example, since the UK was a significant oil producer, and most other European countries were not. But others were more concerned that states would exploit any freedom that they were given to operate an independent budgetary policy to borrow excessively, undermining the credit of the European Union as a whole.

The compromise in the Maastricht Treaty was to leave fiscal policy as a national responsibility, but limit its scope by means of the convergence criteria for borrowing and for the size of the national debt. It could be defended in the following terms:

> The implementation of EMU does not in itself obviously require further political integration. The concept of political union is imprecise unless a discussion is confined to elements which are closely related to the functioning of monetary union, but in this area a norm-based cooperation building on the convergence criteria . . . constitute(s) an attractive alternative to centralization of political authority over budgetary policy at the EU level. Such a centralization is likely to overload cooperation and would imply greater dangers than benefits for monetary stability. (Thygessen, 1996)

The requirement for such 'norms' of fiscal conduct within the EMU, as well as in the preparation for it, was met by the Stability Pact adopted in response chiefly to the concerns of the German government. In effect this required member states to keep to the restrictions placed on government deficits after EMU was in being; penalties were specified for those governments who broke the rules.

The Treaty was a victory for patience, diplomacy and a willingness to compromise. Yet its ratification proved difficult and the extent of popular support for EMU remained in doubt. Within a matter of months from its signature, the whole concept of EMU was called into question again by turbulence in the currency markets (Cobham, 1994). The initial shock was an increase in German interest rates in July 1992 designed to counter the inflationary dangers inherent in the process of German unification. Other countries in Europe did not want to tighten monetary conditions at this time. The markets sensed a potential incompatibility of objectives and expected there to be realignments sooner or later; traders speculated very actively against the currencies that they perceived to be weak. The governments and central banks in Britain, Italy, Sweden and elsewhere mounted a determined defence, making resolute commitments and raising interest rates sharply. The extent to which they were being supported by the Bundesbank was sometimes in doubt, and the support of politicians at home was even more questionable. Amid scenes all too reminiscent of the many previous sterling crises of the twentieth century, Britain, along with Italy, was forced to leave the Exchange Rate Mechanism of the European Monetary System. After the event there was a tendency to claim this as a wise policy adjustment; at the time it was just a humiliating policy defeat. British opposition to EMU hardened as a result.

On this occasion the parity of the French franc survived the crisis, thanks to a narrow vote in favour of the Maastricht Treaty in a national referendum. But the victory over the markets was short lived. In June 1993 the French and German authorities disagreed in public over the appropriate stance of European monetary policy. As the Germans resisted pressure to cut their interest rates, the markets concluded that a devaluation of the franc was likely. This time the defence measures were mounted in vain. Governments could not agree either on how to preserve the existing parities or on how to change them. The only way forward was to redefine the system itself. The margin of fluctuation between currencies was widened from a narrow band of 2.25 per cent to the broad expanse of 15 per cent. One might say that the Exchange Rate Mechanism had in effect been abandoned and that European currencies were free to find their own levels in the markets.

At this stage the opponents of EMU could claim that events were proving their case for them. There did not seem to be sufficient political will to make the system work. The markets would soon detect any wavering of commitment to monetary union and blow it apart. Supporters of the programme, however, could argue against this that fixing exchange rates was now an all-or-nothing decision. Within a monetary union there would be no currency markets in which speculators could take a position against its success. There was a clear choice between monetary union on the one hand and floating exchange rates on the other; intermediate positions like that of the Exchange Rate Mechanism, or the old Bretton Woods system, were no longer viable. European unity had to go either forward or back.

In the mid-1990s it looked as if the direction would be backward, yet, against the odds, the crucial move to introduce the new euro went ahead, on time, at the start of 1999. Moreover the membership of 'Euroland' was much wider than expected. It was, in particular, hailed as a triumph for the Italian authorities when that country was deemed to have met the convergence criteria. The danger that EMU would produce a 'two-speed' Europe had been averted. One could say that the monetary authorities of Europe had won a victory over the markets, proving that disruption of the kind experienced in the course of the decade need not deflect them from their chosen path. One could also say, however, that EMU could come into being only because governments had accepted the constraints on their behaviour that markets nowadays demanded of them.

The UK stayed outside the union, as a matter of choice, reflecting a deep-seated popular opposition to the whole idea of European economic or political union. The Labour government was trying, very cautiously, to change those sentiments, but was reluctant to declare its support for membership of EMU; the Conservatives were moving in the direction of outright opposition. A decision was deferred, and a referendum was promised.

The British ambivalence over EMU highlights a dilemma which faced the world economy as a whole. Britain had important ties, both economic and political, with the rest of Europe, but it had equally important ties, both economic and political with America and the rest of the world. Was the future of the world economy to be regional or global? The successful formation of EMU in Europe suggested the former, but almost everything else that was happening in the 1990s suggested the latter. Trade and capital flows were being liberalised throughout the world. The world as a whole was becoming one market.

The popular term in the 1990s for the formation of a world market was 'globalisation'. It is difficult to give a precise meaning to this word, but it is something more than just the expansion of international trade. It can be seen as the conclusion of a long-term historical trend (Kennard and Longheed, 1999). In the nineteenth century international trade grew faster than total output; capital and labour were both relatively free to move across national boundaries. From the First World War until the 1950s the trend was reversed, with output growing faster than trade as countries adopted policies of self-sufficiency. In the second half of the twentieth century the trend towards integration was resumed, at first in a cautious and controlled manner, then faster and more freely as regulations were relaxed. By the 1990s most of the obstacles to trade and investment had been removed, at least as between OECD countries – although major restrictions remained in respect of agricultural products.

Certainly by the 1990s the major transnational corporations believed that they produced for a global market. The literature of management studies is eloquent on the subject:

> The emerging global order is spearheaded by a few hundred corporate giants, many of them bigger than most sovereign nations . . . The multinational corporation of twenty years ago carried on separate operations in many different countries and tailored its operations to local conditions. In the 1990s large business enterprises, even some smaller ones, have the technological means and strategic vision to burst old limits of time, space, national boundaries, language, custom and ideology. By acquiring earth-spanning technologies, by developing products that can be produced anywhere and sold everywhere, by spreading credit around the world, and by

connecting global channels of communication that can penetrate any village or neighbourhood, these institutions we normally think of as economic rather than political, private rather than public, are becoming the world empires of the twenty-first century . . . (Barnet and Cavanagh, 1994)

At the end of the twentieth century, there was assured peace amongst the major powers of the world economy. All of them were pursuing economic policies on similar lines: the long-standing philosophical and ideological differences seemed to be resolved. Governments and central banks everywhere had learned to respect world markets and to follow policies which would retain their confidence. The authorities in smaller countries actually felt powerless to determine their own economic policies. Against this background the regionalism of the European Union could seem narrow and out-of-date. The slogan of 'One Market, One Money', might seem to be relevant to the whole world, not just to one part of it.

Why then was there not more pressure to unite the world monetary system, to go back in effect to the kind of regime which united the world economy at the start of the century? The idea of a worldwide monetary union was seldom canvassed in the 1990s and attracted little support. It was not that the problem of exchange-rate instability had gone away. Year-on-year the Deutschmark fell against the dollar by 12 per cent in 1995, and rose by 15 per cent in 1997. The effective exchange rate index for Japan fell by 18 per cent between 1995 and 1997, whilst the effective rate for the UK rose by 13 per cent between 1996 and 1998. Swings of this magnitude produced vocal protests either from producers or from consumers; direct investment decision were often made problematic. As differences in inflation rates between the major countries became relatively trivial, it was the exchange markets that caused most of the shocks to international competitiveness.

One writer, sympathetic to the case for a world fixed-rate regime, but doubtful of its political feasibility, summed up the argument as follows:

> . . . it appears that the variability of the exchange rates, and especially the large misalignments that have occurred since the early 1970s have been costly for the world economy. Sizeable adjustments between traded and non-traded goods sectors have been forced on many countries when the currencies moved through cycles of overvaluation and undervaluation. Although hard evidence is difficult to gather, there is a presumption that that these cycles may have stimulated protectionist pressures thereby harming international

trade. Ultimately, this may have contributed to the major slow-down of economic growth observed in the industrialised world since 1973. . . . Thus, there are many reasons to argue for a return to more fixity in exchange rates of the major currencies. Unfortunately, it must immediately be added that although desirable, exchange rate stabilization is unlikely to happen soon . . . Sustainable exchange rate stabilization requires credible commitments, i.e. a commitment that even if the fixity of exchange rates hurts, the authorities will stick to it. The Bretton Woods system and the EMS foundered on the lack of credibility of the exchange rate arrangement. The lack of credibility of fixed exchange rate commitment will continue to exist as long as independent nations pursue domestic objectives that can come into conflict with the exchange rate target.

In addition, fixed exchange rate arrangements require rules governing the system-wide monetary policy. This necessitates either a formidable amount of coordination of policies, or a very asymmetric relation between partners. These conditions do not seem to be satisfied today. (De Grauwe, 1996)

Yet the gold standard endured for a long period. It did not require formal international agreements or the creation of a world monetary authority. Perhaps that was the reason for its success. Gold itself had no nationality and therefore it did not offend the national pride of any of the countries which used it as an anchor. At the end of the century there was no comparable focus for a world monetary regime removed from national policy and competition. No-one took gold itself very seriously any more.

Nevertheless the markets imposed a constraint on national monetary policies not unlike that of the old gold standard. The markets were neither national nor political in character, and they could overturn national policies much as gold flows did on occasion in the nineteenth century. Policies which threatened price stability faced immediate and impersonal punishment. It might be rough justice, but it was respected, and protests against it went unheard.

The lessons of experience

The relative tranquillity of the American and West European economies in the latter half of the 1990s confirmed neoclassical economics as the received wisdom. Firm and consistent monetary policies did indeed subdue inflation, as the textbooks had said that they would. Moreover, the damaging side-effects which had been feared from this treatment were hardly in evidence at all. In the United States especially, output growth was buoyant, actually benefiting, it could be claimed, from the confidence inspired by the success of monetary and fiscal policies. The measures of reform introduced by 'neoliberal' governments of the 1980s had not at first been unambiguously beneficial. At the end of that decade it was still an open question whether they would be sustainable politically, and whether they would be able to demonstrate tangible economic gains. By the end of the 1990s the verdict was much clearer, and more favourable. It had taken a very long time, but they did seem to be working at last. Naturally enough, the ideas behind those reforms were confirmed and given greater plausibility.

The actual behaviour of economies, from year to year, in the 1990s also seemed to be conforming relatively well to neoclassical models. Fiscal contractions did not seem to reduce the growth of output and employment; on the contrary, they produced lower interest rates, and hence more growth. Swings in exchange rates did not seem to have very substantial or lasting effects on competitiveness and trade; on the contrary they seemed to affect mainly the price level, as classical theory would predict. Most significantly, there was not much sign of the Phillips curve: inflation and unemployment could both fall at the same time.

Mainstream economics was chiefly a product of American universities. Perhaps for that reason, it faced no very serious intellectual challenge at the end of the century. There was no pressing need to rethink the accepted framework. It might have been different if the intellectual capital of the subject had been in Tokyo, Moscow or Singapore. The revolutions and counter-revolutions in economics during the twentieth century were the result of tension between the dominant orthodoxy and the evidence of casual observation. No such tension was felt in Chicago or Cambridge, Massachusetts, in the late 1990s. An optimistic assessment could maintain that economics as a discipline had made substantial progress in the course of the century. Economists had learnt from experience, and from the mistakes of their predecessors. After the noisy debates, which had divided the profession from the 1930s to the 1970s, this was a time of quiet self-confidence, not to say complacency.

Yet, despite the claims to have made progress, the mainstream theory of 1999 was not different in essence from that of 1900. There had been no new breakthrough remotely comparable with the advances made during the century in the 'hard' sciences; there was no equivalent of quantum mechanics or molecular biology. In fact economics had gone round in a circle, ending up more or less where it had begun. Nobel prizes were awarded to leading economists, but the advances which they celebrated were often little more than the formal and rigorous statement of propositions already implicit in writings of a much earlier date.

Empirical support for neoclassical economics was not much stronger at the end of the century than it had been at the beginning. This is not, generally speaking, an experimental discipline. Moreover, the concepts of the theory seldom correspond exactly with anything which can actually be observed and measured. If the results do not support the theory, one can always change the definition of 'money' or 'the real rate of interest' or even of 'output' and 'the price level'. In the last decades of the century economists were becoming more self-critical about the philosophical basis of their subject, and methodology was an increasingly popular sub-discipline.

Perhaps economics is not really a science at all. That would explain why it can be so successful without actually making many significant empirical discoveries. One writer put it like this:

> Treating economic theory as a contingent theory about the causes and consequences of choice behaviour will not explain the attachment of economists to the theory, because it is just not a very good explanatory theory of the causes and consequences of economic choice. Over the course of a century it has failed to explain these problems with anything like improving accuracy and precision . . . A theory which cannot predict cannot explain – or at least we have no way of telling whether its explanations are correct . . .
>
> In recent years I have begun to think that we need to seek a non-explanatory rationale for the continuing commitment of economists to neoclassical microeconomics . . . I report two such rationales. First the idea that economic theory is fundamentally a normative discipline; second the notion that economic theory is a branch of applied mathematics. (Rosenberg, 1994)

Such suspicions might well be confirmed by a perusal of the learned journals of economics at any time in the century, but especially in its later years. The axiom of rationality was treasured, not so much for its explanatory power as for its ethical overtones. The elaborate constructs being built on classical economics were rather like those built by the schoolmen of medieval times on the axioms of ancient philosophy. Macroeconomics, which had begun its life with a more eclectic and empirical approach, had been re-assimilated into the neoclassical tradition by the end of the century. The preferred approach to any theoretical problem was always to look at the rational behaviour of one individual – the 'representative agent' – and deduce aggregate behaviour from that. Its 'cognitive status' was no different from that of contemporary developments in what was still referred to as microeconomics.

Monetary theory was imbued with the same axioms. The main challenge to the subject was to reconcile actual monetary experience with the rationality of individual agents. As in other branches of economic theory the most important advances had been made before the century began. The fundamental difference between real and nominal magnitudes was well expressed by the classical writers. The 'quantity theory' of money was familiar in nineteenth-century textbooks. They could also give a reasonably clear account of the influence of credit on the business cycle, as well as the determination of long- and short-term interest rates. They knew that the price level did not adjust instantaneously to eliminate aggregate excess supply or demand, and that variations in the quantity of money had effects on real variables in the meantime. They had already defined the three functions of money, as a medium of exchange, a unit of account and as a store of value. They would have found it very difficult, however, to integrate all these ideas into a consistent and elegant model of general equilibrium.

At the end of the century, monetary theory was still, in some respects, fragmentary and incomplete. There was still no satisfactory theoretical explanation of the degree of inertia in prices, although this is crucial to the design of monetary policy regimes. It still could not be explained, within the axiomatic framework of rational choice by individuals, why prices moved upwards more readily than they moved down. The standard theory was still finding it difficult to explain why anyone held money as a store of value in the presence of alternatives which paid interest. The development of credit cards as a means of payment highlighted the issue of creditworthiness which the classical theory had never adequately addressed. There was plenty of theoretical work still to be done.

Monetary economics at the end of the century was much as it had been at the start because it had unlearned what had once seemed to be the main lessons of experience. What had been called 'modern economics' at the mid-century was deemed to be outdated at the end. A very considerable investment of intellectual effort had been largely written off. The reputation of Keynes and his school at the end of the century was rather like that of Freud and his school in psychology. He was still revered as a great thinker, one of the most influential economists of all time. He still had a considerable number of devotees. But his writings were, for the most part, seen to be relevant, at best, to his own times, and not to the current situation. His claim to have disproved classical economics was now accepted by very few, although many might concede that classical economics did not have a monopoly of the truth.

The argument of this book is that macroeconomics is not the same at all times and in all places. It has few, if any, laws that are invariant across all policy regimes. It is quite possible, therefore, to maintain that the classical economists were right enough in their own day, and also that Keynes was right enough in his. Moreover, the influence of ideas and events may be reciprocal, so that popular belief in an economic doctrine may help to make it come true. This is not to deny that, under any particular regime, there are facts about economic behaviour to observe and to explain. It does mean, however, that lessons learned under one regime may have to be unlearned under the next.

Looking back over the experience of a century we see it from the viewpoint of the end. We see the gold standard at the start of the century as impermanent; we see the attempts to restore it after the First World War as doomed to failure; we see the *General Theory* as the precursor of the postwar golden age; we see the liberal reforms of Reagan and Thatcher as ultimately successful in most of their aims. Any lessons which we may learn with the benefit of hindsight were not so evident to observers at the time.

When we come to the end of the century, however, we are not in such a privileged position. Our interpretation of the 1990s cannot be based on knowing what will happen next. It would be very rash to predict. For the moment a grand narrative for the whole of the twentieth century with a circular pattern seems appropriate: we have been to Utopia and back. We cannot now know, however, whether it will still seem appropriate a few decades hence.

References

Ackley, G. (1961), *Macroeconomic Theory*, London, Collier Macmillan.

Alesina, A. and Summers, L. (1993), 'Central bank independence and macroeconomic performance', *Journal of Money, Credit and Banking*, May.

Angell, J.W. (1937), 'The general objectives of monetary policy', in Goyer, A.D. (ed.), *The Lessons of Monetary Experience – Essays in Honor of Irving Fisher*, London, Allen and Unwin.

Argy, V. and Stein, L. (1997), *The Japanese Economy*, Basingstoke, Macmillan.

Åslund, A. (1995), *How Russia Became a Market Economy*, Washington, DC, Brookings Institution.

Atkinson, P. and Chouraqui, J.-C. (1985), *The Origins of High Real Interest Rates*, OECD Occasional Studies, Paris, OECD.

Barker, K., Britton, A. and Major, R. (1984), 'Macroeconomic policy in Britain and France', *National Institute Economic Review*, November.

Barnet, R. and Cavanagh, J. (1994), *Global Dreams – Imperial Corporations and the New World Order*, New York, Simon and Schuster.

Barro, R. (1984), *Macroeconomics*, Chichester, Wiley.

Bayoumi, T., Eichengreen, B. and Taylor, M. (eds) (1996), *Modern Perspectives on the Gold Standard*, Cambridge, Cambridge University Press.

Beckerman, W. and Jenkinson, T. (1986), 'What stopped the inflation? Unemployment or commodity prices?', *Economic Journal*, March.

Bernanke, B., Laubach, T., Mishkin, F. and Posen, A. (1999), *Inflation Targeting – Lessons from the International Experience*, Princeton, Princeton University Press.

Beveridge, W.H. (1944), *Full Employment in a Free Society*, London, Allen and Unwin.

Black, S. (1977), *Floating Exchange Rates and National Economic Policy*, New Haven, Yale University Press.

Blanchard, O. and Fischer, S. (1989), *Lectures in Macroeconomics*, Cambridge, Mass., MIT Press.

Blaug, M. (1962), *Economic Theory in Retrospect*, London, Heinemann.

Bloomfield, A. (1959), *Monetary Policy under the International Gold Standard, 1880–1914*, Federal Reserve Bank of New York.

Booth, A. (1989), *British Economic Policy – Was There a Keynesian Revolution?*, Brighton, Harvester Wheatsheaf.

Bordo, M. and Eichengreen, B. (1993), *A Retrospective on the Bretton Woods System*, Chicago, University of Chicago Press.

Borschardt, K. (1991), 'Germany's experience of inflation', in Borschardt, K. (ed.), *Perspectives in Modern German Economic History and Policy*, Cambridge, Cambridge University Press.

Brittan, S. (1971), *Steering the Economy*, revised edn., Harmondsworth, Penguin.

Britton, A. (1991), *Macroeconomic Policy in Britain, 1974 –87*, Cambridge, Cambridge University Press.

Bronfenbrenner, M. (ed.) (1969), *Is the Business Cycle Obsolete?*, Chichester, Wiley.

Broughton, J. (1979), 'Demand for money in major OECD countries', *Economic Outlook Occasional Studies*, Paris, OECD.

Brown, A. J. (1955), *The Great Inflation, 1939 to 1950*, Oxford, Oxford University Press.

(1988), 'World depression and the price level', *National Institute Economic Review*, February.

Bryant, R. (1983), *Controlling Money – The Federal Reserve and its Critics*, Washington DC, Brookings Institution.

Bryant, R. , Hooper, P. and Mann, C.L. (eds) (1993), *Evaluating Policy Regimes*, Washington DC, Brookings Institution.

Buchan, J. (1997), *Frozen Desire – An Inquiry into the Meaning of Money*, Basingstoke, Macmillan.

Buckheim, C. (1999), *Fifty Years of the Deutschemark*, Frankfurt, Bundesbank.

Burchardt, F.A. *et al.* (1944), *Economics of Full Employment*, Oxford, Blackwell.

Cagan, P. (1979), *Persistent Inflation – Historical and Policy Essays*, New York, Columbia University Press.

(1986), 'The report of the Gold Commission', in Brunner, K. and Meltzer, A. (eds), *Monetary and Fiscal Policies and Their Application*, Carnegie Rochester Conference Series, Amsterdam, North-Holland.

Calmfors, L. (1993), *Centralisation of Wage Bargaining and Macroeconomic Performance – A Survey*, OECD Occasional Studies, Paris, OECD.

Cargill, T., Hutchison, M. and Ito, T. (1997), *The Political Economy of Japanese Monetary Policy*, Cambridge, Mass., MIT Press.

Cassel, G. (1936), *The Downfall of the Gold Standard*, Oxford, Oxford University Press.

Clapham, J. (1928), *The Economic Development of France and Germany, 1815–1914*, Cambridge, Cambridge University Press.

Cobham, D. (ed.) (1994), *European Monetary Upheavals*, Manchester, Manchester University Press.

Coe, D., Durand, M. and Stiehler, V. (1988), *The Disinflation of the 1980s*, OECD Occasional Studies, Paris, OECD.

Cohen, J.B. (1960), *Japan's Postwar Economy*, Bloomington, Indiana University Press.

Cole, G.D.H. (1935), *Principles of Economic Planning*, Basingstoke, Macmillan.

Cunliffe Committee (1918), *First Interim Report*, Committee on Currency and Foreign Exchanges after the War, Cd 9182, London, HMSO.

Davis, E.P. (1992), *Debt, Financial Fragility and Systemic Risk*, Oxford, Oxford University Press.

de Cecco, M. (1989), *The International Gold Standard*, London, Pinter (Italian edn 1971).

De Grauwe, P. (1996), *International Money*, 2nd edn, Oxford, Oxford University Press.

Dow, J.C.R. (1964), *The Management of the British Economy 1945–60*, Cambridge, Cambridge University Press.

(1998), *Major Recessions – Britain and the World, 1920–1995*, Oxford, Oxford University Press.

Dow, S.C. (1985), *Macroeconomic Thought, a Methodological Approach*, Oxford, Blackwell.

Dowd, K. (1989), *The State and the Monetary System*, London, Philip Allan.

Eccles, M.S. (1937), 'Controlling booms and depressions', in Goyer, A.D. (ed.), *The Lessons of Monetary Experience – Essays in Honor of Irving Fisher*, London, Allen and Unwin.

Eckstein, O. (1978), *The Great Recession*, Amsterdam, North-Holland.

Eichengreen, B. (1995), *Golden Fetters*, Oxford, Oxford University Press.

Einzig, P. (1935), *World Finance Since 1914*, London, Kegan Paul.

European Commission (1989), *Report on Economic and Monetary Union in the European Community*, Committee for the Study of Economic and Monetary Union, the 'Delors Report', Brussels, European Commission.

(1990),'One market, one money', *European Economy*, 44.

(1994), *Growth, Competitiveness, Employment – The Challenges and Ways Forward into the 21st Century*, Brussels, European Commission.

Fearon, P. (1979), *The Origin and Nature of the Great Slump*, Basingstoke, Macmillan.

Federal Reserve Bank of Kansas City (1997), *Maintaining Financial Stability in a Global Economy*, Federal Reserve Bank of Kansas City.

Feinstein, C., Temin, P. and Toniolo, G. (1997), *The European Economy Between the Wars*, Oxford, Oxford University Press.

Fisher, I. (1911), *The Purchasing Power of Money*, Basingstoke, Macmillan.

Flemming, J. (1976), *Inflation*, Oxford, Oxford University Press.

(1987), 'Wage flexibility and employment stability', *Oxford Economic Papers*, March.

Flemming, J. and Matthews, R.C.O. (1994), 'Economic reform in Russia', *National Institute Economic Review*, August.

Foot, M. (1981), 'Monetary targets – their nature and record in the major economies', in Griffiths, B. and Wood, G. (eds), *Monetary Targets*, Basingstoke, Macmillan.

Ford, A. (1989), 'International financial policy under the gold standard', in Matthias, P. and Pollard, S. (eds), *Cambridge Economic History of Europe*, vol. 8, Cambridge, Cambridge University Press.

Friedman, B. (1980), 'Postwar changes in the American financial markets', in Feldstein, M. (ed.), *The American Economy in Transition*, Chicago, University of Chicago Press.

Friedman, M. (1953), 'The case for flexible exchange rates', in *Essays in Positive Economics*, Chicago, University of Chicago Press.

Friedman, M. (ed.) (1956), *Studies in the Quantity Theory of Money*, Chicago, University of Chicago Press.

Friedman, M. and Schwartz, A. (1963), *A Monetary History of the United States 1870–1960*, Princeton, Princeton University Press.

Frisch, R. (1933), 'Propagation problems and impulse problems in dynamic economics', in *Economic Essays in Honour of Gustav Cassel*, London, Allen and Unwin.

Fukai, E. (1937), 'The recent monetary policy of Japan', in Goyer, A.D. (ed.), *The Lessons of Monetary Experience – Essays in Honor of Irving Fisher*, Allen and Unwin.

Fukuyama, F. (1992), *The End of History and the Last Man*, Harmondsworth, Penguin.

Galbraith, J.K. (1954), *The Great Crash 1929*, Harmondsworth, Penguin.

Giersch, H. (1992), *The Fading Miracle – Four Decades of the Market Economy in Germany*, Cambridge, Cambridge University Press.

Gildea, R. (1997), *France since 1945*, Oxford, Oxford University Press.

Goodhart, C. (1988), *The Evolution of Central Banks*, Cambridge, Mass., MIT Press.

Guillebaud, C.W. (1939), *The Economic Recovery in Germany*, Cambridge, Cambridge University Press.

Hansen, A.H. (1932), *Economic Stabilization in an Unbalanced World*, New York, Harcourt Brace.

Harris, S.E. (1947), *The New Economics – Keynes' Influence on Theory and Public Policy*, New York, A. Knopf.

Hawtrey, R. (1913), *Good and Bad Trade*, London, Constable.

Hayek, F.A. (1944), *The Road to Serfdom*, London, Routledge.

Hennesey, P. (1993), *Never Again*, London, Vintage Books.

Hicks, J.R. (1935), 'A suggestion for simplifying the theory of money', *Economica*, February.

   (1937), 'Mr Keynes and the Classics', *Econometrica*, April.

Hirsch, F. (1965), *The Pound Sterling – A Polemic*, London, Gollancz.

Hobsbawm, E. (1995), *The Age of Extremes*, London, Abacus.

Homer, S. and Sylla, R. (1991), *A History of Interest Rates*, 3rd edn., New Brunswick, Rutgers University Press.

Hood, C. (1994), *Explaining Economic Policy Reversals*, Milton Keynes, Open University Press.

Hutchison, T.W. (1953), *A Review of Economic Doctrines, 1870–1929*, Oxford, Oxford University Press.

James, H. (1996), *International Monetary Cooperation since Bretton Woods*, Oxford, Oxford University Press.

Johnson, H.G. (1964), 'Major issues in monetary and fiscal policies in the United States', *Federal Reserve Bulletin*, November.

Kaldor, N. (1938), 'Stability and full employment', *Economic Journal*, December.

Kemp, J. (1995), *Last of the Empires – A History of the Soviet Union, 1945–1991*, Oxford, Oxford University Press.

Kemp M.C. (1964), *The Pure Theory of International Trade*, New York, Prentice-Hall.

Kennard, A.G. and Lougheed, A.L. (1999), *The Growth of the International Economy, 1820–2000*, 4th edn., London, Routledge.

Kettenacker, L. (1997), *Germany since 1945*, Oxford, Oxford University Press.

Keylor, W.M. (1996), *The Twentieth Century World*, Oxford, Oxford University Press.

Keynes, J.M. (1923), *Tract on Monetary Reform*, London, Macmillan.

(1930), *Treatise on Money*, Vol. 2, London, Macmillan.

(1936), *The General Theory of Employment, Interest and Money*, Basingstoke, Macmillan.

Keynes, J.N. (1891), *The Scope and Method of Political Economy*, London, Macmillan.

Kindleberger, C.P. (1973), *The World in Depression*, London, Allen Lane.

Klein, L.R. (1966), *The Keynesian Revolution*, Basingstoke, Macmillan.

Knight, F. (1921), *Risk, Uncertainty and Profit*.

Krause, L. and Salant, W. (eds) (1973), *European Monetary Unifiication and its Meaning for the United States*, Washington, DC, Brookings Institution.

Krugman, P. (1994), *Peddling Prosperity*, New York, Norton.

Kruse, D. (1980), *Monetary Integration in Western Europe*, London, Butterworth.

League of Nations (1920), *Currencies After the War*, Geneva.

League of Nations (1944), *International Currency Experience*, Geneva.

Lerner, A.P. (1944), *The Economics of Control*, Basingstoke, Macmillan.

Liesner, T. (1989), 'One hundred years of economic statistics', *The Economist*.

Lucas, R. (1976), 'Econometric policy evaluation – a critique', in Brunner, K. and Meltzer, A. (eds), *The Phillips Curve and Labor Markets*, Amsterdam, North-Holland.

(1987), *Models of Business Cycles*, Oxford, Blackwell.

MacDougall, D. (1957), *The World Dollar Problem*, Basingstoke, Macmillan.

Machin, H. and Wright, V. (1985), *Economic Policy Under the Mitterrand Presidency, 1981–1984*, London, Pinter.

Maddison, A. (1995), *Monitoring the World Economy, 1820–1992*, Paris, OECD.

Magnifico, G. (1973), *European Monetary Unification*, London, Macmillan.

Marsh, D. (1992), *The Bundesbank*, London, Mandarin Press.

Marshall, A. (1923), *Money, Credit and Commerce*, Basingstoke, Macmillan.

Matthews, R.C.O. (1969), 'United Kingdom', in Bronfenbrenner, M. (ed.) (1969), *Is the Business Cycle Obsolete?*, Chichester, Wiley.

Matthews, R.C.O. (ed.) (1982), *Slower Growth in the Western World*, London, Heinemann.

Meade, J.E. (1936), *Economic Analysis and Policy*, Oxford, Oxford University Press.

Meadows, D. H., Meadows, D.L., Randers, J. and Behrens, W. (1972), *The Limits to Growth*, New York, Universe Books.

Mill, J.S. (1909), *Principles of Political Economy*, book V, 2nd edn, London, Longman (1st edn 1848).

Millward, A.S. (1987), *War, Economy and Society, 1939–45*, Harmondsworth, Penguin.

Mishan, E.J. (1969), *The Costs of Economic Growth*, Harmondsworth, Penguin.

Mitchell, B.R. (1998), *International Historical Statistics, Europe 1750–1993 and the Americas*, Basingstoke, Macmillan.

Mitchell, W.C. (1913), *Business Cycles*.

(1927), *Business Cycles, the Problem and its Setting*.

Moulton, H.G. (ed.) (1936), *The Recovery Problem in the United States*, Washington, DC, Brookings Institution.

Nicholson, J. S. (1906), *Elements of Political Economy*, 2nd edn., London, A and C Black.

OECD (1970a), *Inflation, The Present Problem – A Report by the Secretary General*, Paris, OECD, December.

(1970b), *The Growth of Output 1960–1980*, Paris, OECD, December.

(1975), *The Role of Monetary Policy in Demand Management – The Experience of Six Major Countries*, Paris, OECD.

(1977), *Towards Full Employment and Price Stability*, Paris, OECD, June.

(1988), *Why Economic Policies Change Course*, Paris, OECD.

(1994), *The Jobs Study – Facts, Analysis, Strategies*, Paris, OECD.

(1997–9), *Country Studies* and *Economic Outlook*, Paris, OECD.

OEEC (1961), *The Problem of Rising Prices*, Paris, OEEC.

Patat, J.-P. and Lutfalla, M. (1990), *A Monetary History of France in the Twentieth Century*, English translation, Basingstoke, Macmillan.

Patinkin, D. (1956), *Money, Interest and Prices*, London, Harper and Row.

Phillips, A.W. (1957), 'Stabilisation policy and the time-form of lagged responses', *Economic Journal*, June.

(1958), 'The relationship between unemployment and the rate of change of money wage rates in the United Kingdom, 1861–1957', *Economica*.

Pigou, A.C. (1941), *Employment and Equilibrium*, London, Macmillan.

Radcliffe Committee (1959), 'Report of the Committee on the workings of the monetary system', London, HMSO, Cmnd 827.

Robbins, L. (1954), 'Full employment as an objective' (1949), reprinted in *The Economist in the Twentieth Century*, Basingstoke, Macmillan.

(1976), *Political Economy, Past and Present*, Basingstoke, Macmillan.

Robertson, D.H. (1915), *Study of Industrial Fluctuations*, London, King and Son.

Ropke, W. (1960), 'The economics of full employment', in Hazlitt, H. (ed.), *The Critics of Keynesian Economics*, Van Nostrand.

Rosenberg, A. (1994), 'What is the cognitive status of economic theory?', in Backhouse, R.E. (ed.), *New Directions in Economic Methodology*, London, Routledge.

Rueff, J. (1947), 'The fallacies of Lord Keynes' General Theory', *Quarterly Journal of Economics*, May.

Samuelson, P. (1948), *Economics*, 1st edn, New York, McGraw-Hill.

(1951), *Economics*, 2nd edn, New York, McGraw-Hill.

Savage, D. (1983), 'The assesment of the National Institute's forecasts of GDP 1959 –82', *National Institute Economic Review*, August.

Scammell, W. (1975), *International Monetary Policy – Bretton Woods and After*, Basingstoke, Macmillan.

Schumacher, H. (1937), 'Germany's present currency system', in Goyer, A.D. (ed.), *The Lessons of Monetary Experience – Essays in Honor of Irving Fisher*, London, Allen and Unwin.

Sherwin, S.F. (1956), *Monetary Policy in Continental Western Europe, 1944–52*, Madison, University of Wisconsin Press.

Shinjo, H. (1962), *History of the Yen*, Kobe, Kobe University Press.

Shinohara, M. (1969), 'Japan', in Bronfenbrenner, M. (ed.), *Is the Business Cycle Obsolete?*, Chichester, Wiley.

Sims, C.A. (1980), 'Macroeconomics and reality', *Econometrica*, January.

Skidelsky, R. (1998), 'The growth of a world economy', in Howard, M. and Louis, W. (eds), *The Oxford History of the Twentieth Century*, Oxford, Oxford University Press.

Smith, D. (1995), *Japan since 1945*, Basingstoke, Macmillan.

Stein, H. (1984), *The Making of Economic Policy from Roosevelt to Reagan, and Beyond*, New York, Simon and Schuster.

Stewart, M. (1972), *Keynes and After*, Harmondsworth, Penguin.

Tachi, R. (1966), 'Fiscal and monetary policy', in Komiya, R. (ed.), *Postwar Economic Growth in Japan*, Berkeley, University of California Press.

Takafusa, N. (1994), *Lectures on Modern Japanese Economic History*, LTCB.

Taylor, A.J.P. (1965), *English History, 1914–1945*, Oxford, Oxford University Press.

Taylor, C. (1995), *EMU 2000? – Prospects for European Monetary Union*, London, Royal Institute for International Affairs.

Temin, P. (1996), *Lessons from the Great Depression*, Cambridge, Mass., MIT Press.

Thygessen, N. (1996), 'Should budgetary policies be coordinated further in EMU – and is that feasible?', *Banca Nazionale del Lavoro Quarterly Review*, special issue on EMU, March.

Timberlake, R.H. (1978), *Monetary Policy in the United States – An Intellectual and Institutional History*, Chicago, University of Chicago Press.

United Nations (1949), *National and International Measures for Full Employment*, New York, United Nations.

van der Wee, H. (1987), *Prosperity and Upheaval – The World Economy 1945–1980*, English translation, Harmondsworth, Penguin.

van Dormael, A. (1978), *Bretton Woods – The Birth of a Monetary System*, Basingstoke, Macmillan.

Vaubel, R. (1983), 'Co-ordination or competition among macroeconomic policies?' in Machlup, F. *et al.* (eds), *Reflections on a Troubled World Economy*, Basingstoke, Macmillan.

von Hagen, J. (1998), 'A new approach to monetary policy (1971 –8)', in *Fifty Years of the Deutschmark*, Bundesbank.

Williamson, J. (1983), 'The exchange rate system', Washington D.C. Institute for International Economics.

Worswick, G.D.N. (1944), 'The stability and flexibility of full employment' in Burchardt, F.A. *et al.*, *Economics of Full Employment*, Oxford, Oxford Institute of Economics and Statistics.

Index

Printed in the United States
1198100001B/204